PRACTICE LEARNING IN THE CARING PROFESSIONS

In Memoriam

On 3rd July 1999 Dave died at the age of 54 from oesophageal cancer before seeing this book in print.

During his recent illness he was surprised and enormously comforted to learn just how much he was valued as a friend, as well as a colleague by those with whom he worked.

He spent a lifetime in social work, practising for 14 years before moving into education at Suffolk College, and working ceaselessly for national organisations such as CCETSW, NOPT, Journal of Practice Teaching in Health and Social Work, and BERA, as well as various programmes of learning to which he contributed.

Being part of the early pioneers of the eighties with CCETSW developing the practice teaching award, he wrote the key publications for CCETSW 26.1 'Accrediting Agencies' and 26.3 'Assessing Students Competence to Practice', which remains a mainstay to Practice Teachers.

His commitment to high standards of professional education, emphasising the importance of reflective practice in the curriculum, coupled with his integrity, good humoured support and warmth have helped many colleagues and students, and through them the users with whom they worked. Dave will be remembered as he did make a difference and for this the profession is grateful.

Whatever Dave undertook in life he approached with unstinting enthusiasm and unselfish commitment. He was a loving and encouraging husband and father who will always be much loved in return. Dave enjoyed music, playing the cello in orchestras and quartets, as well as singing bass in choirs. He also loved all sport - playing racket sports in early life and latterly golf.

We will miss him.

Practice Learning in the Caring Professions

Dave Evans

Ashgate
ARENA
Aldershot • Brookfield USA • Singapore • Sydney

Published by
Ashgate Publishing Limited
Gower House
Croft Road
Aldershot
Hants GU11 3HR
England

Ashgate Publishing Company
Old Post Road
Brookfield
Vermont 05036
USA

British Library Cataloging-in-Publication Data
Evans, Dave
Practice learning in the caring professions
1. Human services personnel - Great Britain - Training of
2. Human services personnel - Great Britain - Vocational guidance
3. Human services - Great Britain - Practice
4. Human services - Study and teaching - Great Britain
I. Title
361′.0071

Library of Congress Cataloging-in-Publication Data
Evans, Dave
Practice learning in the caring professions / Dave Evans.
p. cm.
Includes bibliographical references.
ISBN 1-85742-422-0 (hardback)
1. Social work education. 2. Social service - Field work. 3. Nursing - Study and teaching. 4. Human services - Study and teaching. 5. Caregivers - Training of.
I. Title
HV11.E96 1999
361.3'071--dc21 98-52027
CIP

ISBN 1 85742 422 0

Typeset in Palatino by Express Typesetters Ltd., Farnham, Surrey
and printed on acid-free paper and bound in Great Britain

Contents

List of Figures

Acknowledgements

I would like to acknowledge the help, support and influence of a number of people in writing this book. First and foremost, I thank Lesley and Sarah not only for their tolerance and care whilst I have been busy writing but also for their practical contributions to producing the manuscript. I am gratefully aware that a considerable number of colleagues and students have stimulated the development of my thinking, not only in different work places but also within the National Organisation for Practice Teaching. I would also like to thank Jo Campling for her continuing encouragement to write and Kate Trew for her assistance in smoothing the path towards publication.

Foreword

Learning to be a professional necessarily involves *doing* the work of a professional. Listening and watching will not suffice. But how does the aspiring professional gain access to opportunities for doing, appropriate to both their future practice and their current knowledge and experience? In what ways are clients protected from clumsy, ill-informed or insensitive novices; or novices helped to learn quickly from their experience, so that they can take more responsibility for their practice? These issues used to be resolved by the institution of *apprenticeship*. Today's 'solution' is to require aspiring professionals to register as students of higher education and to undertake, concurrently or subsequent to their academic studies, a series of *placements* with organisations providing the relevant professional services. But who is responsible for the quality of these placement experiences, and what features of placements facilitate or constrain the learning of good practice? What kinds of learning are involved in the acquisition of competence and proficiency?

These are but some of the important issues tackled in David Evans' timely review of *Practice Learning in the Caring Professions*. Whilst set in the context of practice learning in general, Evans focuses mainly on learning during the placement components of programmes leading to initial qualifications and professional registration. Greatest attention is given to nursing, school-teaching and social work, whose diverse approaches to placements suggest that many factors other than conditions for learning have shaped their historical development. It is also surprising how often the issues debated by one profession have been tackled quite differently or even ignored by another. The merits of Evans' book derive both from his comprehensive review of the literature on learning in placements: descriptive, evaluative, policy-related, theoretical and empirically researched and from the way in which he makes this material accessible to a wide range of possible readers. Not only does he put practice learning on the map, but his own mapping of this relativelv unexplored territory is of great help to those wanting to come to grips with the key issues, a springboard for the further development of practice and policy.

The culture, organisation and reward systems of higher education are not friendly towards practical knowledge. The recently strengthened research imperative has made it more difficult for university departments to recruit and employ significant numbers of staff with a prime interest in professional practice. Practice learning comes a poor third to research and academic teaching, increasingly handled by strategic alliances with organisations capable of providing placements. These organisations however, do not necessarily give practice learning any higher priority. Their priorities are first to meet the ever-increasing demands of their own clients and second to meet the growing demands for consultation with stakeholders and accountability to local or national government and/or government funded trusts and agencies. Their prime interest in providing placements is likely to be recruitment rather than the provision of learning: in the NHS they are regarded as purchasers of newly qualified professionals rather than providers. The consequence of this marginalisation is that practice teachers/ clinical tutors/mentors frequently find themselves saddled with considerable extra work, little support beyond their immediate line manager (who may or may not be interested in students and their progress) and little recognition or reward. Often it is their dedication and commitment, rather than that of their organisation, which gives the placement its quality, and the converse is equally true.

Evans' book provides a clear framework for thinking once more about the central role of practice learning in professional formation, and how it is organised and facilitated. Practice learning is revealed in all its complexity, and many strategies for supporting it are discussed with full awareness of their strengths and limitations. The analysis is sufficiently clear for readers to use it as a very practical guide to decision-making. Key decisions are treated not only in considerable depth, but also in relation to other linking issues. Ethical and emotional aspects are given high priority. Yet the prevailing ethos is not at all dogmatic. Learning to support practice learning, like practice learning itself, involves a great deal of learning from experience. Evans suggests how this may be shared with others – colleagues, students and even clients – and also raises our awareness of a wide range of learning activities, issues that need to be discussed and things that can easily go wrong. On the one hand he advocates an overt learning model of planning and negotiating agreements, which give parity of esteem to professionals, students and clients, clarity of purpose and principles of procedures; while on the other hand there is continuing recognition of how much learning is implicit, unplanned or opportunistic. The overt learning agenda helps to sustain practice learning as the main purpose of a placement, to consider different approaches to learning and different types of knowledge, and to periodically review progress and give students general, as well as incident-specific feedback. Yet learning is still recognised as elusive and unpredictable, and never complete, as the uniqueness of clients and situations prevents certainty and closure.

At a time when practical support from universities and placement organisations is increasingly threatened, it is ironic to find theoretical support for practice learning increasing. Such support, however, appears to rely on a rather romantic view of apprenticeship, bolstered by references to 'communities of practitioners' and 'learning organisations'. These terms are rarely deconstructed nor linked to the realities described in a generally positive, though grounded, way by Evans. This appears to be a somewhat belated attempt by the literature on apprenticeship to recognise that most professionals today are not autonomous professionals, but employed or contracted professional workers (Johnson 1972). Placements are with organisations rather than individual practitioners, although practice teachers may be expected to take on the responsibility formerly accorded to apprentice 'masters' without the concomitant power and authority. These become less problematic when the duties can be shared amongst a community of practitioners or the learning climate deserves the epithet 'learning organisation'. But how many placements offer this kind of support? In the best examples, the converse is often true. Managers see the presence of students as part of a strategy for moving towards a learning community. Although rarely specifically stated, this is the direction in which Evans' advice is moving. He frequently mentions the learning benefits to practice teachers of having students and emphasises the need for students to share experience and discuss issues with a wider range of colleagues than their designated practice teacher. This should be a joint strategy of the practice teacher and her/his manager, negotiated with the student and periodically reviewed. The danger that a student may be passed around like an unwanted parcel to unwilling practitioners or 'difficult' clients also has to be avoided.

Nevertheless, in many placements, a designated, responsible practitioner provides the emotional and cognitive hub of a student's experience, around which excursions to the periphery can be planned, negotiated, supported and reviewed. Evans describes this relationship as a 'reflective apprenticeship' and discusses its differences from the traditional model. This entails discussing in considerable detail the processes of students observing and being observed, then going on to discuss joint working and 'live supervision'. His chapter on assessment succeeds, remarkably, in maintaining the spirit of the rest of the book. The contractual requirements and problems facing practice assessors are discussed in some detail; but he also emphasises ways in which the assessment process can be empowering rather than disempowering for students.

I have tried to express my delight in getting an early opportunity to see this book, a fore-read as well as a fore-word. It has provided me with many new perspectives on practice learning and a framework with which to connect them, with my prior knowledge of this central, though often hidden, dimension of professonal education. Evans' more sophisticated, yet still very practical review of practice learning has been needed for some time. This book needs to be urgently read by policy-makers in this area and by those concerned about developing the futures of their professions. It is also well suited for use in courses preparing practice teachers for their roles and helping experienced practical teachers to reflect on their experience and further develop their practice. Though not addressed to theorists, its theoretical range is wide and stimulating, and many original ideas of theoretical significance are discussed. The book is a useful antidote to a repetitive diet of two or three fashionable authors. It will help both practitioners to use their heads and theorists to keep their feet on the ground.

Professor Michael Eraut, University of Sussex, 1999

Introduction

Practice learning is considered by many to have an important role in the education of the caring professions. During this current phase in the development of education for the caring professions (Bines 1992), most professional regulatory bodies insist that a substantial proportion of the educational programme takes place in a practice setting, often 50 per cent or over. There is, moreover, a burgeoning literature on many aspects of practice learning. Wilkin (1997) cites 33 books in initial teacher education alone, with comparable developments in health and social care, including the *Journal for Practice Teaching in Social Work and Health*, newly launched at the time of writing. Furthermore, Central Government seems poised to attempt to reinforce this position through its focus on work-based learning and assessment, not only by extending the remit of the then National Council for Vocational Qualifications to include the professions, but also by conducting a consultation exercise on higher level vocational qualifications (DfEE 1996), ostensibly to expand the NVQ framework within the professions.

However, the actual position of practice learning does not appear to be as substantial as these signs might suggest. Positions of substance require substantial funding. Several professions (HCPEF 1997) indicate major problems in resourcing practice learning, which are evident in a number of areas, including: placement availability, workload relief from service delivery for practice teachers and basic practice learning materials. In the case of social work, at least, these chronic problems have been reported since the early 1980s (Folliard 1983; Evans 1996).

This lack of funding can be explained to a large degree by the peripheral position which practice learning occupies in almost every sphere and which reduces its bargaining power in the allocation of resources. Within the partnerships of professional education, the processes of professionalisation (see Chapter 1), including an emphasis on a professional knowledge base, help maintain the lead role which higher education institutions hold and the subsidiary position of practice agencies. Within the higher educational institutions themselves, the needs of income generation and other scholarly activities reduce the priority attributed to any form of teaching, never mind practice teaching, although the Dearing report (1997) has set an agenda for some reprioritising. Even in the practice agencies, practice learning has only a marginal existence, since the primary focus is on service delivery. Managers tend to allocate resources to service provision rather than training of any form, while their practitioner employees tend similarly to prioritise clients' needs above students'.

The aim of this book is to help improve the position of practice learning in the education of the caring professions in three main ways: by fully acknowledging the importance of practice learning, by contributing to the development of the practice and theory of practice learning and by encouraging others to achieve a more substantial position for practice learning. Many people who consider practice learning to be important, none the less consider that learning in the academic setting is more important. A common misconception is that learning takes place in the higher education institution and is then 'put into practice' in the practice agency, a misconception which underpins many features of curriculum design. There is, however, clear evidence that students do learn directly in the practice agency, often as much as in the higher education institution and sometimes more, depending on the profession to be learned and the individual learner. Part I of this book seeks to establish the important function of practice learning in the education of the caring professions.

Wilkin (1997) notes tentative beginnings to the generation of theory about practice learning as a discrete domain of knowledge. Practice learning is not synonymous with, or even a subset of, adult learning, in part because adults can learn without reference to professional practice and also because it is possible to envisage an increased emphasis in secondary education on *learning* for and from work experience and not merely undertaking it. Generating theories of practice learning progresses beyond a phase in which theory has been borrowed from other disciplines, such as psychology, to inform practice learning practice, a progression which mirrors many caring professions themselves. Many books on practice learning, including Jarvis and Gibson (1985), Sawdon (1986), Thompson et al. (1990), and Shardlow and Doel (1996) indicate, for example, how adult learning theory and learning style theory can influence the processes of practice learning. However, none of these particular books would claim to offer a theoretical explanation of how practice learning works or why it is effective. Part I of this book also includes some contribution towards theorising the nature and operation of practice learning.

The context for practice learning is constantly changing. The fact that it spans both the world of higher education as well as the world of agency practice means that it is subject to change from at least these two directions. The educational world is grappling with issues such as competence-based education and training and the impact of modular structures on professional education, while accountability and managerialism are major preoccupations of practice agencies. At times of such change on multiple fronts, it is important that the practical know-how of practice learning has a contemporary relevance and a contextual awareness. These are major aims of the three remaining parts of the book, which become more detailed and concrete by subdividing the whole territory of practice learning into three major processes - learning, teaching and assessing. Although their main emphasis is on practical know-how, these three parts maintain some foundation in theory, both *of* as well as *for* practice learning. Perhaps the centrepiece of these three parts is an exploration of the notion of 'reflective apprenticeship' (Chapter 6), which would seem to be at the heart of practice learning.

The third aim of encouraging others to achieve a more substantial position in professional education for practice learning is perhaps more likely in a political pamphlet or a discussion document for a lobbying group than in a book. However, the boundary between professional and political interests is somewhat permeable. Practice teaching is undoubtedly a political as well as a professional act, since the formal assessment of students is part of a process of accountability to the public for the quality of those accepted into the profession. It would seem somewhat inconsistent for anyone concerned to improve the quality of their practice teaching through training, reading and reflection to ignore the impact on that quality made by policies and resourcing at a number of levels. Whilst this aim is a subtext throughout the bulk of this book as some aspects of the political context of practice learning are explored, the final section addresses some specific strategies for action.

The overtly inter-professional aim of this book places it firmly within a political context which has recognised for more than two decades the potentially harmful impact professional and agency tribalism can have on effective service delivery and has led to an increasing number of Government initiatives in recent years, including the NHS and Community Care Act (1990) and the White Paper on health, current at the time of writing (NHS 1997). An inter-professional perspective would seem to aid all three aims for this book by facilitating a sharing of current knowledge and know-how between caring professions, none of whom have a monopoly on good practice. It does this largely by lifting practice learning as an educational process out of the specific practices of the professions which engage in it. While the content of practice learning – what a student learns on placement – is mainly specific to a given profession, the processes of practice learning are in large part common to all caring professions. It is often the content of practice learning which motivates practitioners to become involved. However, this has correspondingly reduced the focus on the processes of practice learning. A recent research project sponsored by the Health and Care Professions Education Forum (HCPEF 1997) would appear to recognise this communality between caring professions, while the Centre for the Advancement of Interprofessional Education (CAIPE 1997) similarly reports on the development on interprofessional training courses in practice teaching.

Another important contextual feature of any book is the position of the writer. My own conviction about the central function of practice learning in the education of caring professions began with the experience of being educated for two professions, teaching and social work, and discovering that I learned more for both professions from my time in the practice settings than in the higher education institutions. This has been reinforced by the anecdotal experiential evidence of many of the students I have encountered in professional education and by the literature I have read, initially in two full-time practice teaching posts and subsequently working in a higher education institution. Ten years in joint appointments straddling academic and practice agencies has, moreover, confirmed an interest in both the practice and the theory of practice learning. Whilst my main experience as a practice teacher and in the politics of practice learning has been in social work education, I have also been involved in teaching and training practitioners and practice teachers from a range of other professions and have been developing an interest in inter-professional working and learning since a period of time working in a postgraduate teaching hospital and in family therapy.

Terminology

Unfortunately, there is no commonly recognised language for practice learning throughout the caring professions. The two-word phrase 'practice teacher', for example, is commonly accepted in social work education in the UK to describe the main person who facilitates student learning in the practice setting. In other professions and countries (Doel and Shardlow 1996), however, the first word may be 'clinical' or 'fieldwork' while the second word may be 'educator', 'supervisor' or 'instructor'. In yet other professions, this person may be referred to as the 'mentor' (initial teacher education), the 'tutor constable' (police) and the 'trainer' (general practice). My own grounding in social work is therefore the sole explanation for adopting 'practice teacher' and much of the other terminology throughout this book, with no sense that this terminology is to be preferred. Most of this terminology is, I hope, intelligible to readers with other professional backgrounds. I have used the term 'client' to describe the recipient of agency services, not because it is currently common in social work (Evans and Kearney 1996), but because it has been a traditional term in many professions for this person, though clearly not in teaching, medicine and nursing.

I have sought to avoid language which is gender-specific and potentially sexist, unless there is a particular reason for not doing so. The English language is helpful in achieving this aim when using the plural ('they', 'their', 'them'), but unfortunately less so in the singular ('she', 'him', 'her'). I have therefore moved between singular and plural forms in a way which is becoming reasonably familiar in written texts and, I hope, perfectly intelligible.

Two terms from the book title require further explanation. 'Practice learning' has two meanings in the book. One delineates the whole territory of learning for and from professional practice and is largely the usage in Part I and the final section of the book. The other meaning specifies student learning, recognising that this is not synonymous with the teaching they receive ('practice teaching'). This meaning is adopted particularly in Part II of the book. Practice learning, in both senses, typically refers to processes within professional qualifying education. Qualifying education is of particular importance in the socialisation of professional practitioners and in the accountability of the professions to the public and is hence the dominant focus of this book. However, as an educational process, practice learning clearly occurs at all levels of occupational learning on a continuum from pre-qualifying to post-qualifying education and includes learning which occurs in the work place, independent of any award level. Some of the contents of this book will have relevance across this wide range of contexts.

'Caring professions' are taken in this book to be those professions in which a human relationship has a relevance to the delivery of a service to the client. However, the degree of relevance varies considerably, for example, from the brief contacts of diagnostic radiography to the sustained and intimate relationships of some forms of nursing and social work. This is assumed to include not only all the health professions and social work but also teaching, considering the pastoral care element in compulsory education and the importance of care in early years 'educare' (Taylor and Woods 1998). This book tends to concentrate mostly on social work, nursing and teaching, since they are the professions of which I have most experience, although reference is made to several others.

The phrase 'human services' is often used to describe these professions and their activities, but this tends to neutralise the emotional dimension of these professions somewhat. Hugman (1991) makes a useful distinction between professions which care *for* and those which care *about* other people. It is in the professional activities which show care *for* others in practical and direct ways that feelings are most pronounced: what Allott and Robb (1998) refer to as 'emotional labour'. This emphasis on feelings which occur as part of a human relationship is also reflected in the processes of practice learning, which usually take place in the context of a fairly close working relationship and often focus on the affective aspects of professional work as well as the cognitive. This congruence between the affective processes of learning and the affective content of learning is one of the main reasons for concentrating on the caring professions in this book. However, other facets of practice learning are clearly relevant to professions other than the caring professions.

PART I

1 The Importance of Practice Learning

The position of practice learning, it would seem, is reasonably well established in the education of the caring professions. Students expect a substantial proportion of their learning to take place in practice settings, certainly in the UK although not consistently throughout Europe and the rest of the world (Doel and Shardlow 1996; NOPT 1998). Regulatory bodies seek to ensure that practice settings of sufficient quantity and quality are available. The image of practice learning as one of the 'twin pillars of professional education' (Walker et al. 1995; Evans 1987a) reinforces this impression of substance.

However, for a number of conceptual and practical reasons, this position is far from assured. Conceptually, the learning which takes place in Higher Education Institutions (HEIs) is often accorded greater prominence than that which occurs in practice placements, for reasons discussed below. Indeed, the first two directors of the Central Council for Education and Training in Social Work (CCETSW) are on record as conceiving the learning to take place primarily in an HEI and then 'put into practice' in the practice placement (Gardiner 1989). Practically, the problem of resourcing practice placements, particularly of releasing busy practitioners to supervise, teach and assess students, threatens to diminish the practice learning component of professional education. Early CCETSW drafts of revisions to the Diploma in Social Work in the mid-1990s speculated over the possibility of not having placements in the first of two years. Some social work education departments are now offering degrees without a practice component (Evans 1996).

This chapter, therefore, seeks to assert the important, perhaps central role, that practice learning plays in education for the caring professions, partly as a bulwark to prevent further erosion of practice learning in a climate of financial stringency but more proactively to persuade all those involved in professional education to place a high value on practice learning.

What is practice learning?

From the growing literature on practice learning in the caring professions, it is difficult to extract a clear and succinct understanding of the distinctive nature of practice learning. Much of the literature (Jarvis and Gibson 1985; Brooks and Sikes 1997; Bogo and Vayda 1987; Thompson et al. 1990) seeks to aid practitioners in taking on the mantle of teacher and assessor and hence, understandably, concentrates on the roles, responsibilities and tasks of practice teaching and assessing – 'teacher' or 'teaching' usually having prominence in the title. Where 'learning' features prominently in the title (Butler and Elliott 1986; ENB 1996) the nature of practice learning seems to be taken as self-evident. Shardlow and Doel, however, elevate learning above teaching in their title and furthermore provide a definition of 'practice learning': 'This term is used to refer to the learning that occurs whilst a student is on placement ... It refers to the context of learning in the practice agency' (1996: 5). For Shardlow and Doel, practice learning is thus defined by the setting in which it takes place. Whilst setting clearly has a major impact on the processes of learning, as will be discussed below, it is possible to delineate processes inherent in practice learning which are independent of setting.

Practice learning essentially takes the specific practice event as the central source of learning. The phrase 'practice event' implies work not only directly with, but also indirectly on behalf of, the client, both of which are intended to ensure delivery of a service. It also includes the cognitive and feeling aspects of that work as well as the behavioural. Eraut (1994) uses the phrases 'professional action' and 'professional performance' to describe this event. The practice event is 'central' in three main ways. It is the principal source of stimulation to learn. It is also central in that the learning has a primary aim of improving practice and not merely of benefiting the learner in some other, vague way. It is this aim which requires an emphasis on supervision and accountability and not just teaching and learning (see Chapter 5). Finally, the practice event can be seen as *chronologically* central: learning can take place *before* the event as part of the process of planning, *during* the event as part of the process of adjusting the practice to a changing or unexpected context and *after* the event, particularly as part of reflection (see Figure 1.1).

In order that learning can focus centrally on the practice event, it is helpful if it is in close proximity to that event. The importance of temporal and spatial proximity is stressed in the literature (Eraut et al. 1995) and supports

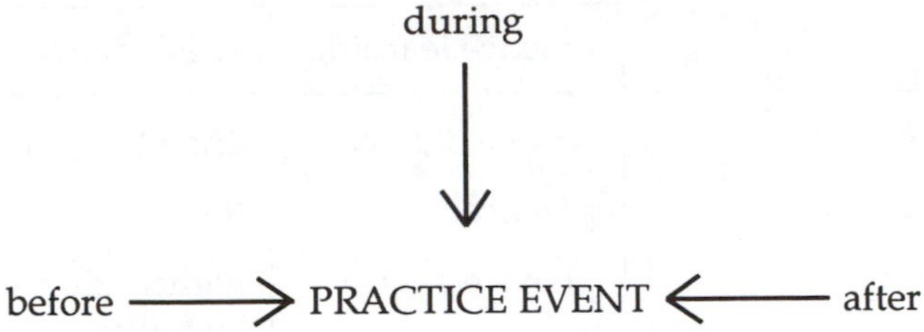

Figure 1.1 Practice learning

Shardlow and Doel's (1996) emphasis on setting. However, there is also a need for conceptual proximity, whereby the thinking about the event is at some point reasonably concrete and is not constantly at a high level of abstraction.

Proximity in both practical and conceptual senses is clearly a continuum. At one end of the continuum, learning during a specific practice event which focuses on the practical delivery of an effective service is clearly practice learning. At the other end, learning which precedes any practice events by many weeks and is at a high level of abstraction with no reference to specific practice events is clearly not practice learning. The latter is a form of learning which takes place in many front-loaded professional education courses. In between these two extremes, it is possible, particularly on concurrent college/placement courses, for a teacher in an academic setting to facilitate learning from a recent specific practice event or for one that will shortly occur. Under such circumstances, I would suggest, practice learning can take place in a setting other than the practice agency.

It is possible to contrast practice learning with academic learning – that is, learning designed to acquire theoretical knowledge and understanding (see Figure 1.2).

The different primary aims, sources and settings of practice and academic learning have already been discussed above. The two forms of learning are also differentiated in how they proceed to connect the primary source to a secondary source. Practice learning tends to move inductively from concrete practice to abstract theory while academic learning tends to move from abstract theory to concrete practice (see Chapter 4). However, it has to be said that the literature (Eraut et al. 1995) indicates how both practice and academic teachers are often reluctant to move away from their primary source of learning.

The final suggested criterion distinguishing between practice and academic learning is one of focus. Academic learning focuses mainly on the content of learning – the syllabus. In practice learning, the unpredictability

	Practice learning	Academic learning
Major aim	service delivery	knowledge acquisition
Primary source	practice	theory
Main setting	practice agency	higher education institution
Main process for relating theory and practice	inductive	deductive
Main focus	process	content

Figure 1.2 Practice learning and academic learning

of practice events renders the syllabus difficult to control, although the concept of 'practice curriculum' (Doel 1987; Phillipson et al. 1988) has sought to introduce a measure of control over the syllabus. Instead, the literature of practice learning seems to concentrate on key processes such as: the practice teaching session, the relationship between practice teacher and student and the support offered the student by agency staff. Gray and Gardiner (1989) make a similar distinction between content and process in their first two levels of learning.

This comparison between practice and academic learning has developed a form of archetype for the two which inevitably oversimplifies and distorts what takes place in both practice and academic settings. There are some academic teachers, for example, who attend carefully to the processes of learning and rather neglect the content while there are practice teachers with the reverse priorities. None the less, the analysis is a definition by contrast and is offered in an attempt to elucidate a number of characteristics of practice learning, in addition to the one identified by Shardlow and Doel (1996).

The importance of practice learning: the evidence

Research evidence would also seem to support the view that practice learning has an important role in the education of the caring professions. A number of consumer studies of social work education undertaken in the late 1970s and 1980s (Shaw and Walton 1978; Davies 1984; Coulshed 1986; Faiers 1987; Davies and Wright 1989) all suggested that social work qualifying students tended to put more into practice placements and gain more from them than from college-based learning. It would seem that the only study of that period which discovered a more equal pattern of student satisfaction was of Ruskin College social work students, who the researchers acknowledged have a particular motivation towards 'intellectual stimulation' and 'academic adventure' (Bryant and Noble 1988). Social work educational studies in the 1990s seem to eliminate this contrast in settings from their research designs, despite major changes in both settings. None the less, two major studies in the UK (Walker et al. 1995; Marsh and Triseliotis 1996) and one in Australia (Fernandez 1998) still report a high level of student satisfaction (over 80 per cent) in their practice placements.

Research into nurse and teacher education, likewise, does not seem specifically to contrast learning in academic and practice settings. However, a similar pattern of high levels of student satisfaction seems to emerge. Macleod Clark et al. (1996) report that a few months after qualifying from Project 2000 courses, nursing ex-students cited clinical placements as the single most influential aspect of their course. This seems consistent with their finding that during the second part of students' training, when more time is spent in the practice setting, students were finding mentors in the practice setting more influential in their understanding of nursing than academic teachers. Phillips et al. conclude similarly from their study of three and four-year nursing degree courses: 'Quality in clinical learning is central to the whole strategy of professional development' (1996: 79).

Following a review of two major studies of initial teacher education, Tomlinson (1989) advocates the value of an emphasis on the practice setting for student learning. Back and Booth (1992) surveyed opinions of both students and school teachers about practice teaching ('mentoring') and presented a generally enthusiastic response. Hill (1997a) compares the responses of articled teachers, whose training was predominantly in the school, with those of students who were trained predominantly in a higher education institution. Whilst the pattern of satisfaction with their education and training is mixed, one of the most conclusive findings was a considerably greater satisfaction on the part of the articled teachers with the emphasis on practice teaching and learning ('teaching practice') in their education.

These studies confirm an appreciation, particularly by students, of the major role learning in the practice setting plays in the education of a number of caring professions. This is not to deny the important contribution of learning in the academic setting, which is examined somewhat below (see Chapters 3 and 4). Moreover, it is likely, as Becher (1994a) suggests, that some caring professions, such as medicine, will tend to place greater emphasis on the academic setting, partly because of the more substantial physical science component in their education and partly due to the restrictions on students' practice caused by levels of risk. However, the academic institutions tend to be the leading partners in professional education and it is tempting for them to overplay the role of academic settings and underplay the role of practice settings in student learning. This overview seeks to redress such a tendency.

Towards a theory of practice learning

It is possible to identify a number of theoretical explanations for the key role that practice learning plays in students' educational experience. Three of these are intrinsic to the students: the fact that they are adults, the distinctive learning styles of caring professionals and the motivation of caring professionals to learn. Three explanations, however, are more a product of the context within which practice learning typically takes place: the opportunity to observe professional role models, the involvement in a community of practice and the opportunity to learn within a developing relationship. Some of these, such as adult learning and learning style theory, are discussed in depth in the literature on practice learning (Jarvis and Gibson 1985; Thompson et al. 1990; Shardlow and Doel 1996), although usually with the aim of informing the roles and tasks of practice teachers, rather than explaining the importance of practice learning. Others, such as situated learning and social learning theory, have as yet had less impact on practice learning. In this section, I shall briefly outline the main features of each area of theory and indicate how it tends to reinforce the important role played by practice learning in the education of the caring professions

Adult learning

A number of writers (Knowles 1978; Cross 1981; Rogers 1983) have stressed that adults tend to differ from children in both their reasons for learning and also the ways in which they learn best. Whereas children learn as part of their biological development, adults need to have a particular purpose to encourage learning. Knowles contrasts the assumptions of adult learning, 'andragogy', with those of traditional 'pedagogy' in Figure 1.3 below.

Knowles (1978) also emphasises the importance of mutuality and negotiation in adult learning while Rogers (1983) stresses the importance of active involvement.

Whilst there have been creative attempts to develop the curriculum in academic settings according to andragogical principles (Burgess and Jackson

	andragogy	pedagogy
self-concept	increasing self-directiveness	dependency
experience	learners are a rich resource	of little worth
readiness	developmental tasks of social roles	biological development, social pressure
time perspective	immediacy of application	postponed application
orientation to learning	problem-centred	subject-centred

Figure 1.3 Andragogy and pedagogy (from Knowles 1978: 110)

1990), there is a strong case that practice learning has inherently a greater orientation towards adult learning than much academic learning. Certainly, the centrality of the practice event gives an opportunity for active involvement and for the immediate application of learning to a specific task required as part of the professional role. Humphries (1988) usefully criticises the notion of mutuality in adult learning on the grounds of the real power differentials which exist between teacher and learner. None the less, it is likely that the student is more able to negotiate an educational experience which meets their learning needs in the one-to-one relationship of much

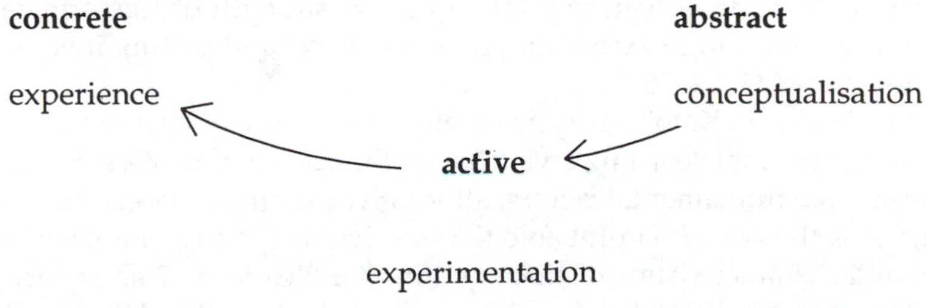

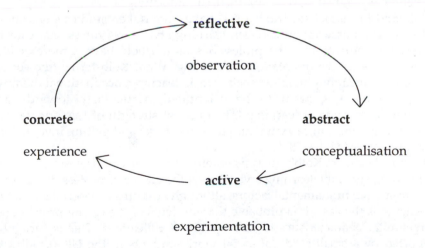

Figure 1.4 Kolb's learning cycle

practice learning than in the one-to-many context of much academic learning.

Learning style research

Learning style theory recognises the different approaches which individuals can take towards learning. The literature suggests a range of different learning styles. Smith (1984), for example, outlines 17 inventories which seek to discover different aspects of individuals' learning style. Two learning style theories (Kolb 1984; Witkin 1950) seem particularly relevant to the processes of practice learning.

Kolb's (1984) analysis of learning style is based upon a breakdown of the experiential learning process into four phases: concrete experience, reflective observation, abstract conceptualisation and active experimentation. These four are based on two axes, concrete/abstract and reflective/active and are sequentially connected in a learning cycle (see Figure 1.4).

Four basic learning styles stem from different strengths within this learning cycle. Thus, the convergent learning style relies mainly on abstract conceptualisation and active experimentation; the divergent learning style relies on the opposite strengths of concrete experience and reflective observation; the assimilative learning style relies predominantly on abstract conceptualisation and reflective observation, and the accommodative learning style relies on concrete experience and active experimentation. Honey and Mumford (1995) use different terms to describe the same styles, respectively: pragmatist, reflector, theorist and activist.

Kolb and his associates (Kolb 1984) have undertaken studies suggesting that there is an association between learning style and professional career. The studies indicate that the professions as a whole have a more active rather than reflective orientation to learning. What Kolb terms 'the social professions', including nursing, social work, teaching, occupational therapy and physiotherapy, seem to be orientated particularly towards an accommodative style of learning: 'The greatest strength of this orientation lies in doing things, in carrying out plans and tasks and getting involved in new experiences' (1984: 78).

It is not clear from Kolb's analysis whether the choice of profession shapes the learning style, the learning style shapes the choice of profession or both stem from more fundamental factors, although he seems to assert the former. Whichever is the case, it is probable that students of the caring professions share similar characteristics to their qualified colleagues. This is certainly supported by a small study of social work students in the UK (Bradbury 1984). Cavanagh et al. (1995) in a rather larger study of nursing students in the UK also found a dominant focus on learning from concrete experience, with a slightly increased frequency for the divergent style. Practice learning is, therefore, likely to have much to offer students in these professions, which academic learning may not.

Witkin (1950) proposes an alternative analysis of learning style based upon the one dimension of what he calls 'field-dependency'. People with a field-independent style of learning tend to perceive elements independent of their context, to be analytical, whereas field-dependent learners see situations as a whole, with individual elements in context. Tennant (1997) suggests a number of associations with a field-dependent style: relying on a social frame of reference in formulating beliefs and attitudes, and greater awareness of and sensitivity to other people. He also cites Witkin et al.'s (1977) comprehensive analysis of the educational implications of this style and their suggestion that field-dependency is more likely to be characteristic of people who work 'with people', for example in the caring professions. It is probable, therefore, that students in the caring professions will tend to value the more contextualised learning which takes place in the practice setting, rather than the more analytical, less applied learning of the academic setting.

Motivation to learn

Maslow (1954) suggests that the highest level in a hierarchy of motivational forces is the need to realise to the full our potential as people (self-actualisation). Professional people, Johnson (1972) suggests, tend to share an altruistic commitment to the service of others, a 'collectivity-orientation' rather than a 'self-orientation'. In the case of the caring professions, the commitment is to show concern for other people through the performance of relevant tasks (Hugman 1991). It could be argued, therefore, that people in the caring professions achieve considerable self-actualisation in the performance of tasks which show concern for others and that this achievement constitutes a major motivation to learn. If this is the case, it is likely that learning in the practice setting, where students are able to achieve this professional goal by caring directly for clients, will harness that motivation well.

The evidence of the value of live supervision (see Chapter 6), when learning is most closely associated with the delivery of an effective service, both in time and in its practical orientation, suggests this is indeed the case. Students speak of the powerful impact which suggestions for effective practice have had when they have been floundering as to the next course of action and the client was still present, requiring a service.

Social learning

Social learning theory differs from much behaviourist theory in its concentration on human learning in social contexts. Bandura (1977) suggests that an important process of learning in social situations is observational learning. Learning takes place by observing a model and later imitating that behaviour. Observational learning can be intentional or unintentional and comprises four major subprocesses: attending to the model, retaining the observed behaviour, reproducing the observed behaviour and motivation to reproduce the behaviour.

This approach to learning can be criticised (see Chapter 6) for its emphasis on an uncritical acceptance of an 'expert's' way of practising and the need to make sometimes confidential and private practice accessible to others. An emphasis on evaluative reflection and informed consent can mitigate these weaknesses in observational learning. It is clearly a mode of learning which is particularly relevant to the practice setting, where not only the practice teacher but also other colleagues in the setting can model effective practice. Its importance in practice learning is alluded to in some of the literature (Shardlow and Doel 1996; Brooks and Sikes 1997). Whilst staff in academic settings can be models for some desired behaviours, they are less likely to model professional practice.

Situated learning

This theory of learning has been developed in recent years (Lave and Wenger 1991; Chaiklin and Lave 1993) on the basis of a number of studies of apprenticeship, particularly in the US. It emphasises the importance of the work context in learning, stressing the participation of the individual within a whole community of practice. Learning is integral to the processes of work, and cannot, it is claimed, be de-contextualised or abstracted. Lave and Wenger (1991) also suggest how situated learning can be enhanced, that is, when the relationships between learners and experienced workers are not strongly asymmetrical and when the learners have less responsibility and demands on their time.

This body of theory asserts strongly that the practice setting is the only legitimate arena for occupational learning. It is of significance, however, that their studies were focused on apprenticeships and did not include the more complex forms of professional education, including the role of the higher education institution. The extreme view that learning cannot be de-contextualised or abstracted poses a challenge not only to the teaching of the theory of professional practice but also to the concept of transfer of learning from one work setting to another, inherent in most professional educational designs. Nevertheless, the emphasis on the whole community of practice in the workplace finds an important echo in the concern, particularly by professional regulatory bodies, to ensure quality throughout the workplace and not simply within the practice teacher (see Chapter 2).

Relationship and learning

Both social learning and situated learning theories suggest that particular aspects of relationships can assist the processes of learning. There is also some evidence that relationships have a more general connection with the processes of learning. Winnicott (1971) explores how early family relationships provide a context within which a child can learn and develop. Other writers suggest how similar processes of transference and counter-transference (Salzberger-Wittenberg et al. 1983) and emotional 'holding' (Hinds 1998) influence learning in adults. Rogers (1983) suggests that the relationship between the learner and the person who facilitates their learning has a major impact on learning at all ages, in particular through three personal characteristics of the facilitator: realness or genuineness, prizing or accepting, and empathic understanding.

One of the processes of practice learning which contrasts most with academic learning is that it usually takes place in the context of a developing and often quite close relationship between the student and the practice teacher. The literature of practice learning attests to the importance of this relationship in the learning process (Jarvis and Gibson 1985; Walker et al. 1995; Brooks and Sikes 1997). Whilst students can form important relationships with staff in academic settings, particularly personal tutors, much of their learning will be facilitated by a range of staff with whom they develop little relationship, due to modular structures and specialist lecturer inputs. The consistent relationship of the student and practice teacher can, thus, provide a coherence to learning in the practice setting which the academic setting can often lack.

The exposition of these six areas of theory provides some explanation of why practice learning is much valued by students within the education of the caring professions. While this brief analysis does not seek to compare the archetypes of practice and academic learning within each area, it is clear that practice learning more readily offers a number of advantages than academic learning. In addition to explaining the important role of practice learning in student learning, it is hoped that these areas, particularly those which have hitherto received less attention in the literature, may assist in the development of an understanding about practice learning.

The history of practice learning in the education of caring professions

Bines (1992) postulates a progression of three phases in the development of professional education: the pre-technocratic, the technocratic and the post-technocratic. This delineation of phases owes much to Schon's (1983, 1987) critique of the over-emphasis by higher education institutions on the scientific component in professional education

> The professional schools of the modern research University are premised on technical rationality. Their normative curriculum still embodies the idea that practical competence becomes professional when its instrumental problem solving is grounded in systematic, preferably scientific knowledge. (Schon 1987: 8)

The pre-technocratic phase, Bines suggests, was that of the apprenticeship, when professional education occurred largely in the workplace. The pupil-teacher arrangement (Taylor 1969) and the Nightingale nurse training (O'Brien and Watson 1993) of the second half of the nineteenth century are good examples of this model, which stretches back to the mediaeval craft guilds (see Chapter 6). This was a phase in which experience in the practice setting undoubtedly dominated. However, the practice learning potential of that experience came increasingly under attack. Murphy and Torrance (1988) suggest that apprenticeships were increasingly seen as time-serving, with learning not maximised. Whatever learning did occur was seen as conservative, lacking critical appraisal of current practices or scope for innovation (Payne 1977). This critique has some validity but also, unfortunately, obscures some of the strengths of apprenticeship, notably the potential for modelling and learning within a relationship, which will be re-examined later in Chapter 6.

Bines (1992) suggests that the second, technocratic, phase has emphasised the systematic knowledge base which is contributed by the traditional academic disciplines. As Schon (1987) suggests, pure sciences take precedence over applied sciences and applied sciences over the distinctive knowledge bases of the professions. It is possible to see the development of this phase as largely due to a process of professionalisation whereby 'an occupation passes through predictable stages of organisational change, the end-state of which is professionalism' (Johnson 1972: 22). Professionalism can be seen as an ideal state wherein occupations are accorded rewards and privileges by society in exchange for socially valued expertise and service.

Most commentators (Johnson 1972; Watson 1992; Eraut 1994) agree that the establishment of a systematic, sometimes exclusive, knowledge base for professional practice is one of several key criteria in developing towards the ideal of professionalism. This knowledge base is typically gained through a publicly authenticated and visible educational process, which has increasingly been associated with HEIs and has attracted their awards. Nursing and teaching have both progressed from apprenticeship through specialist colleges to HEIs and the award of their diplomas and degrees. Social work has similarly, in recent years, raised the academic level of its award to diploma and, in some cases, degree level. Becher (1994b) suggests that many other countries in Europe, North America and Australasia have followed a similar pattern for a range of caring professions.

The key role of HEIs in this second phase has undoubtedly contributed significantly to the expansion and promulgation of the professional knowledge base (Lorenz 1998). However, those institutions have a strong territorial interest 'in the "sale" and "production" of knowledge as a commodity' (Eraut 1994: 14). This tight grip on the territory of knowledge may well have had an adverse effect on the development of practice learning during this phase. Practice learning typically takes place outside the HEI and often concentrates on the acquisition of skills and more applied, often local, knowledge. This renders it somewhat marginal to the HEIs and of lower status.

Bines (1992) suggests that in the early 1990s the second phase was still the dominant model. Since this suggestion, progression towards a third, post-technocratic, phase has continued to accelerate. The main characteristic of this third emergent phase in the development of professional education, Bines (1992) suggests, is an emphasis on competence. This emphasis can be seen to have its roots in the dominant climate of economic ambition of the past two decades, which would seem to have led to a new vocationalism throughout education:

> Countries facing major challenges to restructure, to re-energise to achieve greater competitive strengths, of which Britain is a notable example, have turned to education and training as instruments of social and economic reform. The extent to which education is vocationalised becomes a new measure of economic and social performance. (Skilbeck et al. 1994: 23)

This emphasis on producing a more economically effective workforce has fostered the rise of competence-based education and training and modes of work-based learning and assessment (NCVQ 1986). Despite broad and detailed criticism of this approach to professional education (see Chapter 7), three of the recent national reports on education (Fryer 1997; Dearing 1997; Kennedy 1998) have emphasised the importance of work-based learning and have found strong support from Central Government (DfEE 1998a, 1998b). This political emphasis on learning and assessment in the workplace and the vocational relevance of education has clearly reaffirmed the potential importance of practice learning within the education for the caring professions. The renewed focus on practice learning in this third phase, however, does not constitute a return to phase one. The progression is illustrated in Figure 1.5.

Phase	pre-technocratic	technocratic	post-technocratic
Dominant influence	practice setting	academic setting	partnership

Figure 1.5 The progression of practice learning in professional education

Partnership between practice agencies and higher education institutions is a dominant feature of this third phase and is now enshrined, to a greater or lesser degree, in the requirements of many regulatory bodies. However, 'partnership' has been something of a 'buzz' word over the past decade, which can obscure real conflicts between the participants in a partnership over aims, structures and processes (Evans and Kearney 1996). These conflicts have perhaps been most pronounced in initial teacher education over the extent to which the educational programme should be based in schools or higher education institutions (Williams 1994a; Cohen et al. 1996; Baty 1997a, 1997b). Social work education, on the other hand, has presided over a reduction of the practice learning component from a half to a little over one-third of the total programme (26 out of 72 weeks) with very little debate, let alone conflict. At times, too, the reality of partnership can fall well below the rhetoric, when some higher education institutions persist in retaining maximum control over most aspects of their professional programmes. Moreover, the focus on the two major types of institution seeking to work together can easily reduce the voice of another important partner who lacks institutional power - the student.

There have been substantial gains for practice learning within this period of partnership, particularly as higher education institutions have lent their support to the development of the practice learning component, notably in helping develop the knowledge base of practice learning and in training and supporting practice teachers.

However, much of this activity can also be seen from an alternative perspective of territorial advance. The vested interest of higher education institutions in the production and sale of knowledge, noted by Eraut (1994), can be seen to have taken them onto the relatively fertile and under-cultivated soil of practice learning. It would seem that academic staff have generated most of the research and much of the existing literature on practice learning. They also would appear to have a strong role in training practice teachers, despite the existence of experienced practice teachers with a well-developed knowledge of practice learning, both theoretical and practical. The practice curriculum (Doel 1987; Phillipson et al. 1988) has often been a means for higher education institutions to control, through the validation process, much of the content of learning in the practice setting. Even reflective practice learning, a well-established mode in the practice setting, is becoming part of this territorial advance of higher education institutions (Elliott, 1997a). In the face of this advance, the key questions those most actively involved in practice learning might ask themselves include: how much does the involvement of higher education institutions advance the cause of practice learning in professional education? What would be the gains and losses if practice teachers and other practice learning staff were to take more control over these processes?

The position of practice learning in this post-technocratic, or competence-based phase, in professional education would seem to be seriously weakened by one major factor – its marginality. Within the practice agency, the dominant focus is on service delivery. Training and staff development of all kinds usually attracts a very small proportion of the total agency budget, of which practice learning in qualifying education will then attract only a share. Practice teachers in many caring professions have to put the pressing demands of clients, both in terms of quantity and urgency, above those of students (Weinstein, 1992; Davies et al. 1995). Within the higher education institutions, increasing demands for income generation through research and other activities lessen the focus on educational programmes as a whole and certainly on the practice learning component of those programmes, an area over which they have little control and for which they are not deemed fully accountable.

This marginal position of practice learning would seem to contribute to two other difficulties: resourcing and disorganisation. The resourcing of practice learning is a widespread difficulty throughout the caring professions. It shows itself, particularly, at the level of educational programmes in a shortage of placements and at the level of the individual practice teacher in problems of workload relief. One study of practice learning (HCPEF, 1997) suggests that resourcing difficulties are widespread throughout the ten caring professions surveyed, including nursing, social work and several of the professions allied to medicine. Teaching has encountered similar difficulties (Dunne et al. 1996). Other professions, however, would seem to be rather better funded, notably medicine with high levels of per capita funding to teaching hospitals (Richards 1995) and GP clinics (Evans 1997).

The problem of resourcing can be seen to derive from a number of other factors, mainly stemming from the essential marginality of practice learning. First, several of the caring professions have been slow to make explicit the actual costs of practice learning, particularly of releasing staff from service delivery tasks to attend to student learning. Two factors inhibit this costing: the political undesirability of revealing a level of funding which is not directly providing a service to the public and the difficulty in weighing costs against the benefits of students, including their contribution to service delivery and to staff recruitment and retention and their general positive impact in the practice agency. Social work moved somewhat beyond this position when making its case to Central Government for three years' training (CCETSW 1987), although most social work agencies continued not to include the full costs of practice learning in their budgets (Thompson and Marsh 1991). The NHS (1996), however, would seem still not to have moved beyond this initial position.

A further resource difficulty stems from the fact that some of the resources available to higher education institutions for practice learning, for example through the additional level of LEA mandatory grant for courses with placements and under the Pattern agreement for schools (Tysome 1994), would seem not to have consistently reached their intended goal. Moreover, in social work education, particularly, tension between central and local government has restricted the availability of ear-marked central government funds for practice learning.

Twenty years ago, a study of practice learning in social work (Syson and Baginsky 1981) revealed a relatively high level of disorganisation in many aspects of practice learning, including the selection, training and support of practice teachers and the provision of placements. The number of recommendations about the organisation of practice learning made by the latest large-scale survey (Walker et al. 1995) suggests that the situation has not changed sufficiently. Similar difficulties are experienced within other caring professions. Such difficulties frequently stem from a lack of resource: where dedicated staff within the practice agency or the higher education institution are employed to organise the practice learning experience, it often leads to greater efficiency. Repeated reductions to local government funding have contributed to a decrease in such posts for social work education, for example, and a consequent diminishing of organisation.

Even in a political climate of support for work-based learning and assessment, it can be seen, therefore, that practice learning is not thriving as it might or even as it deserves, if the above arguments for its important role are valid. There are two directions which those interested in advancing the cause of practice learning might turn in seeking some way forward - the protection and promotion of professional regulatory bodies and the development of the position of practice learning by those involved within it.

The role of the professional regulatory bodies in practice learning

The discussion in this section is based largely on three comparative studies of practice learning in the caring professions, all conducted independently and at approximately the same time. Franks (1997) interviewed a small number of staff involved in practice learning in her local area, while the Health and Care Professions Education Forum (HCPEF 1997) and Evans (1997) used a combination of documentary evidence from the professional regulatory bodies and interviews with key people in the professions. All three included nursing, social work, occupational therapy and physiotherapy in their sample. The HCPEF (1997) additionally included six other professions allied to medicine - dietetics, orthoptics, clinical psychology, radiography, speech and language therapy, chiropody and podiatry - while Evans (1997) included teaching, policing, radiography and general practice in both the UK and New Zealand. Between them, the three studies cover 14 different caring professions. All three studies investigated the three main areas which constitute the broader territory of practice learning: practice teaching, practice learning in the practice setting and practice assessment. It must be recognised, however, that all caring professions periodically review their regulatory frameworks: one such review is currently, at the time of writing, under way for the professions allied to medicine. The picture presented therefore is cross-sectional during 1997 only.

Practice teaching

Nearly all the professions investigated stipulate criteria for the selection of their practice teachers. Most common are the requirements that practice teachers should be qualified in that profession and have had at least one year's experience since qualification. Teaching, however, makes a somewhat vaguer specification, that 'all those involved in training understand their roles and responsibilities and have the knowledge, understanding and skills needed to discharge these competently' (DfEE 1997: 46).

CCETSW (1995) includes a variant on this theme by allowing certain exceptions, such as people from another caring profession with a professional qualification or people with no professional qualification but with at least four years' experience in social work practice. The key issue in the selection of practice teachers would seem to be how much should the practice teacher, who contributes considerably to the socialisation and selection of new students into a profession, themselves be qualified and experienced in that profession, an issue of both fitness for purpose and professional self-regulation.

The training of practice teachers is considered important by all the professions consulted, particularly in view of the importance of practice assessment. However, only a minority *insist* upon training, including nursing, orthoptics and general practice. The HCPEF (1997) suggest that the CCETSW also require practice teacher training, but although they recommend two levels of training, with an expressed intention of requiring the more rigorous level at a future time, they do not, in fact, insist on any at the time of writing. The training offered varies considerably in terms of length from one or two days to the more extensive training offered to some community nurses, social workers and police. It also varies in terms of process. Most are theoretical with only a minority (social work and community nursing) including a practice learning component. Moreover only a minority, including nursing and social work, assess the outcome of the training or make a recognised professional award. There is also a growth in inter-professional training for practice teaching, particularly crucial for new programmes which qualify students jointly and simultaneously for nursing and social work (Weinstein 1994).

One key issue concerns the effectiveness of practice teacher training. Two surveys of social work education (Walker et al. 1995; Marsh and Triseliotis 1996) reported little impact on practice teachers' effectiveness made by the more extensive training which leads to the CCETSW's Practice Teaching Award (CCETSW 1996a). However, the data collection periods for both these studies were quite soon after the start of this CCETSW initiative and neither focused on this area in depth. It would seem important to discover the most cost-effective length of practice teacher training and whether effective practice teacher training requires a practice learning component, which a consideration of congruence between course design and content would suggest.

There is also a variable pattern of financial rewards offered to practice teachers to undertake the task. In some professions the practice teacher is rewarded, in some the practice agency and in some neither. General practice would seem particularly well rewarded, with a standard fee of £3,500 per student in the UK and NZ$7,000 plus the trainee's earnings from patient consultations in New Zealand. In both countries the income goes to the GP training practice in which the trainer has a financial interest. Nevertheless, there are clearly intrinsic rewards in being a practice teacher. Walker et al. (1995) indicate an unusually high level of satisfaction among social work practice teachers (89 per cent), derived particularly from the pleasure of providing learning experiences for able, hard-working and committed students. Enhanced promotion prospects can also be an additional extrinsic reward. For many practice teachers, however, the task is an increasingly onerous one, given mounting pressures for increased service delivery from the agency and for more rigorous assessment from the educational programme. Given that most of these professions come under the jurisdiction of the same central government department – the Department of Health – the recommendation from the HCPEF (1997) study for greater equity in financial rewards between the caring professions would seem a reasonable one.

There is a clear recognition in the literature of the problem of workload relief for practice teachers (Weinstein 1992; Davies et al. 1995). There would seem to be a similar pattern of variability across professions in providing workload relief, with an apparent dearth of strategies and little regulation. CCETSW (1991) included a requirement within its ambitious attempt to approve agencies for practice learning, but only a minority of social work agencies underwent this process and its impact on workloads would seem, from Walker et al.'s findings (1995), to have been minimal. Clearly, effective practice teaching and assessment relies on people in the practice setting having the time to undertake these tasks. However, the service delivery workload continues to grow. Caring professions could perhaps work together with the Department of Health to develop coherent strategies. One suggested strategy (Evans 1996) is for funding to follow students into placements to purchase a level of workforce replacement, as potentially occurs, for example, in teaching hospitals.

Many practice teachers benefit from support while undertaking this activity, particularly when they have had little or no prior experience or when they are encountering major difficulties, for example, when a student is failing (Evans 1990a). Several professions organise peer group support for practice teachers, sometimes within larger agencies (Clapton 1989), sometimes organised by higher education institution and sometimes at a more regional level. CCETSW (1991) included this among its criteria for agency approval, with limited impact. It is to be hoped that as the caring professions recognise the need for support for practitioners over the demands of service delivery, they will also recognise and provide for the increasing demands of practice teaching.

Practice learning in the agency setting

All the professions investigated require students to spend some time in practice settings for learning and assessment. As with other areas, there is considerable variation between the professions in the length, proportion and pattern of placements. Many of the professions seem to rely on a number of block placements in different settings, thus gaining experience of a range of different client groups. Whilst this helps prepare students for a variety of later posts, as befits generic professional qualifications, it places both the learning and assessment in relatively short placements under considerable time pressure. The minimum assessed nurse placement, for example, lasts for only four weeks, while the minimum 50-day social work placement is also criticised for being too short. This brevity runs counter to the expressed desire of students for longer placements (Walker et al. 1995; Macleod Clark et al. 1996; Hislop et al. 1996). Moreover, while block placements have the advantage of complete immersion in one setting, they also have the disadvantage of potentially hindering the integration of theory and practice, a factor which has influenced initial teacher education to move from block to concurrent structures (Furlong 1997). The proportion of time spent in placements during the course varies considerably, according to the HCPEF (1997), from 12 per cent to 60 per cent, while GPs in New Zealand spend 80 per cent of their time in placement (Evans 1997). Perhaps the most alarming feature of these variations is that they seem to be based on custom, hunch and preference rather than any more reliable source of understanding.

All the professions involved in the studies support the notion of monitoring the quality of the practice learning setting. However, there is again considerable variation over two main factors: whether this occurs before or after a student is placed there; and whether the monitoring is performed internally to the programme or externally. It would seem to jeopardise the experience of individual students, perhaps even their career prospects, if placements are agreed without prior monitoring. However, the evidence is that only a minority of professions insist on this and then often only as part of a general initial validation process rather than monitoring specific settings. CCETSW's agency approval process would seem to have limited impact in this area.

Several, though not all, professions insist on regular monitoring of the practice learning setting once the programme is underway. The tendency is for monitoring to be undertaken internally (by the programme itself) according to the programmes' own criteria and executed by the higher education institution. There is clearly a value in internal monitoring, but it would seem sensible for practice agencies to be engaged actively in this process, as well as or instead of the higher education institution, as part of their own quality assurance systems (Thompson and Marsh 1991), since they are best placed to respond to the information generated. A few professions ensure external monitoring either through professional regulatory bodies or the inspectorate, as is the case in teaching and the police. General practice in both the UK and New Zealand would appear particularly rigorous in its monitoring system, with external monitoring both before student placement and regularly thereafter, using external criteria. Even if external inspection is not feasible, it would seem appropriate that external statutory bodies seek to clarify the minimum requirements in this area, including timing and monitoring criteria, which individual programmes then implement internally.

The general practice monitoring criteria specify three key features in the learning environment: good practice in the setting, appropriate learning opportunities for the student and appropriate equipment for the student. Several other professions focus on these features but vary in how they do so. Notable variations include: the quality of other staff in the practice setting (nursing and general practice), the requirement that students are supernumerary (nursing), the value base operated in the setting (social work) and the availability of theoretical material in the practice setting (general practice). Even in such a concrete area as equipment, there can be a lack of clarity over what is required or, in some professions, no requirement at all. One monitoring criterion omitted by nearly all professions is that of learning opportunities for staff. A student is more likely to learn if placed within a culture of learning, certainly if the situated learning thesis is correct (see above).

Practice assessment

There does not appear to be any one factor in the assessment of practice which is required by all the professions studied. Most require an assessment of practice separate from theory and conducted by someone in the practice setting. Sometimes, the criteria for practice assessment were set by the regulatory body at a national level with an expectation that they would be developed and applied by individual programmes. Consistent with Bines' thesis (1992), however, there seems to be a movement towards the development of national competences or standards to which all courses must adhere. Some (teaching and social work) are fully competence based, while it is the intention of others such as general practice and the police to develop a competence framework.

Specific methods of assessing practice are not required by all the professions, although most specify observation and a report from the practice teacher/assessor. A few professions are developing the use of portfolios, although only nursing would seem to require them at the time of writing. Video recording offers considerable potential to make professional practice accessible outside the practice setting to a second internal assessor or an external assessor (Evans and Langley 1996). However, while social work allows this as an alternative to some observation, only general practice in the UK seems to require it. Other important assessment methods such as client feedback, evaluation of practice outcomes and student self-assessment, the advantages of which are discussed in Chapter 7, are apparently rarely required (HCPEF, 1997).

Conclusion

The considerable variation between the 14 caring professions in nearly all the areas studied is scarcely surprising, given their different histories and the current differences in how they function. These differences include: the nature and size of their work settings, the range of client needs to which they attend, the proportion of work time spent in direct contact with clients, the level of qualified staff within the workforce, the funding base, and the relationship between professional regulatory bodies and the inspectorate. None the less, it would seem that some of the variation, at least, emanates from differences in the determination of the regulatory bodies to ensure a reasonable quality of practice learning experience for every student seeking to enter their profession.

The regulatory framework of practice learning by general practice in both the UK and New Zealand (The Royal New Zealand College of General Practitioners 1997; Anglia Regional General Practice Education Committee 1996) would seem to be particularly robust. Both practice teacher and practice setting are externally inspected using well-articulated external criteria before any student is placed with them as well as at regular intervals subsequently. Practice teachers receive regular support in that activity and practice assessment has progressed to make use of new information technology. The main deficiencies would seem to be in the minimal time required for initial practice teacher training and the criteria for practice assessment. While some of these strengths can be explained by the generally higher levels of funding attracted by medicine than many other caring professions and the fact that GP training is specialist, post-graduate training, the quality of the general practice setting, as opposed to the hospital, has been clearly identified as a significant contributor to the effectiveness of the training and considerable effort has been invested over many years in ensuring it.

Initial teacher education (DfEE 1997), on the other hand, would seem to have developed a somewhat sparse regulatory framework governing quality in the practice setting. There seem to be no clear requirements for practice teacher selection, training or support. Although there is a requirement for internal monitoring of the practice setting, rather imprecise national criteria are offered for this and there seems to be little attempt to ensure a satisfactory learning environment before any student is placed within it. Whilst copious standards are set, against which students should be assessed, there are no standards for the methods by which this should occur in the practice setting. Unlike most professions, teaching does not even delineate practice learning as a specific area for regulation.

This position can be explained in part by the understandable assumptions that schools should be appropriate settings for learning and that trained teachers should be able to teach students as well as pupils. However, schools can be as busy as any other work setting with sometimes poor practice occurring, thus giving little time for reflection and inadequate models for learning. Moreover, teaching and assessing adults in professional competence is somewhat distant from teaching and assessing children in more academic achievements. The considerable pressure from Central Government to clarify the content of initial teacher education may also have deflected attention away from the processes which are so essential to achieve that content. Moreover, the Ofsted inspection regimen would seem to offer a potential second arm in monitoring the quality of schools as practice learning settings. However, these provisos would seem not to exonerate the Teacher Training Agency, in conjunction with the Department for Education and Employment, from the responsibility to attempt to regulate practice learning more rigorously.

It would seem advisable that the bodies regulating the education of the caring professions seek to inform themselves as fully as possible about what constitutes an effective practice learning experience, including its relationship with the academic learning experience. This could be done partly through effective collaboration with other regulatory bodies, discovering different strategies to resolve common difficulties, and partly to undertake research into the practice learning component, possibly in conjunction with other similar professions. The Health and Care Professions Education Forum would seem to be proceeding in both these directions, although their research project (HCPEF 1997) did not attempt to investigate the effectiveness of any of the processes surveyed.

In the absence of such information and still seeking to discharge their responsibility for quality, it might be better if the regulatory bodies sought to ensure reasonable minimum standards rather than strive for the optimum. Practice teacher training provides a clear example. The 150 hours' training required for the CCETSW's Practice Teaching Award and the two-year part-time course, including 30 days' theory, required for ENB registration as a Community Practice Teacher would seem perhaps more than a satisfactory minimum, whereas the one- or two-day courses available to many professions, including some social workers, would seem less than satisfactory. Furthermore, the effect of severe resource constraints is such that for every practice teacher receiving more than the minimum training, another practice teacher in the same or another profession will receive less than the minimum, possibly nothing. Optimal training schemes, however, can still be encouraged through the dissemination of exemplars.

There is also a strong argument (Evans 1996) that the caring professions should attend to quantity in practice learning provision at least as much as quality. A larger pool of practice settings would give students greater choice in meeting their learning needs, rather than being sent to the only available placement. Moreover, students clearly seek longer placements (Walker et al. 1995; Macleod Clark et al. 1996; Hislop et al. 1996). The brevity of some placements imposes an unrealistic expectation on both students and practice teachers of settling into a new learning experience, performing well, being assessed and leaving, all within very few weeks: an expectation which is hopefully not to be transferred to the students' later employment career.

Developing practice learning from within

Whilst it is reasonable to expect professional regulatory bodies to seek to ensure an effective practice learning experience for all students, there are inevitable limitations to their influence. The people most able to influence practice learning might well be those most actively involved in it. Clapton (1996) exhorts others involved in practice learning to follow his example in effecting improvements: 'Practice teachers need not only to effect a consciousness shift, but also to start to campaign. Practice teachers should make known the value of what they do and what they offer, but first they have to recognise this themselves' (Clapton 1996: 13).

Perhaps the single most effective way for practice teachers and others to improve the position of practice learning is to develop and promulgate its knowledge, skills and values. Just as one of the traditional routes to professionalism is through the published knowledge base, practice learning can, as Bridge (1996) suggests, improve its own position through its knowledge base. Wilkin (1997) has, for example, collated an impressive list of recent publications on practice learning in initial teacher education; other professions, including social work, have seen a similar burgeoning in recent years. As indicated above, much of this literature is written by academics, sometimes with the assistance of practice teachers as research subjects or as subsidiary writers. None the less, experienced practice teachers themselves are at the cutting edge of developing practice learning in a changing workplace and yet are often reticent to write these experiences down for others. They could enhance their own contribution to the knowledge base by co-writing with experienced academic writers, by undertaking action research as part of higher degrees, or by gaining writing experience through newsletters, such as the National Organisation for Practice Teaching's, or in appropriate journals. The recently formed *Journal of Practice Teaching in Social Work and Health* is, at the time of writing, seeking to develop policies which will encourage the involvement of busy practitioner/practice teachers in all its activities.

Many practice teachers prefer to influence others in person rather than through the written word. The importance of training and support for practice teachers has been emphasised above. Experienced practice teachers are well placed to provide these services for their less experienced colleagues. This can be informally within work-based networks but also by asserting their readiness to contribute to the formal training courses which are often run and staffed by academic institutions.

A developing sense of professional competence in practice teaching is, however, not in itself sufficient. Practice agencies need to be persuaded of their essential role in providing an appropriate learning environment for students. Practice teachers can combine to form a persuasive voice within their agency to achieve aims such as securing proper workload relief, appropriate rewards for the task and agency ownership of practice learning. Some groups of practice teachers in social service agencies have collectively achieved some successes with the first two aims. Thompson and Marsh's study (1991) made an eloquent case for social care agencies to own the responsibility to manage the practice learning environment as they manage other services. However, it is likely to take a ground-swell from those involved in practice learning to alert managers in the settings of all the caring professions to this need.

One effective strategy to raise awareness and levels of competence within practice agencies is to create a specialist post in that area. Practice learning has had a history of such posts in many agencies, for example, clinical teachers in nursing and radiography, and student unit supervisors in social work. Curnock (1975) traces the history of social work student units from tentative beginnings in the 1930s to a position of considerable strength at the time that she wrote. This continued to grow, with the support of CCETSW, until well into the 1990s, when financial pressures and some apparently unhelpful decisions by CCETSW (Joint University Council, Social Work

Education Committee 1997) accelerated their rapid decrease. Other professions have found similar difficulties in sustaining such posts. However, one specialist post-holder, through their competence and commitment, can help sustain the part-time activity of many other practice teachers. Furthermore, specialist practice learning posts can also help foster a general climate of learning throughout the workplace, for example, by assisting in staff continuing professional development and contributing to the work-based learning and assessment of students at a range of different levels. Non-specialist practice teachers are well placed within the practice agency collectively to voice this potential.

As well as working together within agencies, practice teachers can also work towards collective action outside their agency. Community practice teachers in nursing, for example, have created some networks which lobby local courses. Perhaps the most well-established national forum for practice learning is the National Organisation for Practice Teaching (NOPT), established in the late 1970s through the initiative of committed social work student unit supervisors to promote the position of practice learning in professional education. It has subsequently been expanding to meet the needs of non-specialist practice teachers and others interested in practice learning at both pre-qualifying and post-qualifying levels. Whilst its current focus is on practice learning in social work, the growth of inter-professional practice teacher training could herald a further expansion into other professions. Alternatively, other professions may seek to develop comparable organisations promoting the position of practice learning in professional education.

PART II

Practice learning

2 Learning in the Practice Setting

Learning and teaching

In the previous section, the term 'practice learning' has been used mainly to denote all those processes which help students learn from and for practice. In the next three sections, however, it is necessary to distinguish the three processes – learning, teaching and assessing. There is of course considerable overlap between these three. All teachers hope that teaching leads to learning. The literature on assessment (Rowntree 1987; Evans 1990a) suggests that its key functions include facilitating learning and informing teaching. Nevertheless, they are separated hereafter as the focus shifts from a more global appreciation of the position of learning for and from practice within professional education as a whole to a more detailed exploration of specific processes.

It is particularly important to differentiate learning from teaching. The simple difference is that teaching requires at least two participants, a teacher and a learner, whereas learning requires only one, a learner. Furthermore, even when a teacher is teaching, it does not guarantee that learning takes place. Figure 2.1 shows a simplified matrix with four principal possibilities.

Possibility 1 is the one which many practice teachers and students like to think is occurring much of the time. However it can never be taken for granted. Both parties need to check whether learning has in fact occurred, often by assessment/self-assessment on subsequent occasions. The considerable advantage practice teaching enjoys over academic teaching is that there are usually many more one-to-one contacts between teacher and learner in which to assess learning. Moreover, these contacts are usually two-way, involving dialogue. Academic teachers are often reliant on just one

	teacher teaches	teacher does not teach
learner learns	1	2
learner does not learn	3	4

Figure 2.1 Teaching and learning possibilities

assignment to assess learning, which is usually one-way and often excludes significant dialogue, to explore the student's learning.

Over a period of ten years as a full-time practice teacher, I came to a humbler appreciation of the extent to which Possibility 2 occurs and Possibility 1 does not. In a practice setting, there are considerable opportunities to learn from a well-constructed workload and from other staff, without explicit teaching from the designated practice teacher. However, a number of influences can minimise these opportunities. The higher education institution may seek to liaise with only one person in the practice setting and focus on that person as the major source of learning. The agency team may be overwhelmed with service delivery pressures and wish the designated practice teacher to retain sole responsibility for the student's learning and assessment while they are on placement in that team. Practice teachers may be experiencing for the first time the pleasure and responsibility of helping another person develop and may wish, or feel obliged, to keep this experience largely to themselves. The important issue here is that the practice teacher may not be the main source of student learning on a placement and has some responsibility to organise other learning opportunities beyond their own availability. Furthermore, the student may not wish them to be their main source of learning, for example when student and practice teacher have significant differences in approach.

Possibility 3 can be a major source of concern, particularly when the practice teacher is unaware that the student has not yet grasped an issue of accountability or risk which has been taught to them. The onus remains on the practice teacher to check whether important learning of this nature has in fact taken place. Most placements also benefit from Possibility 4, when both practice teacher and student are 'off duty' and can diversify somewhat within their relationship. Indirectly, the development of a more rounded, human, and therefore reciprocal, relationship between them may foster some of the trust and respect which can lead to future learning.

The distinction between teaching and learning can be sustained to a greater or lesser extent according to the paradigm of teaching espoused.

Teaching can be construed as something which is 'done' by a teacher to a learner. This is typified by the sight of the teacher speaking and the learner listening: the teacher possesses some information which is imparted to the learner in a process called 'teaching'. The emphasis is on the *content* of what the teacher says. What the learner does with the information thereafter is of lesser concern. This may well be because of an assumption that the teacher has kept their part of the bargain by transmitting the content: what the student then does with the content is up to them. One student used a culinary analogy, 'the jug and mug' method, to describe this paradigm, where the pun on the word 'mug' seems particularly apt.

The principal danger of this paradigm is that it is often the one which both practice teacher and student have most absorbed during their formative experiences in primary and secondary education and hence it is comparatively easy to slip into again. The change of situation from a classroom to a practice agency may provide some safeguard against this modelling, but it may not entirely. The student does not primarily need to hear the practice teacher's journey towards being an effective practitioner: they need to undertake their own. A further danger rests in the assessment of practice teachers, for example on practice teacher courses, when it can be tempting to focus on the activities of the practice teacher which might lead most directly to learning, without first ascertaining whether learning has in fact occurred, or second, recognising activities which more indirectly lead to learning.

An alternative paradigm of teaching concentrates on the processes within the learner. What the teacher does is of interest only to the extent that it encourages helpful processes within the learner. Thus, the teacher is 'facilitating' the student's learning (Rogers 1983), that is, 'structuring' or 'managing' a context within which learning can take place (Peters 1977; Dearing 1997). Its pedigree is lengthy, since Socrates' teaching through questioning was of a similar orientation. The emphasis here is on the *process* the teacher adopts in order to encourage learning. A contrasting culinary metaphor might be of adjusting the heat to bring a pan of milk to the boil. The content is primarily within the learner: the teacher merely seeks to encourage its optimal development. In linguistic terms, the first paradigm involves a transitive verb where something is done to an object, while the second paradigm involves a causative verb which concentrates on what is caused by the action.

The attraction of this second paradigm is that it focuses full attention on the learner and their learning: all eyes are on the milk boiling. The teacher by contrast has a more humble even peripheral role: 'Such a vision puts students at the centre of the learning and teaching process and places new challenges and demands upon teachers' (Dearing 1997: 114).

No practice teacher adopting this paradigm will be content to sit back having done their part. They will be constantly enquiring: whether the student understands or not, what they wish to learn and how they can best learn it. Their stock sentence is a question, not a statement. Moreover, the teacher is seeking to help the student learn how to learn so that learning will continue beyond the presence of the teacher. Heron's (1975) description of 'oppressive over-teach' is a salutary reminder for all teachers of the dangers of slipping too far into the first paradigm.

Doel (1993) helpfully cautions against totally rejecting the first paradigm in favour of the second. There are many times when a student simply needs to be told: when they are totally ignorant on a topic or extremely anxious about undertaking an unfamiliar activity. Gardiner's (1989) delineation of three levels of learning suggests that the reliance on an external authority becomes superseded by a higher, self-determining level. However, I would argue that everyone, no matter how experienced, knowledgeable and wise they are, will, in certain circumstances, need to be told by someone else who knows the answer.

The learning itself can be conceptualised in different ways. The influence of behaviourism in learning theory has promoted the conceptualisation of learning as 'permanent changes in behaviour' (Gross 1996: 155), although psychologists have increasingly emphasised cognitive as well as behavioural change. These two strands would seem to underpin the understanding in the Dearing report (1997) of learning as both an intellectual and practical activity. Other commentators (McGill and Beaty 1995; Rogers 1983) would suggest that learning also involves affective change, a dimension of particular interest for those involved in the caring professions. Rogers (1983) goes further to advocate a totally holistic view of learning, incorporating these three with other dimensions.

A number of implications arise for practice teachers from this three-fold conceptualisation of learning. The current emphasis on assessing students by observing their behaviour runs the risk of omitting to investigate exactly what they are thinking when they behave in a certain way. The student may or may not behave as they intended and similarly may approve or disapprove of what they did. Practice teachers in the caring professions also need to encourage and monitor how students feel towards their clients. More often than not, this is to encourage students to become somewhat less emotionally involved in their clients' lives and adopt a certain emotional distance, both for their own and the client's sake. Sometimes, however, it is necessary to encourage students to be more empathic towards their clients. One student who had suffered considerably as a child needed careful help, even in their early thirties, in opening themselves to the different distress suffered by the children they worked with.

The 'onion' model of practice learning

Practice learning can be seen as a number of concentric layers, with the most crucial at the centre and the least crucial on the periphery (see Figure 2.2).

The student

It has been suggested above that the student is at the heart of the learning process. The student is an active participant in practice learning, continuously construing meaning for all the practice events they experience, whether directly or indirectly. It can never be assumed that their meanings are the same as the practice teacher's or any other worker's in that practice

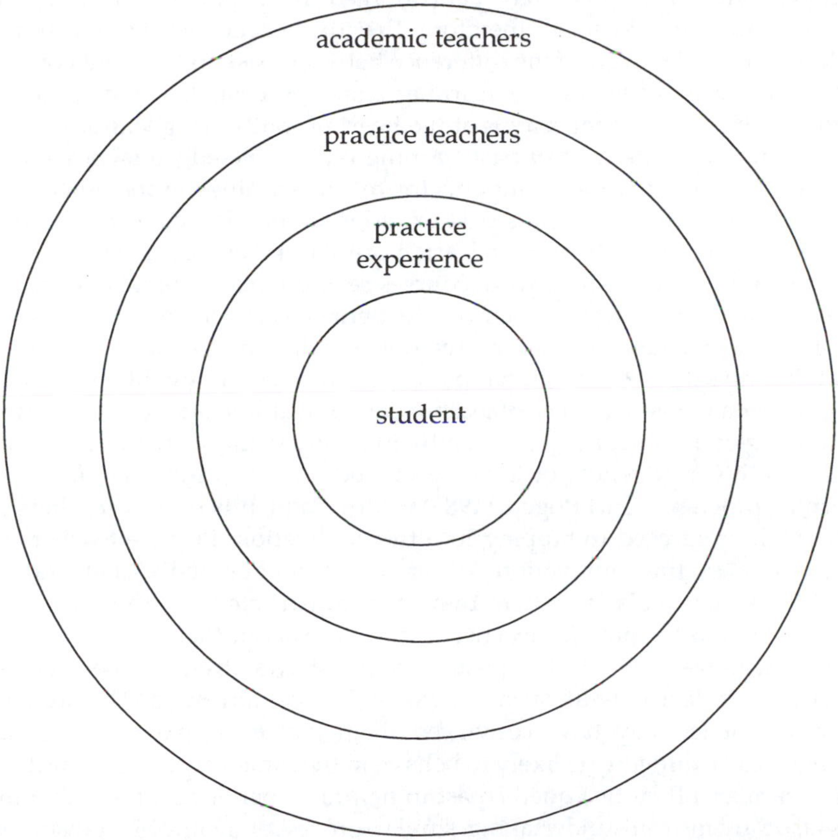

Figure 2.2 The 'onion' model of practice learning

setting. Some commentators (Rogers 1983; Doel 1993) contrast this active, participatory role with a more passive, receptive role which is traditionally allocated to learners.

The adult student brings with them a vast range of prior learning from their personal and occupational life which forms the baseline for subsequent practice learning. This baseline includes an existing repertoire of knowledge, skills, values and aptitudes, some of which will be relevant to the current practice setting. The practice teacher will need to discover this repertoire, partly in order not to belittle or patronise the student by attempting to teach them what they already know and partly to help them transfer that learning to a new context. Many teachers talk of the unavoidability or even desirability of students 'unlearning' past learning or feeling 'deskilled'. However, it can be argued that past learning has occurred in a different context, one which may have encouraged poor practice or unhelpful approaches. It would seem, therefore, that the practice teacher's task is to help the student recognise the difference between past and present contexts, rather than simply to dismiss learning from the past. This recognition of difference as well as similarity is at the heart of transferring learning.

The student's repertoire of past learning is a double-edged sword. On the one hand, it can provide an impetus for future learning: on the other, it can inhibit learning. The student's past experience of caring or being cared for will often form the motivation to learn more about that sort of experience for other people. Several social work courses set students an initial assignment, which asks them to explore their own experience of social need and usually explores major sources of their motivation to help others in need. I am aware that for myself a rather unhappy experience of family life as a child stimulated a whole sequence of learning about children and families, both in qualifying education and subsequently in family therapy practice. Similarly, past positive experiences of learning can become a springboard for future learning processes. Carl Rogers (1983) writes eloquently of how teachers can either fail or succeed in tapping into this motivation. Practice teachers can often harness this motivation within the student's individual learning objectives, particularly when they are constructed as the placement progresses and the practice teacher learns more about them.

The negative side of this past learning shows itself in the student's reluctance to learn about certain areas and in certain ways. The student's past experience may have convinced them that everyone with a certain mental health difficulty is likely to behave in the same way as their aunt who has a similar difficulty. Equally, past unhelpful experiences of learning may dissuade them from undertaking similar processes again. Megginson and Boydell (1979) outline four types of block to effective learning within the student - perceptual, cultural, emotional and intellectual - which the practice teacher needs to be alert to and prepared to overcome with the help of the student.

The practice experience

It is often motivation from the student's prior experience which leads them into professional education. Once within the educational programme, it is the engagement with the practice experience which then provides a major motivation to learn (see Chapter 1). The practice experience has three main aspects: the direct work with clients, the indirect work on behalf of clients and the participation within a community of practice (Chaiklin and Lave 1993). Some students, as well as some experienced practitioners, consider the direct work with clients to be the most central aspect of practice. However, preparing for the encounter with the client and working with others, within that work setting and the wider welfare network, to deliver a better service are all key aspects of practice, the more so as professional tasks and institutional infrastructures increase in complexity.

Once practice teachers perceive the central position of the practice experience, they can recognise the importance of realising that potential to the full (see Chapter 6). The choice and monitoring of the workload assumes considerable significance. They will also recognise the value of ensuring that the student is thoroughly accepted by other staff within the setting – practitioners, managers and administrators – thus achieving an authentic experience of working in a practice setting, albeit with the protection of not being a full-time employee but 'supernumerary', as nurse education terms it.

The practice teachers

Here I include all members of staff in the practice setting who consciously take it upon themselves to help the student learn about the practice experience and not just the one person who is usually designated as the student's main practice teacher. The designated practice teacher's particular contribution will be examined in detail in Chapter 5. This conscious effort to help the student to understand what is going on in the practice setting and to perform appropriately is beyond that contribution which they make to the student's learning simply by accepting them within the setting, namely by constituting part of the student's practice experience. Many staff will make this extra effort willingly: some will not. Even those who are willing, will not always be able to venture beyond being part of the practice experience, as the pressures of service delivery overwhelm them. In one of the student units where I worked, most of the staff valued the regular through-put of students and contributed considerably to their learning, though there was one long-standing member of staff who was unwilling for some years to make such a contribution. However, they could not escape being part of the practice experience, since students would notice that practitioner's attitude towards many aspects of the work, including students, and learn how it had arisen.

This teaching by any member of the practice agency staff, including the designated practice teacher, draws most of its potency from its proximity to the practice experience: in time, in place and in ethos. Students can usually turn to some member of staff to meet their intellectual, emotional or practical learning needs just when they need to, often immediately before or after a significant event, such as an encounter with a client or a meeting with staff. Sometimes they can temporarily leave the encounter with the client to seek support or advice from a nearby staff member before returning better equipped. This learning can be considerably facilitated by ensuring that students are accommodated close to some other staff whilst on placement, although these do not have to include the designated practice teacher. Pressure on accommodation in work settings has at times led to students being placed in the 'broom cupboard' or other places rather remote from staff, which can render such learning less accessible. Likewise, practice settings which accommodate numbers of students at a time sometimes have an invidious choice between placing students all together, thus enhancing the opportunity for peer learning and a critical perspective on agency practice, or dispersing them amongst the agency staff and encouraging this proximal learning from staff.

Practice teachers, in this broader sense, are also close to the practice experience in that they understand its agency context. They know how the setting operates, they can empathise with its frustrations and they are for the most part in sympathy with its purposes and ethos. Often they have had similar experiences to the student's, sometimes with the same client. For this reason, they are able quickly to tune in to much of what the student is experiencing, with the proviso that the student's experience is not exactly their own, because of how the student construes it.

The academic teachers

The very advantage which practice teachers enjoy in contributing to students' practice learning can also have its disadvantage. Practice teachers can often be too close to the practice experience. They can have lost a critical perspective on agency practices which they might once have held, particularly when they first joined the agency and had not been fully assimilated into its culture. They may be over-tolerant of poor practice on the part of the student, because they identify with the student's position.

Academic teachers, on the other hand, are more distant from the practice experience and this distance can become a strength in practice learning. They can encourage a realistic critique of the student's practice, of other staff's practice within the agency and of the functions which the agency fulfils within the welfare network (Hill 1997a). They are also in a position to step back from the setting and make connections from beyond its boundaries. These connections need not be limited to theoretical and research material, often seen as the major focus of academic teaching, but can also include other practice settings. Conceptualising the similarities and dissimilarities between practice settings is an important aspect of transfer of learning. From this more distant position, academic teachers can therefore encourage students in three crucial learning skills, based on practice: critical evaluation, relating theory and practice, and transfer of learning.

Full-time practice teachers can often combine the advantages of both the closer and the more distant positions. They are often employed by the practice agency and hence have an understanding of and some sympathy with its culture and practices. Yet their educational role keeps them slightly removed from day-to-day service delivery and often takes them out of the agency into other settings, both practice and academic. The delicate balance between the two positions is emphasised when the practice teachers are jointly appointed by practice and academic institutions (Jack 1986; Bastian and Blyth 1989), although in a climate of increased managerial accountability and financial stringency, such appointments seem unfortunately to be diminishing.

A detailed exploration of how academic teachers can develop practice learning from their perspective is not within the province of this book. However, practice teachers need to be aware of this potential in academic teachers and to seek to harness it when working in partnership with their academic colleagues.

The placement as a learning experience

As discussed in Chapter 1, the placement is clearly recognised as making a major contribution to student learning for the caring professions. It would not be oversimplifying excessively to suggest that professional regulatory bodies recognise it as *a* major contribution, while students consider it to be *the* major contribution. Within this contribution, however, it is difficult to determine which aspects have the greatest influence on learning.

There is some evidence of the major role exercised by the designated practice teacher. In social work education, Fernandez (1998) suggests that satisfaction with the practice teacher is the best predictor of satisfaction with the placement as a whole, while Walker et al. (1995) similarly report that two of the three factors which correlate with placement satisfaction are characteristics of the practice teacher. Macleod Clark et al. (1996) also report how nurse students found the practice teacher to be the single most influential person, although they do not associate this finding with their other finding of the pre-eminence of clinical placements in the students' educational programme. The importance of the practice teacher is also indicated in the suggestion that one of the main factors leading to placement difficulties or breakdown is the relationship between the student and the practice teacher (Burgess et al. 1998). None the less, there is clear evidence, including from the above studies, that other aspects of the placement make a significant contribution to learning. This section explores many of these other aspects.

Establishing a learning culture in the practice setting

A growing understanding of the economic impact of an accelerating rate of change in society has contributed significantly to an increasing recognition of the importance of learning at all levels. Dearing (1997) writes of the 'learning society', while at a lower level Senge (1990) explores the implications of the 'learning organisation'. It would seem self-evident that students are more likely to learn in practice agencies which have a more general commitment to learning as an organisation, so that their service delivery will continue to develop in response to internal and external change.

Senge defines a learning organisation as 'an organisation in which people at all levels are, collectively, continually enhancing their capacity to create things they really want to create' (O'Neil, 1995: 20). This definition somewhat underplays the real differences of power between employers, employees and consumers to determine organisational priorities. However, it does indicate the importance of collectivity within the organisation, which can be encouraged particularly by communication. Honey and Mumford (1996) and the English National Board (1994) similarly emphasise the importance of organisational communication in all directions - upwards, downwards and sideways. Organisational capacity is further enhanced partly through a commitment to the more formal training and supervisory processes which Sawdon and Sawdon (1987) and the English National Board (1994) consider so important in a practice learning setting and partly through an acceptance that the organisation has a need to develop and an openness to new ideas which can help that development occur.

These broad approaches within a practice agency clearly provide an environment from which students can benefit. The emphasis on the whole organisation is congruent with the emphasis on total agency commitment to practice learning in qualifying education, not only by professional regulatory bodies such as CCETSW (1996b) but also within the professional literature on teacher education (Wilkin 1992; Brooks and Sikes 1997). Within the practice agency, it is helpful if staff from different sections discuss good practice together, if managers listen to workers and workers listen to clients and if supervision and critical reflection are experienced by all staff. A 'climate of learning' (Elliott 1990) such as this is likely to respond easily to the learning needs of students. My own experience of working within a post-graduate teaching hospital, where students from a number of professions were easily accommodated within a staff programme of seminars, shared practice and visiting specialists established for staff to learn, has contrasted considerably with my predominant experience of social service departments, which infrequently encourage the sharing of practice or critical debate about practice and the professional literature and within which practice teachers, students and their teams often have to establish a form of learning 'counter-culture'.

The approach of the practice agency to students, in particular, is likely to provide the springboard from which the students' learning will progress. Davies et al. (1995) reported a tension within the practice settings of nurse education between service delivery and student learning, which is experienced similarly by other professions. When client demands increase, do the needs of students recede? Certainly, it would be difficult to sustain a placement if clients were thought to be damaged by the presence of students. In this sense, practice agencies have a primary duty, often enshrined in statute, to their clients. Most students and practice teachers are quite clear about this. However, it would not seem disingenuous to suggest that the more the agency develops a climate of learning in its overall approach to service delivery, the easier it is to offer the student an opportunity to learn which is similar to that offered to other staff. Where, for example, supervision is highly valued by staff, it is unlikely to be interrupted by anything other than urgent client need, whether the supervisee is a full-time employee or a student.

It is useful if the practice agency articulates its expectations of the student's role and function while they are working there. This is particularly the case in agencies for whom student placements are more frequent, usually large statutory settings such as hospitals and social service departments but also some small voluntary agencies contribute greatly to the pool of placements in social work education. At one level, this involves a fundamental consideration of 'studenthood' within the agency, that is, the extent to which students are members of the establishment like other staff with the same or similar working hours, uniforms, ID cards, police checks on safety, and so on, and the extent to which they are different from other staff, including how clients will know them and any restrictions on the work students can undertake. These are important considerations if the authenticity of the practice experience is to be maintained and if the aim of professional education is to produce practitioners who can perform a wide range of tasks once qualified.

One such issue of 'studenthood' which seems to receive insufficient attention is the extent to which the agency's clients are given any choice in whether a student or a paid employee works with them. If clients choose a student there are certain possible consequences: they may be asked to contribute to the student's learning or assessment, and the work is likely to be closely monitored by the practice teacher, including being observed. In addition, the student may be less experienced than a staff member but may bring more time and enthusiasm to the task. Any one of these consequences may be perceived as an advantage or a disadvantage by a given client. It would seem important to allow clients to choose, particularly when there is a significant difference between the choices. If it is not possible to give a choice, however, clients would need to be informed first of the reasons for the lack of choice, and second of the circumstances under which they can have access to a paid employee, or even a student if that is their preferred option.

In the two student units where I have worked, staff were familiar with the pattern of student placements and developed more informal expectations of students. Certain aspects of work would be orientated towards the forthcoming presence of students in the agency: students would be eagerly anticipated as co-leaders of groups or as leaders of various projects, including research, which paid staff might be prevented from undertaking due to busy workloads.

Thus far the emphasis has been on how a student can learn from the agency. However, learning can often be a much more reciprocal process. Many staff, both practitioners and managers, attest to the value of students being in their agency: their interest, enthusiasm, new ideas and creative approaches, as well as their questioning and challenging of existing practices and procedures and their contact with higher education institutions. Fernandez (1998) reports how students are disappointed when this reciprocity does not occur and agencies are unable to respond to their ideas. However, I have known a number of social work teams who routinely integrate into the placement student feedback to the agency about how the agency functions. This can occur by whatever process most benefits both student and agency, for example, feedback at a team meeting, anonymous questionnaire, brief written report. In such processes, students contribute to the development of a learning climate as well as benefiting from one.

This reciprocal learning process also occurs over issues of practice.

Sometimes students enter a placement with experience of work which is largely unfamiliar to most of the staff. One social work student was able to take their prior experience of voluntary work with adolescents into a drugs advisory service and help develop services for this client group. They subsequently took the experience of working with adolescent drug abusers into a second placement within a youth justice setting, with similarly creative results. Such exchanges reinforce the student's status as an adult learner with useful past experience to contribute.

However, it is the reverse process – the agency's practice which is likely to influence the student's learning – which concerns many of the professional regulatory bodies, including for initial teacher education, nurse and social work education, and GP training. The requirement in teaching (DfEE 1997) is a general one that good models of teaching should be available to students but without further specification. Other professions make a few more specific requirements: for rigorous monitoring of practice standards in nursing and general practice (ENB 1997; Anglia Regional General Practice Education Committee 1996); for upholding the value base of the profession in nursing and social work (ENB 1997; CCETSW 1991, 1996b); for management, recording and communication within the GP practice setting (Anglia Regional General Practice Education Committee 1996). Fernandez (1998) reports how strongly students respond to the practice around them, both when it is of a high standard and when they find it unacceptable. Experiences of other countries where practice is generally developing from a low level, for example, social work in eastern Europe (Doel and Shardlow 1996), also highlight the importance of the standard of practice which surrounds students whilst they are learning.

Practice teachers and students are not well placed to influence the overall standard of practice within the practice setting, certainly as individuals, although collectively they may wield more influence. As individuals, however, they can take pains to discover which workers within the practice agency demonstrate good practice within a given speciality. Usually the agency grapevine can convey this information. However, it is a function of how much staff share practice, either through evaluative discussion or co-work, that it will be more widely known whom to approach for good practice in which specialism. In this way a learning climate generates further contexts for learning.

A final way in which the practice agency can develop a climate for student learning is by offering a context within which the designated practice teacher can fulfil their role effectively. Nearly 20 years ago, Syson and Baginsky (1981) reported that the selection, recruitment, support and training for practice teachers in social work education was somewhat haphazard. Now, despite urgings from those involved in practice learning

(Sawdon and Sawdon 1987), and the CCETSW's subsequent attempts (1991, 1996b) to ensure consistency and quality, this inconsistency, as reported in the latest major survey of social work practice learning (Walker et al. 1995), is far from resolved. Davies et al. (1995) report a similar situation in community nurse education.

Much of the responsibility for the necessary systems rests on agency upper managers and the higher education institutions who rely on the placements for the students they enrol. However, the marginal position practice learning occupies for both these constituencies, as has been explored above in Chapter 1, mitigates against such systems being widely established. However, we shall explore below the contribution other key people within the practice agency can make to improve the position of practice teachers.

Choice of placement

Following the principle of student-centredness in practice learning, it would seem important that students exercise some choice in their placements. Walker et al. (1995) indicate how lack of student choice predicts decreased satisfaction with social work placements and that quite high proportions of students (40 per cent in their main study) felt they had no choice.

The value of choice would seem unquestionable in caring professions which currently stress the importance of empowering their clients. Two studies of social work placements in Australia and New Zealand respectively (Cooper 1995; Walker 1996) emphasise the anti-oppressive value of choice in placement selection, particularly for ethnic minority students in those countries. De Souza (1992) describes how some black students have been knowingly sent to racist placements and might wish to choose placements which provide an environment which does not alienate them through its physical environment, resources and materials, staffing, equal opportunity policies and in generally not validating the black student's experience. Phillips (1998) makes similar claims on behalf of the disabled students she investigated and similar claims could be made for all students whose structural position places them in a position of disadvantage which the placement agency can either ameliorate or exacerbate.

The other main reason for student choice in placements is the increased possibility of meeting the students' individual learning needs (Walker et al. 1995), since students are usually more aware of their learning needs than anyone else. These are mainly determined by comparing their past learning achievements and gaps with the desired outcomes of the educational programme. All students in the caring professions are adult learners with significant past experiences to build on. Even professions which recruit heavily from school-leavers, such as nursing and teaching, may find their students are becoming older and more experienced in a climate which encourages life-long learning (Dearing 1997). However, individual learning needs can also derive from a consideration of the future: what sort of posts the student hopes to achieve once qualified. In social work education, the second and usually longer placement is often for the specialism in which the student anticipates seeking employment and will frequently be a subject of much student lobbying.

Student choice of placement is constrained by a number of factors, some helpful, some unhelpful. Perhaps the least helpful is the chronic shortage of placements which is affecting most of the caring professions in many countries (Weinstein 1992; Davies et al. 1995; Cooper 1995; Dunne et al. 1996; Rogers, 1996). A restricted pool of placements inevitably leads to reduced choice, no matter how well staff juggle that pool to meet specific student needs. Furthermore, the current emphasis on ensuring the *quality* of placements in all the caring professions, laudable in itself, nevertheless places an additional restriction on the *quantity* of placements available. If student satisfaction is related to choice and choice implies sufficient quantity, there is clearly a difficult balance to be achieved between quantity and quality in the provision of placements (Evans 1996).

The process of matching students and placements can involve a complex consideration of many perspectives, of which the student is only one, albeit an important one. Staff at the higher education institution, particularly the personal tutor if such a system is operated, will gain an impression through time, including from the student's performance in earlier placement(s), of what their developing learning needs are. Staff in the practice agency will be aware of what the placement has to offer, what characteristics they are looking for in a student and whether other internal factors such as staff shortages or workload pressures even preclude a placement altogether. Agency staff may, for example, specify some relevant prior experience before the student can be placed in a highly specialist agency. Some placements serving far-flung rural communities may require that any student owns a car.

It is also possible that the agency's clients, particularly in smaller closed units, may also wish to have a say in whether a student should be placed with them and if so whether the student should have certain characteristics. Davies et al.'s (1995) study revealed that a high proportion of complaints in community nursing placements concerned male students providing care to women. Similarly in social work, the clients may determine the choice of student, for example, women's refuges will only accept women students and some agencies undertaking developmental work with ethnic minorities will require students of a corresponding ethnic minority.

The process of matching students and placements can be considerably facilitated by an initial exchange of information between the three key participants - student, placement and practice teacher - before the placement is agreed. Student and practice teacher profiles will be explored further below. The agency profile could include information such as:

- The philosophy, aims and ethos of the agency
- The range of work on offer, including projects as well as client groups
- The range of approaches and methods available
- Other activities students might participate in
- Equal opportunity and other relevant policies
- Basic details of size and composition of staff and clients
- Resources available for student use.

Profiles of this sort are particularly useful for more unusual placements of which the student may have had no prior knowledge, or for smaller settings within large statutory organisations, for example, specialist units within hospitals, social service departments and schools, which may have a distinctive approach in delivering a service.

Workload

The historical shift in the caring professions towards a greater focus on teaching in the practice setting and away from simply providing students with an opportunity to practise has been outlined above in Chapter 1. One corollary of this shift is that much of the current literature tends to emphasise the processes of teaching (Jarvis and Gibson 1985; Shardlow and Doel 1996; Brooks and Sikes 1997) with relatively little focus on the practice which becomes the springboard for learning and teaching. In a book first written in the 1970s, Danbury (1986) devotes a chapter to what she calls 'selecting cases'. Such a focus supports the prioritisation of the 'onion model' of practice learning presented above, in which the practice experience, particularly the practice with clients, has a more central role in learning than the encounters with the practice teacher. Fernandez (1998) also indicates the importance students attach to the tasks which they undertake on placement.

There are a number of factors which can influence the workload which a student receives on a placement. Hopefully, the student's educational needs will be at the top of this list. The student's individual learning objectives can usefully be matched against the practice opportunities which will assist in achieving them, often in a written placement agreement (see Chapter 5). Increasingly, the student will need to demonstrate key competences or standards for assessment purposes (CCETSW 1995; DfEE 1997), for which appropriate practice opportunities will be required. Sometimes, learning or assessment needs may not be met within that particular agency setting, but can easily be arranged within another setting, thus creating what can be called a 'complex', 'integrated ' or 'network' placement (see Chapter 5).

The actual pacing of an appropriate workload for a student is a complex process. Some academic social work tutors have asked me 'How many cases will the student have on the placement?' As my confidence in practice teaching grew, I would politely refrain from answering this question. One of the imponderables towards the start of a placement is the student's style and rate of learning. Some students are keen to get involved with any number of new experiences, what Honey and Mumford (1986) call 'activists' or Kolb (1984) 'accommodators', while others like to reflect at length on what they have been doing or even on what they have been observing other practitioners do, before they become involved themselves. Some students will learn all they need from one performance of a particular task, while others may take a number of attempts before they achieve a similar level of learning.

Another related factor influencing the work a student undertakes is the student's response to stress and anxiety. The literature on stress (Hanson 1986; Davies, 1998) suggests that there is an optimal level of arousal for effective functioning which is neither too little nor too much. Without sufficient challenge a student will become bored and less able to make use of what learning is available. On the other hand, too much anxiety can become a block to learning. Two social work students started their placements suffering from considerable anxiety. One was a black student who had been told they had barely passed their previous placement, apparently due to racist judgements; the other was very young with no prior experience of social work whatsoever. Both students required a much slower rate of exposure to practice than most, as they gradually gained confidence, not only in their ability but also in the opinion of those around them.

Vygotsky (Crain 1992) posits the notion of the 'zone of proximal development', that is, the extent to which a given child is able to be encouraged to develop beyond their current ability. A similar approach may be useful when choosing the next practice task for a student: if it is to extend the student, it should not extend them too far. Some tasks, on the other hand, will be chosen to reinforce prior learning.

Rather than talking of numbers of cases or tasks for a student, it seems more useful to think of the level of stress generated by the workload in terms of some form of reverse U-curve (see Figure 2.3).

In this analysis stress is caused by a combination of the number of tasks/cases and their severity. The stress level builds up slowly as the placement progresses but diminishes as the placement draws to a close. In this way the stress derived specifically from the workload dovetails with other stresses inherent in beginning and ending a placement (see Chapter 5).

Whilst discussion has so far concentrated on characteristics of the student

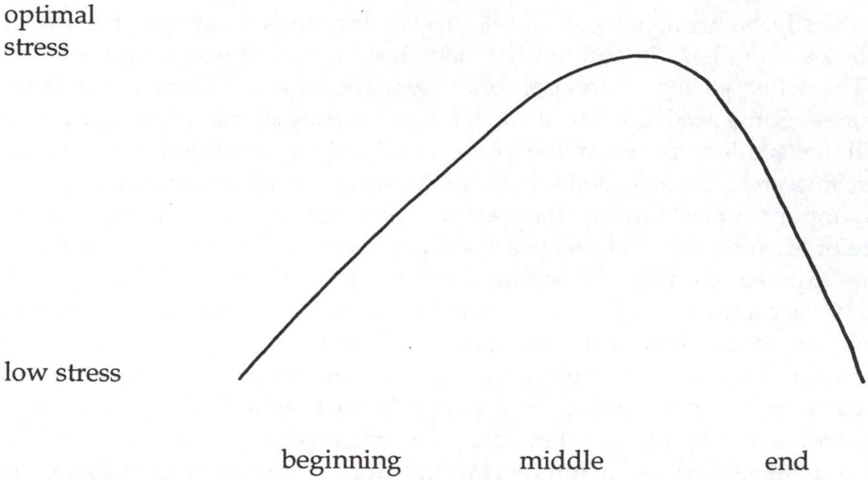

Figure 2.3 Pacing the workload through the placement

which determine the workload, there are also many influential factors within the practice agency. One factor which cannot be totally predicted is the learning potential of a given practice task. What may seem like a straightforward piece of work may develop into something which absorbs much of the student's time and energy and stretches their capacity to the full. Another young social work student embarked upon a reasonably well-defined piece of work on a child care difficulty which subsequently escalated into the child being accommodated by the local authority. A second student became involved in this increasingly complex and demanding piece of work which provided them both with a major source of learning throughout the placement. Sometimes, of course, the work proves more than a given student can cope with and the work needs to be reallocated to another worker to ensure an appropriate service.

When a student steps into a placement, they encounter a number of assumptions and expectations about what students can and cannot do, what they should and should not do. Often there are 'student cases' or 'student tasks' which are traditionally given to the student because of their simplicity or low risk, particularly in settings where students are continually on placement. These attitudes can deny certain clients of any continuity of service, as they are handed from one student to another, or of any service from a more experienced worker. These attitudes can also fail to take into account the vast range of ability which differentiates students. Experienced students may need to start with more complex, demanding pieces of work.

Many people in professional education make the mistake, in my view, of equating student experience with the length of time in qualifying education: any student in their second or third year is seen as necessarily more experienced than a first-year student. However, this can negate the experience of adult learners prior to the qualifying programme, particularly in those caring professions for which this is common.

There may be staff in the practice agency who find it difficult to allocate full responsibility for a piece of work to the student. This may be for reasons of accountability, particularly when a new practice teacher has not been used to taking responsibility for another person's work. One experienced child care social worker who had not previously been a practice teacher refused to allocate work directly to the student, even if the work appeared quite straightforward, but ensured that they were allocated the work themselves and then they closely supervised the student. This deprived the student of the experience of being as fully responsible for a piece of work as they could have been. Another reason for insisting on sharing work with students can be financial. In private practice, for example in GP training in New Zealand, staff may be loath to risk losing income by allocating work totally to the student (Harre-Hindmarsh 1998)

A further pressure from the practice agency occurs when the student's arrival corresponds closely to the departure of a staff member, who has thus just relinquished their workload en bloc, what some community nurses call 'the empty caseload'. It is tempting for the agency to turn to the student to absorb this workload, without any regard for the student's learning needs and it can take some firm assertion on the part of the student, practice teacher or academic tutor to resist this pressure.

Practice teachers are also not immune from exerting their own pressure on students to undertake work. They may have on their workload certain clients whom they have felt unable to help or simply do not like. There may be certain tasks which they will avoid if possible. Moreover, practice teachers can have an eye to the reallocation of the student's work on leaving the placement, when the residue of the student's work can often be taken on by the practice teacher, now in their practitioner role. They may wish to ensure that certain tasks do not come their way at that time.

The resolution of all these conflicting pressures, needs and demands shaping the student's workload is best achieved by negotiation, particularly between the practice teacher and the student, but also including the agency team manager, if they are responsible for allocating work to the student. In both my jobs as a student unit supervisor, I spent considerable time in discussion with team managers and students seeking to determine what work might best provide the student with the learning they needed at that particular time on the placement. This process might include advocacy on behalf of the student that they are now at a stage when they can be entrusted with an increased level of risk or, alternatively, that the proposed work is currently beyond them. These processes also hinge on an accurate assessment of the student's ability and the way in which power differentials between practice teacher and student are managed (see Chapters 7 and 6).

People and resources

The organisational context of the practice agency varies between caring professions and also between different settings within professions. However, most practice contexts have a number of human and material resources, beyond the designated practice teacher, which can contribute greatly to the student's learning. The practice teacher is usually part of a wider team comprising: peer practitioners, a line manager responsible for their practice and other relevant resources, some administrative staff and material resources which assist them in their work. Other key people in all practice agencies are the clients.

The team members

Walker et al. (1995) and Macleod Clark et al. (1996) both report the value students attached to team members other than the designated practice teacher in, respectively, social work and nurse education. Team members can have a role directly with the student both in their learning and their assessment (see Chapter 7). Often this is by virtue of being present when the practice teacher is not available and being willing to offer support or advice. It can also be through the special attributes of the team member, for example, they may have developed an area of specialism in their practice which the practice teacher has not, or they may be the only team member of the same gender or ethnic origin as the student. Often they simply offer an alternative perspective about the agency and its practices to the practice teacher's.

The process of professionalisation (see Chapter 1) often encourages undue emphasis on a student's learning with and from staff who are already qualified in the student's profession. However, there are often other members of the team. Unqualified staff can sometimes have been practising in that team for longer than the qualified staff and be a fount of local knowledge: administrative staff are often more available than professional staff and usually have a better grasp of procedures, and staff from other professions in a multi-professional team can bring another perspective to the activities of the agency and an outside view of the profession to which the student aspires.

For these various contributions to be maximised, both the practice teacher and the student will need to encourage them and welcome them. The practice teacher will need to make it clear that they wish to share facilitating the student's learning with other staff, who out of deference may not wish to interfere. For some practitioners, becoming a practice teacher represents a developmental shift, in which being responsible for another person's work as well as their own is akin to changing from adulthood to parenthood, and for some parents it is an effort to share their new charges. Students can often enjoy a somewhat more relaxed relationship with team members who make less contribution, if any, to their assessment. They may also need to compromise their workload needs by performing occasional tasks for team members in order to encourage them, reciprocally, to be more involved in the student's own learning.

Team members can also contribute to the placement more indirectly by facilitating the practice teacher to perform their job. One significant way is to help the practice teacher with their workload as a practitioner, so that they have a little more time for the student. Some teams rotate the task of practice teacher so that this reciprocal sharing benefits them all equally. However, this process can mitigate against anyone gaining much experience in being the practice teacher and can be prohibitively expensive if practice teachers are required to receive lengthy training. Another way team members can help is by substituting for the practice teacher, not just when they are absent but also when they are unable to perform a certain function. As a full-time practice teacher, I was often asked to take students who were judged to be likely to fail or were repeating a placement which was already failed. The stress of such assessment sometimes made it difficult for a student to receive support from myself as the principal assessor, but they could often receive it more readily from team members with little or no assessment role.

The team manager

The significant role which a team manager can play in practice placements is recognised in the research literature of both nurse and social work education (Davies et al. 1995; Thompson and Marsh 1991). Indeed, in one form of social work education when the student remains in employment throughout the educational programme (CCETSW 1980, 1984) this role has been considerably heightened. As with other team members, the team manager's role can be directly with the student, or indirectly with the practice teacher and other team members.

The team manager can have access to the student's work at key times of decision making about the service to clients: in allocating work to the student, in deciding whether resources should be allocated to the clients or not, and in determining whether the student should proceed with a course of action or not. At these times, there is an opportunity for learning which the team manager can enhance, by explaining the agency and client parameters which influence their decision. The practice teacher can facilitate this learning, by encouraging the student to approach the manager directly on such issues, rather than mediating between the student and the manager, including advocating to the manager on the student's behalf.

The team manager has often been one of the first people to encourage a practitioner to continue their professional development by becoming a practice teacher (Syson and Baginsky 1981). Once in that role, the practice teacher can look to the team manager for support particularly in the difficult area of workload adjustment, for example, discussing with the team how to relieve the practice teacher of some of their service delivery work.

The team manager can also offer support to the practice teacher by discussing aspects of practice teaching as well as service delivery and by allowing the practice teacher time to attend other opportunities for training and support as a practice teacher, both within the agency and outside it, for example at a higher education institution. All these forms of support are more likely to be forthcoming from the manager if the practice teacher and the student emphasise the importance of practice teaching and learning in the agency as well as service delivery.

The clients

In a climate which has increasingly recognised the contribution clients can make to the planning and delivery of current services, it is also possible to extend their influence into the professional education of the next generation of practitioners. Peter Beresford (Beresford and Croft 1990; Beresford 1994; Beresford, 1996) has for some time campaigned to increase client involvement in social work education and other professions such as nursing have begun to involve their consumers in planning programmes and teaching.

The consumer perspective is of particular importance for the caring professions, since they all need to understand how human beings are responding to the services they deliver. It is possible for a student to gain this perspective in three ways: their own experience of other people's practice, often before coming on an educational programme; their own experience of their own practice, for example, doctors (Swain 1996), nurses and masseurs can perform some aspects of practice on their own bodies; and finally, other people's experience of their practice. It is this last which is most likely to be harnessed in a practice placement.

Beresford (1996) suggests that clients can contribute in three main ways: planning the programme, teaching on a number of topics related to their needs and the services they have received, and teaching on the specific topic of client involvement. Whilst he is writing mainly about whole educational programmes, these three all potentially apply to the practice placement. When the practice setting is a residential or day-care setting, there are usually processes for involving groups of clients in a number of activities. The prospective arrival and subsequent learning of a student could be one such activity – suggesting the student's role with different clients, and giving the client group's perspective on the agency's policies and practices and on the student's performance. In settings where contact with clients is usually on a more individual basis, it is still possible for the individual student to seek feedback from the individual client. Evans et al. (1988) describe a project whereby social work students sought to learn from their clients, in particular, at different stages in their contact with them, including at follow-up. Davies et al. (1995) confirm the clients' enjoyment of making such contributions in community nurse placements.

Resources

Many statutory bodies in professional education recognise the importance of physical resources to a successful placement. Although the CCETSW (1996b) and the English National Board (1997) are somewhat general in their requirements for social work and nurse education, other professions are more specific. General practice training (Anglia Regional General Practice Education Committee 1996) is clear about the importance of appropriate space being available for the student to both practise and learn, a requirement which is echoed by social work students (Walker et al. 1995). In many settings this comes down to a desk or other comparable space where the student can store relevant belongings, think, write and read. Such a space is also important for the student's need for some territory of their own particularly when the placement is unfamiliar and for a sense of accepted status within the practice agency.

The Anglia Regional General Practice Education Committee (1996) also specify the importance of books and information technology equipment for learning purposes, as do the Department for Education and Employment (1997), although without clarifying whether these need to be available in the practice or the academic settings or both. The most useful literature is often that which gives theoretical support and guidance for the practice methods and approaches of the practice teacher and other practitioners involved in the student's learning. If practice teacher and other staff have such literature easily to hand in the setting, they can facilitate the relationship between theory and practice for the student (see Chapter 4). One item of IT equipment which can greatly enhance the student's reflective practice learning is the tape recorder, either audio or video, depending on the type and location of the practice to be recorded (see Chapter 6).

The Anglia Regional General Practice Education Committee (1996) also requires the availability of written guidelines on good practice. Many agencies have a range of documents, such as policy statements, resource directories and procedural manuals, which inform the practice of paid employees and which should be kept easily accessible to students.

3 Reflective Learning

Experiential learning

This chapter and the next focus on two aspects of learning which are of considerable importance to the student and the practice teacher. 'Reflective learning' and 'relating theory and practice' are both conscious learning processes which the student can deliberately undertake, with or without the help of the practice teacher. However, these do not represent the total learning experience for the student on a placement: the student also benefits from learning which is neither conscious nor immediately accessible to either party.

The literature on experiential learning so appreciatively summarised and carefully furthered by Kolb (1984) stresses two aspects: that experience and learning are separate processes, and that conscious reflection is integral to experiential learning. Kolb's learning cycle (Kolb 1984: 40 ff) clearly delineates the two processes of concrete experience and reflective observation. However, Schon's (1983, 1987) conceptualisation of reflective practice is founded on a view of professional practice as a complex activity which inherently entails learning in order for it to be effective. It will not be sufficient to have learned from scientific rationalism ('technical rationality') and then simply to apply that learning to complex practice situations. MacLeod (1996) and Chaiklin and Lave (1993) likewise emphasise that learning is intrinsic to the process of practice. It may well be that the familiar Cartesian dualism, separating the practical body from the thinking mind, has contributed to a somewhat unhelpful sense of division.

It would also seem clear that much learning which occurs through or within experience is unconscious. Freud's major contribution to Western thinking has been to establish that unconscious learning from childhood experience shapes adult life. While classical learning theorists have been much criticised for their lack of emphasis on conscious thought in the process of learning, later social learning theorists who have recognised a more prominent role for cognition still suggest that learning processes such as modelling can occur unconsciously as well as consciously (Gross 1996). It would seem to be counter-intuitive to suggest that all that we have learned from experience, including a wide range of basic life skills, has necessarily involved a conscious reflective process: we would have spent much more time on conscious reflection and much less on experience. MacLeod (1996) and Greenwood (1993) both emphasise the learning about professional practice which takes place through everyday, taken-for-granted experience, but which the learner may only become aware of at a later stage.

None the less, the literature does stress that experiential learning takes place in conscious learning processes which are separated from the experience (Kolb 1984). It is not too hard to perceive how this emphasis should arise in a literature predominantly contributed by writers from institutions of learning, that is, higher education institutions. The view espoused by Chaiklin and Lave (1993) that occupational learning occurs predominantly during the practice in the workplace and supported less radically by Schon (1987) and MacLeod (1996) poses some difficulty for people who require learning to take place in an entirely different institutional context. It becomes crucial for practice experience to be separable from the learning process.

As a willing teacher in such an institution of learning, I do not hold the most radical position that occupational learning only occurs in the workplace. However, I am aware of the considerable learning which can only occur in the practice setting. Moreover, there is a considerable body of learning which is unknown even to the teachers in the practice setting since it is also unknown to the student. It is for this reason that I have sought to emphasise above (in Chapter 2) the many contexts for learning in the placement, such as an instructive workload and colleagues willing to share their practice, which the practice teacher may help to arrange, but which will subsequently lead to both unconscious and conscious learning within the student alone. Likewise, I have included this arranging of learning opportunities as a major function within the responsibilities of the practice teacher (see Chapter 5).

Defining reflective learning

The philosophical tradition of empiricism stretching back to Aquinas has always emphasised the importance of experience in acquiring knowledge. Within the caring professions, Kolb (1984) suggests that Dewey had a profound influence on the importance given to experiential learning in the sphere of education, an interpretation reinforced by Warnock's 1996 review of Dewey's contribution to education. By 1991, Adler (1991) suggests that reflection is the dominant discourse in teacher education. Seminal, general works on reflection in the mid-1980s (Schon 1983; Boud et al. 1985a) stimulated a significant growth in the literature on reflection in nurse education, including major texts such as Reed and Proctor (1993) and Palmer et al. (1994). Social work education, however, has been rather slower to recognise the value of the general literature on reflection and to develop its own (Yelloly and Henkel 1995; Gould and Taylor 1996).

The existing plethora of literature on reflection in the caring professions has inevitably led to considerable variety in how the term is understood. Boud et al. define reflection as 'those intellectual and affective activities in which individuals engage to explore their experiences in order to lead to new understandings and appreciation' (1985b: 3).

This definition emphasises three important characteristics of reflective learning: that it includes feelings as well as thoughts, that it focuses on experience and that it brings about change. The first of these is of particular importance in the caring professions which by definition recognise aspects of human beings and relationships which extend beyond the rational. The focus on experience in professional education is often equated with a focus on professional practice, although students and teachers forget the other aspects of experience – at home, at school and in other occupations – at their peril, since they will also have an influence on professional learning. If 'reflect' means to 'cast back', like an image from a mirror, then it is usually professional practice which the student's thinking is 'cast at' and 'caught back' from. In this sense, therefore, reflective learning can be thought of as the conscious, deliberate component of practice learning.

A fourth aspect of reflective learning would seem to be captured in Dewey's emphasis on the 'active, persistent and careful consideration' (1933: 9) which constitutes the activities alluded to by Boud et al. (1985b). Reflection would seem to be more purposive and sustained than an accidental, fleeting thought. It is a deliberate attempt to broaden understanding, refine meanings and develop professional practice by devoting some time and attention to the process.

The great strength of reflection would appear to be its capacity to generate learning from both unconscious and conscious experience. Sometimes, reflection can help a student become aware of aspects of their experience of which they were hitherto unconscious. As Thompson et al. (1990) suggest, this can be of considerable importance when students' implicit values, including potentially discriminatory prejudices, can become open to scrutiny and possible change. Reflection may also help the student recall key factors of a practice experience of which they had been hitherto unaware, although they were stored in their memory. At other times, reflection can help the student explore in detail practice experiences of which they were already aware but did not fully understand.

Reflection can also help students move outside their personal experience by connecting details of their own practice with other people's experience and understanding. This can include the very different perspectives of their peers as well as the understandings of formal theory. One-to-one discussion and small group learning with student peers and teachers can greatly extend students' understanding of their practice. This occurs through the juxtaposition of their own experience with the broadening influence of others' experience (see Chapter 5), a matching of like with like.

However, it is in the connection between own experience and formal theory, generated by people of whom students have usually had no personal experience, that reflection succeeds in matching like with unlike. Gadamer suggests that 'experience itself can never be science. It is in absolute antithesis to knowledge and to that kind of instruction that follows from general theoretical or technical knowledge' (1975: 319).

The sense of antithesis between scientific knowledge and experience derives from a number of dimensions: the former would seem to be an external, public and objective authority, while the latter is an internal, private and subjective authority. Some writers (Perry 1970; Gardiner 1989) suggest that learners can develop from a greater reliance on the former to the latter. However, through its processes of conceptualisation, reflection can assist in spanning the extremes of highly personal, private experience and publicly available knowledge.

Whilst this understanding of reflective learning may be relatively new to some academic teachers more accustomed to other teaching and learning processes, it comes as no great discovery to most practice teachers who are well used to encouraging students to reflect about their practice. England (1997) suggests that practice teachers themselves might be particularly skilled in this form of learning within their own practice. The value of this chapter lies not so much in bringing reflective learning to the attention of practice teachers, but in exploring it in some detail with a view to helping them expand their repertoire of 'reflective teaching'.

A model of reflective learning

Many writers (Boud et al. 1985a; Kolb 1984; Boyd and Fales 1983; Schon 1983,

1987; Steinaker and Bell 1979; Atkins and Murphy 1993; Johns 1995; Brookfield 1996; Smith 1997) have delineated a number of different stages and processes within reflective learning. This section seeks to synthesise these many analyses, and includes my own perspectives as appropriate. Reflective learning is a complex process entailing considerable creativity as well as discipline in response to experience. The simplified model offered here (Figure 3.1) comprises four major phases, five reflective processes, potentially one or more participants and the dimension of time.

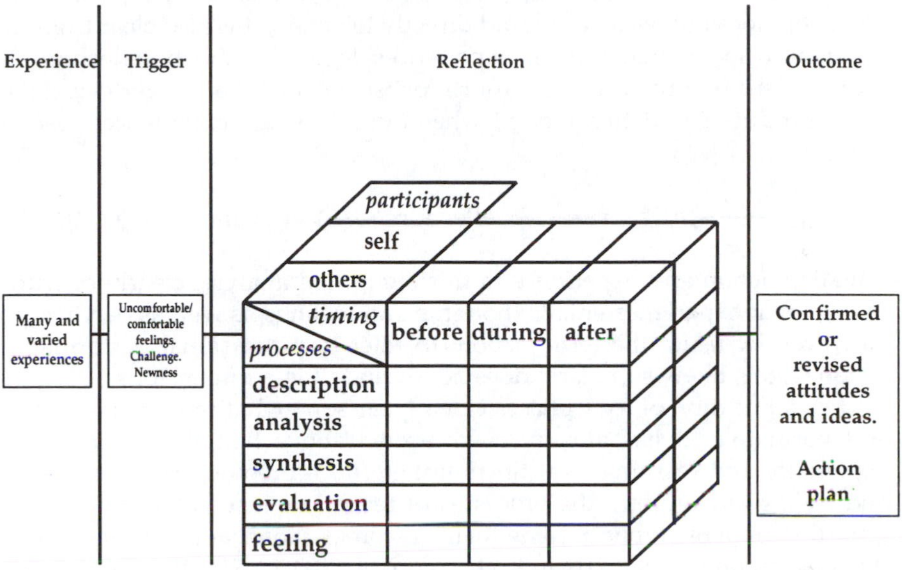

Figure 3.1 A model of reflective learning

The four phases

Schon's analysis (1983, 1987) would seem to be founded on two basic phases - reflection and action - whereby action (1) leads to reflection and hence to subsequent action (2):

action (1) ⟶ reflection ⟶ action (2)

Pilalis (1986) largely supports this duality, although indicating that they are intrinsically interrelated. Boud et al.'s (1985b) analysis is extended to include the possibility of a third phase, namely an outcome which is not necessarily a subsequent action or experience. They suggest that cognitive and/or affective change may occur which may in turn lead to further action/experience. Kolb (1984) also posits a third phase, abstract conceptualisation, which mediates between reflection and action, although his phase focuses solely on cognitive change. The model is therefore expanded as follows:

action (1) ⟶ reflection ⟶ outcome ⟶ action (2)

Just as Boud et al. (1985b) and Kolb (1984) recognise the possibility that reflection does not necessarily lead directly to action, it is also clear from the discussion above that not all experiences lead directly to reflection. To represent the filtering process, a fourth phase – called the 'trigger' – is therefore introduced into this model, whereby only some experiences lead to reflection:

action (1) ⟶ trigger ⟶ reflection ⟶ outcome ⟶ action (2)

Equating action and experience in this simplified analysis clearly obscures the fact that experience entails thoughts and feelings as well as behaviours. However, by using the term 'action' to refer to professional performance, Schon (1987), likewise, clearly does not exclude these dimensions.

This delineation of four phases can appear somewhat reductionist, linear and normative. It has already been argued above that the separation of experience and learning is at times unhelpful. Moreover, trigger thoughts and feelings merge into the processes of reflection, just as the processes of reflection imperceptibly become their outcomes (Boud et al. 1985b). Whilst the recognition, particularly in Kolb's model (1984), of a feedback into action prevents an entirely linear analysis, there are other possibilities of recursion. It is quite common, for example in reflective apprenticeship contexts (see Chapter 6), for reflection to lead directly to further action, when the constraints of time and the immediate need to deliver a service do not permit more general abstraction: this can occur with greater deliberation at a later time.

James and Clarke (1994) suggest that an overemphasis on reflection can inhibit the practitioner's capacity to act quickly. However, it is clear that there will be times when it is necessary to omit the reflective phase. There is an oral account of a social work experience in which a female practitioner interviewing a male client intuitively felt very unsafe and left the building at once, only to discover subsequently that he had just murdered his wife. The trigger led directly to action, omitting any reflection. However, the danger for professional practice would seem to me the reverse of James and Clarke's (1994) suggestion, that practitioners all too often jump from one experience to another without adequate reflection, not only in their particular profession of nursing but also in other caring professions.

Phase 1 – Experience

Through her most illuminating study of the practice of ten highly experienced nurse practitioners, MacLeod (1996) concludes that while most writers tend to treat experience as 'unproblematic', she considers it to be a complex phenomenon: in its range from everyday to what she terms 'watershed' experiences; in its different facets using different senses; and in the extent to which it involves theorising. Experience includes not only the full humanity of the person experiencing – perceptual, intellectual, emotional, moral and spiritual – but also aspects of an experience which occur outside the person undergoing the experience, for example, the behaviour of clients and colleagues. Nevertheless, the whole experience is constructed by that person, by the meanings and understandings they have gained from their past experiences which they bring to the current experience (Brookfield 1996). Student and practice teacher may both have been present at the same event, yet clearly will have undergone different experiences due to differences in what they observed, felt and understood. Much useful learning takes place, for both parties, as these differences are explored.

Phase 2 – Trigger

How is it, then, that from a vast array of experiences, we select only a small proportion for reflection? Even a student with, hopefully, a manageable workload will have too many experiences in a given day in the practice setting to be able to reflect on them all. Nor would this be useful, since one of the learning-to-learn skills a student needs to acquire is when to reflect and when not to. It would seem that reflection can be triggered both emotionally and cognitively.

Schon particularly identifies the feeling of surprise as a trigger for reflection:

> All such experiences, pleasant and unpleasant, contain an element of surprise. Something fails to meet our expectations. In an attempt to preserve the constancy of our usual patterns of knowing-in-action, we may respond to surprise by brushing it aside, selectively inattending to the signals that produce it. Or we may respond to it by reflection ... (Schon 1987: 6)

Dewey (1933: 12) similarly writes of 'a state of doubt, hesitation, perplexity', and Burrows (1995) of surprise, puzzlement and confusion. These emotions are closely related to a cognitive state, an awareness of newness, unexpectedness or strangeness. Knapp (1963) suggests that it is quite common for emotions to be inextricably interwoven with other processes such as thoughts. Likewise, it would be difficult to disentangle the emotional from the cognitive in Heidegger's example of thought being provoked by a doorknob sticking (MacLeod 1996: 120).

However, it is often strong emotions which predominate in triggering reflection. Boyd and Fales (1983) mention 'inner discomfort', while others can include fear, anxiety and distress. The saying goes that we learn by our mistakes and hence these emotions are often unpleasant. However, we can also learn by our successes, when the triggering emotions are likely as Schon (above) and Brookfield (1996) suggest, to be pleasant. The evolutionary view of emotions is that they predispose people to act in a way which aids their survival (Knapp 1963), so it is scarcely surprising that emotions trigger students to examine crucial experiences, particularly those that go awry, so that they will not repeat them and fail! When a group of trainee sonographers were asked to reflect on a piece of practice, it was noticeable that they all chose a situation with complications in pregnancy which had evoked strong, uncomfortable feelings in them.

There are, however, occasions when the trigger for reflection is largely cognitive. Knowledge and understanding can help the student recognise circumstances which require further careful thought – a knowledge of the signs of serious child abuse or disease, for example. An awareness of the considerable impact of structural inequality can trigger them to reflect how circumstances of structural inequality have influenced other aspects of an experience.

Whilst most triggers for reflection will occur within the student, particularly the emotional ones, it is also likely that their reflection will be triggered externally by other people such as practice teachers. Practice teachers will often have a conceptual understanding of key aspects of an experience of which students are ignorant. At times, though, practice teachers will also feel a sudden pang of alarm or a nagging worry that a student has neglected a major aspect of a situation, which then precipitates an extended reflective dialogue.

There would seem to be a progression in the extent to which practitioners are triggered to reflect, not only within the course of a placement but also throughout their career. Butler and Elliott (1985) describe how beginnings tend to be associated with feelings of anxiety. Students are inclined to feel both the worry and excitement of newness at the beginning of a placement and will have much to reflect on at such times. Both Benner's (1984) and MacLeod's (1996) accounts of nurses' learning would also suggest that they tend to practice more intuitively as their careers progress, with fewer watershed experiences which trigger major reflective processes.

Both the student and the practice teacher need to become aware of the typical triggers for the student's reflection. Some students, through their personal emotional life, may be more attuned to some emotions but tend to ignore others. Some may have a well-developed understanding of the importance of certain factors but be ignorant of others. Some students may tend to operate more effectively at a feeling level than at an intellectual level. The aim would be to develop the student's self-awareness and to encourage an increase in the options for triggering reflection.

Intuition can also be a significant trigger to further reflection: an intuitive sense that something is not quite right which then stimulates often a process of analysis to determine exactly what it is. Others (Benner 1984; Butler and Elliott 1987; Johns 1995) recognise the important role of intuition in professional learning and practice.

Phase 3 – Reflection

In this model, it is proposed that there are three dimensions to reflection: five reflective processes can take place, with one or more participants in the processes and at different times in relation to the experience. These three dimensions are mentioned in the literature, as are their constituent aspects. However, no other writer seems to conceptualise all three dimensions as being of comparable significance. Most writers concentrate on the reflective processes and often on subtle nuances within these processes. However, it would seem to me that the growing emphasis on supervision in the caring professions (Hawkins and Shohet 1989; Bond and Holland 1998) is one indication of the importance to hard-pressed practitioners in the caring professions of the other two dimensions, having the opportunity to spend time reflecting with another person. The five reflective processes are discussed below.

1. Description Description is the process of entering into the detail of an experience. Usually when the experience is past, this particularly involves remembering but it also entails some elements of selection, through analysis and feeling, since not all the details of the experience will require description. While some writers (Atkins and Murphy 1993; Smith 1997) use the same term, description, for this process, Boud et al. refer to it as 'returning to experience': 'Returning to experience is simply the recollection of the salient events, the replaying of the initial experience in the mind of the learner or the recounting to others of the features of the experience' (Boud et al. 1985b: 26).

However, words such as 'salient' and 'features' reveal how this process is not quite as simple as they claim. What is salient to a student may seem quite unimportant to a practice teacher, who will then need to encourage further description in other areas to uncover more important features of the experience. As a regular practice teacher in child care settings, I was frequently alerted to a possibility of child abuse by some chance, descriptive detail which the student did not see as at all salient. I would then need to direct the student to recall other details such as the physical appearance of the child, the parent and the dwelling which had seemed quite unimportant to the student. Sometimes, the reverse would occur when a student, cognitively triggered to reflect extensively on the possibilities of abuse, would need to be encouraged to describe quite different aspects of the experience. One of the criticisms levelled at reflective learning by Newell (1992) is possible problems in the initial selection of data, but which guided returns to the original experience of this sort can help obviate.

Whilst this process is generally associated with the past, it can also apply to the future. When students are apprehensive about a future task, because of its newness or difficulty, they can be encouraged to anticipate the details of the event, with questions such as 'how is it likely to go, then?' The practice teacher's experience of similar events can help in fleshing out the scenario. By envisaging the possible detail of the event, including through role play, students can gain confidence in their ability to respond appropriately in circumstances which have lost their total strangeness.

Several writers (Atkins and Murphy 1993; Boud et al. 1985b; Smith 1997) place description first among the processes of reflection. This is probably because it is often chronologically the first, particularly when describing past events, although as we shall see, this is not necessarily the case. Moreover, in some circumstances when the practice teacher and the student have both just been present at the same event (see Chapter 6), there will be less need to re-enter the experience or to recount many features to each other.

2. *Analysis* Analysis involves two key sub-processes: identifying the constituent parts of an experience and conceptualising them at a level of abstraction which moves beyond the concrete detail. A student might, for example, analyse an experience as follows: 'There was a considerable power differential between us, due to age and size, and some difficulty in resolving our conflicts.' The student identifies two key aspects – power differential and conflict resolution – at an abstract level which, in fact, gives us little clue as to the precise nature of the encounter. Was the other person a client, a colleague or someone else? Who was older/bigger? What exactly did they disagree about? What happened to the disagreement?

A description, on the other hand, would supply all those concrete details. It might include:

> I went to see Emily Smith yesterday evening. She is 83 years old and only 4 foot 3 inches high. She had been referred to us for some extra day care but I didn't think it was appropriate. I explained this to her, but she looked rather uneasy and um-ed and ah-ed a bit. So I said it again and she said rather vaguely 'Well, my daughter thought I might qualify.'

Description is very much a blow-by-blow account of an experience rather like a child's narrative: 'I did this and then I did that ...'. Analysis, on the other hand, seeks to abstract certain themes and issues and is not bound by chronology. Of course, the distinction between the two processes is not always so clear, largely because both processes involve words and most words involve a degree of abstraction - some words and phrases are simply more abstract than others.

It is important for students to be able to progress from description to analysis, since it is at the level of analysis that the student accesses key learning to learn skills (Smith 1984; Resnick 1987; Dearing 1997), such as transfer of learning and relating theory and practice, which will help them develop their practice for the future. They will probably never again meet another 83-year-old woman who is 4 foot 3 and who is hesitant and unassertive in quite the same way, never mind Emily Smith herself. They need to know the key aspects of the situation which may be replicated or varied on another occasion, so that they will know how to react themselves. Similarly, it is unlikely that the theoretical literature will discuss Emily Smith herself. However, concepts such as power differential and conflict resolution will be covered in the literature. I usually encourage this progression from description to analysis by asking students to step back from the concrete detail and to look for the main themes and issues.

The movement between description and analysis is not all in one direction, however. At times students will have reached a succinct analysis of an experience, which is, none the less, somewhat premature and does not account for other crucial features. In the above example, it may be that the encounter ended with the older woman threatening to complain to her daughter, the local MP. These details lead to a rather different analysis. In such circumstances, the practice teacher may need to encourage the student back into the detail and away from their somewhat inaccurate analysis. Questions such as 'what exactly did she say/do?' will often achieve this.

The connection between analysis and theory is also two-directional. Not only does analysis provide conceptualisations which form signposts pointing to certain literature, theory also helps shape the whole process of analysis. An abstract knowledge of power differentials and conflict resolution helps alert the student to the possibility of analysing how much these processes occurred in this particular event. As discussed in Chapter 4, the key issue is how much does the theory helpfully structure thinking and how much does it unhelpfully place it in a strait-jacket. How much will the student be flexible to construe the event for themselves, as is suggested by Kelly's personal construct theory (Gould 1989), thus possibly identifying elements not previously indicated in the literature? Or will they see only through the blinkers of those aspects of formal theory of which they are already aware? The practice teacher can have a role in both respects, suggesting existing theoretical perspectives and freeing them to think for themselves.

3. Synthesis In the sense that synthesis also involves abstraction, it is like analysis. However, it entails drawing discrete ideas together to form a whole picture, reaching a conclusion or summarising the situation, which is the opposite of separating the picture into component parts as achieved through analysis. It is suggested (Kolb 1984: 49) that whereas analysis is a function of the more logical, rational left-side of the brain, synthesis is a function of the more creative, intuitive right side. The progression from description to analysis to synthesis is not unlike the view from a rocket during its journey: initially on the ground picking out all the details of the plants, buildings and so on, then quite quickly only seeing the fields and villages and eventually seeing the much broader picture of territories and countries.

Synthesis is identified by several writers as an important reflective process. Atkins and Murphy (1993) use the same term, while others refer to it in other ways. Boyd and Fales, for example, describe a process of resolution in which 'The individual experiences a "coming-together" or creative synthesis of various bits of the information previously taken in, and the formation of a new "solution" or change in the self – what might be called a new gestalt' (Boyd and Fales 1983: 110). Their conceptualisation includes within one process both the reflective process of synthesis and also the outcome to that process – a change in the self.

Boud et al. describe a process of integration which not only involves seeing the relationship between those aspects previously analysed but also in 'drawing conclusions and arriving at insights' (1985b: 32). The importance of this process rests partly in the fact that most professional decision making rests upon the ability to make an overall judgement having analysed the component aspects of a situation. Does the patient need to go to hospital or the client into a residential establishment? Analysis may take the student to the brink but the creative leap to an overall judgement still needs to be made. Synthesis is also important because of its contribution to learning to learn.

Having synthesised the overall view of an experience, the student is well placed to transfer that view to other different contexts in the future.

One strategy which sometimes helps students achieve this whole picture is to place the experience as a whole within a wider context. How does this way of working with a client compare to how you worked in your last placement/job? Questions such as these encourage the student to seek the essence of the experience. Systems theory also provides a useful analogy: a system can be analysed into its component sub-systems, while as a whole (synthesis), it forms part of a larger supra-system.

4. Evaluation Evaluation means simply placing a value on something: is it 'good', 'effective', 'right', 'appropriate' or not? It is possible to describe, analyse and synthesise an experience without placing a value on it, but usually some degree of valuing suffuses those processes. 'Critical analysis' is a common term in the literature combining analysis with evaluation, while overall judgements often entail evaluation as well as synthesis.

Evaluation is an important reflective process for students to develop for the same two reasons as analysis and synthesis. It will be required of them in their practice that they can distinguish good from bad and in so doing they will need to analyse the difference in values attributed by the range of people involved in their practice – clients, other workers, managers, key figures in society such as politicians and the media, and of course themselves. Having a sense of the value of a given piece of practice is also essential in learning for the future. It will not do to replicate bad practice in a future similar context. Inherent in the process of transferring learning, then, is a recognition of effective and ineffective practice.

Evaluation would seem to take place at two main levels: locally and societally. At a local level, students need to be able to evaluate the practice of themselves and their colleagues and also the policies and procedures of their practice agency. At this level, students can encounter a number of difficulties. Some find the whole process of placing a value worrying, perhaps in case their evaluation conflicts with the practice teacher's or a manager's, while others are only too keen to designate a particular way the 'right way', when no such way exists. Some students when reflecting on an event are quite firm in evaluating the actions of others, for example, the workers of another agency, without assigning a value to their own actions. Distant blame can be more comfortable than personal guilt. Other students are able to evaluate their own practice, but may dwell overly on either their strengths or their weaknesses. Many students seem to need reminding of the particular importance to the client and the practice agency of evaluating the outcome of their practice (Evans et al. 1988) and not just its constituent processes.

There is also a tradition of evaluating the deeper presuppositions and assumptions within society as a whole, the practice agency in particular and students themselves, all of which constitute the context for local practice. This is respectively called 'critical consciousness' (Freire 1970), 'critical inquiry' (Habermas 1984), 'critical thinking' (Brookfield 1987) and 'critical reflection' (Mezirow 1990). This form of critical evaluation can help the student understand the internal and external meanings and values which frequently constrain their practice. Two nursing studies (Powell 1989; Richardson and Maltby 1995) indicated that nurses tend not to have developed this level of critique, but to concentrate on evaluating local practice.

The key issue here would seem to be to develop awareness and understanding. However, there are limits as to how far any students of the caring professions can be expected to proceed from this understanding into action. Clearly they can monitor and adjust their own actions to prevent personal discrimination. However, it is less clear how much they can influence others to change, particularly when their practice agency is itself an arm of the state and may be required to implement oppressive policies. Moreover, students are generally of low status in practice settings and they are rendered vulnerable by the assessment process. In requiring social work students to counter inequality, injustice and discrimination, CCETSW would seem to recognise this vulnerability in their phrase 'using strategies appropriate to role and context' (CCETSW 1995: 18).

5. Feeling At the heart of all the caring professions is a human relationship in which one person cares for another, not just in their behaviour but also emotionally. In reflecting on an experience, it is important to ensure this human facet receives due consideration and not to concentrate solely on cognitive processes. Boud et al.'s (1985b) particular contribution to an understanding of reflection has included their emphasis on 'attending to feelings', although other writers (Kolb 1984; Brookfield 1987) also acknowledge the significance of feelings.

The focus on feelings often starts with the trigger and the subsequent reflective process entails accepting, understanding and constructively utilising them. Glasman (1998) uses the term 'emotional literacy' to describe these processes within oneself as well as being attuned to the feelings of other people. Often students seem to think that it is not appropriate to be experiencing emotions, having an expectation of being the objective, uninvolved professional worker. I usually seek to encourage the acceptance of feelings by indicating that clients generally want to be helped by a friendly, warm person and not a faceless automaton, and by suggesting that their emotional involvement in caring may well have been a major strength which brought them into this profession in the first place.

Understanding feelings can help in the process of utilising them. The literature on emotions (Solomon 1993) suggests that many emotions involve a cognitive process of identifying and comprehending them. One common feeling experienced by students is a sense of guilt when something goes wrong for the client they are working with, for example, the client might suddenly die or experience a major trauma. Often with help they can come to recognise that guilt is a natural concomitant of loss and that professional workers experience loss and disappointment as well as clients. This understanding can help to place this feeling in perspective and understand that nothing they could have done would have prevented the trauma.

Boud et al. (1985b: 36) make a distinction between 'utilizing positive feelings and removing obstructing feelings'. While some feelings clearly do predispose us to act helpfully while others may temporarily prevent us, it is difficult to distinguish 'positive' from 'negative' feelings: anger may lead to destructive violence or energetic campaigning, grief to debilitating sadness or accurate empathy. Wallace (1996) suggests that it is the strength of feeling which needs monitoring: too little or too much can inhibit the subsequent practice. However, this is not a universal guide. Some students' natural range of emotional experience is much narrower than others. Often, too, it is the student's great enthusiasm and emotional commitment to a task which carries it through in a way that experienced qualified workers have lost.

Often what students need is space and time to come to terms with strong feelings, sometimes by themselves and sometimes in the company of someone who recognises and accepts their feelings. Sometimes, more detailed reflection is necessary. Many students have a tendency, particularly in the early stages of their career, to identify or empathise too strongly with the client's own distress. They can be assisted to introduce a boundary between the client's world and their own, as they gradually recognise the limits of their responsibilities and the need for them to appreciate the extent of their client's feelings without being similarly affected by them.

Sometimes, however, students are simply not in touch with how they feel about an experience, perhaps because they are concentrating their efforts on rationalising their response or because they have a vague sense of discomfort, without being able to identify exactly what they feel. At such times, the reflective process also includes becoming aware of feelings. This can be encouraged through cognitive processes: how would you expect to feel in such circumstances? Alternatively, the practice teacher can suggest how they themselves might be feeling in those circumstances.

Hulatt (1995) is critical of how reflection, particularly in group contexts, can at times awaken distressing feelings, without then dealing with them adequately, and urges the importance of ground rules. This is also a salutary reminder for one-to-one contexts. Practice teachers and students need to be clear how much reflection on feelings will develop beyond the initial feelings evoked by the experience. Feelings from work can easily connect with strong personal feelings and neither party may wish to pursue the connection. In responding to feelings sensitively, the practice teacher may need to deploy some counselling skills, initially to indicate they have tuned into the student's feelings and accept them. They may also help the student release strong feelings in what Heron (1975) calls a cathartic intervention. However, it is generally not appropriate for the student and practice teacher to develop a fuller counselling relationship, since this can conflict with the essential function of assessment. If emotional difficulties persist for the student, it is advisable to refer them elsewhere, for example, to the college counselling service.

Recognising, accepting and utilising feelings is one major facet of self-awareness. Self-awareness is recognised as an important reflective process (Burnard 1992; Atkins and Murphy 1993) primarily because in professions which rely on human relationships, the professional worker is inevitably part of the relationship. Professional workers are not objective observers who then act on a situation external to themselves: they are intrinsically part of the situation. In such circumstances, students need to be aware of what they themselves are contributing to the situation and what comes from elsewhere.

Self-awareness, however, entails analytic, evaluative and synthesising processes as well as feeling. Boyd and Fales (1983), Boud et al. (1985b) and Steinaker and Bell (1979), for example, all explore the various ways in which a new experience becomes synthesised into our continuing awareness of ourselves. These four processes can be directed, like a spotlight, internally at ourselves as well as externally at the world around us. Students' motivation to help others often encourages them to concentrate on those others to the neglect of themselves: practice teachers can help them recognise that for the sake of those others they also need to consider themselves.

The participants in reflection Much of the literature on reflection focuses on the individual practitioner as the main participant in the reflective process. This is consistent with a student-centred approach to learning. It is, moreover, a realistic appraisal of the greater number of opportunities for the student to reflect by themselves than with other people, for example, on car journeys in community placements. However, some students find it difficult to stop 'doing' and to reflect, particularly when the practice agency culture is one of furious activity and sitting reflecting is interpreted as not working. They may need encouragement to take themselves off into a quiet place to reflect.

However, reflecting with other people can bring important extra dimensions to the process. Other people can help us evaluate our contribution to an experience from another perspective. This may be to counter the self-serving attributional bias (Gross 1996), whereby many people tend to think better of themselves than they do of others. For students, this is particularly tempting since they are being assessed and would wish others to see them in a positive light, too. Greenwood (1993) uses the term 'ego protection' to describe why people might think of themselves in this overly positive way. This serves as a reminder to practice teachers of the protective care they must take in gently persuading many students of a less positive evaluation of their practice. However, some students have the opposite tendency - to think ill of themselves and their practice, through low self-esteem - and may need careful and detailed feedback about their strengths (see Chapter 7).

Other people can often be more emotionally removed from an experience which has had a considerable emotional impact on the student and can help them achieve a resolution of their feelings. They may simply have more frameworks for analysing a situation than the student, whether through formal theory or their own practice wisdom.

Students may seek to reflect with one other individual or with a group. Both are useful learning skills and can be relevant to different work cultures. Some settings do much of their work in teams, including reflection as well as work allocation and agency internal communication, with little regard for individual supervision. Other agencies have a much more individualised culture, often through a respect for confidentiality. Students need to be able to learn how to maximise whatever opportunities are available. One of the disadvantages of concurrent college/placement designs is that students can miss opportunities for team discussions on certain days of the week. Group reflective discussions will be explored in Chapter 5.

The practice teacher is one individual with whom the student will expect to reflect. However, there may be characteristics within their position or within themselves which inhibit the student's reflection. The practice teacher is in a position of authority and although Schon (1987), for example, concentrates on reflective conversations which occur largely with someone in a position of authority, not all students are as comfortable with authorities as peers. This may be particularly if they wish to reflect on aspects which indicate their uncertainty or their inadequacies or it may be through some basic orientation, as Gardiner's (1989) analysis of learning levels might suggest. Smith (1997) and Vygotsky (Crain 1992) likewise support the value of a critical peer perspective. The practice teacher can encourage a student to seek out this perspective, particularly if there are a number of students in the placement at the same time, or alternatively within their college network.

There may be other reasons why a student might seek to reflect with someone other than the practice teacher. The literature (Evans 1990b;

Burgess et al. 1992; Anonymous 1994) suggests the value of ethnic minority students having the opportunity to develop their professional identity through reflecting with a black consultant. A woman student may prefer to reflect with another woman, particularly on their shared experiences as women (Hanmer and Statham 1988). Boud and Miller (1996) use the intriguing term 'animator' to describe the person who helps another person reflect on their experience, presumably through a capacity to help animate or enliven the experience.

Although most reflection with other people takes place in their presence, it is also possible for students to use other people's frameworks when reflecting by themselves – a sort of halfway position between reflection by oneself and reflection with another. An ex-colleague in practice teaching prepared a checklist which she gave students to use when listening to themselves on tape, so that they could use her analytical framework on more occasions than she could be present with them. Many of the published critical incident analyses and learning log summaries (see below) provide a similar checklist for reflection. Gradually the student can internalise the helpful features of these checklists in developing their ability to reflect by themselves.

Time Schon (1983, 1987) posits two points in time for reflecting on practice: reflection-in-action occurs during the practice; reflection-on-action occurs after it. However, he does not emphasise a third important time, *before* the practice, an omission also indicated by Greenwood (1993).

Greenwood's emphasis on 'reflection-before-action' stems from a sense that

> ... much of the suffering in the world, including that caused through nurses' errors, could have been avoided had practitioners stopped to think about what they intend to do and how they intend to do it before they actually did it. (1993: 1186)

While somewhat overstating practitioners' influence in the world, this underlines the value of all the above reflective processes in *planning*, an important phase in the work process for all caring professions (Lippitt et al. 1958; Evans and Kearney 1996). Phillips (1997) also indicated the value of reflection before the experience as a way of imagining or visualising it. Much of the work practice teachers do is helping students prepare for situations which they have not yet encountered. One method is to encourage the student to explore what they have already learned from past similar experiences which may be transferable to this forthcoming situation. Such exploration can both validate the student as an adult learner and increase their confidence through the affirmation of existing competence.

The point of time *during* practice is in a sense the most illusory, since it can be reduced to reflecting retrospectively on what has immediately just happened and prospectively on what is just about to take place. Many of the strategies for helping students reflect by themselves during practice are in fact designed, as it were, to 'stretch' that brief point in time. Time-out, described in more detail in Chapter 6, is in effect a way of suspending the practice while a more considered reflection can take place before the practice proceeds. I sometimes suggest to students that if they recognise that an important event has occurred or statement been made, but they are unable to reflect on its precise significance at that moment, they jot down a word or two which triggers their memory of it and then return to it either later during the practice or after the practice has finished. Students can also indicate to clients that they cannot immediately think of a way forward, say that they need to discuss it with an experienced colleague and return at another time.

One strategy which does not 'stretch' time but the thinking space is to suggest to students that they slightly disengage from the process of engaging with the client to give themselves space to think. This is a delicate balance since to disengage too far would risk losing the necessary rapport with the client. None the less, it can gain the students valuable thinking time. Social workers and therapists used to use the expression 'the third eye' to describe this reflective disengagement. Strategies which involve another person are explored at length in Chapter 6.

One key issue in reflecting on past experiences concerns the functioning of the memory. Newell (1992) and Burrows (1995) are both critical of the role of memory in reflective processes. Newell (1992) indicates a number of factors which can inhibit accurate recall of an experience, including the length of time between the experience and the reflection, changes in the setting from experience to reflection and changes in the internal state of the individual. Most of these factors are significantly reduced if the reflection takes place immediately after the experience, as can occur in the various forms of reflective apprenticeship explored in Chapter 6. This immediate reflection can establish key learning points or 'markers' which can be developed at greater length at another time and in another place, particularly if the student and/or the practice teacher have another pressing commitment.

Sometimes it is not possible for the student to reflect immediately after the experience, either by themselves or with another person, such as their practice teacher. In such circumstances, it is helpful if the student can at least note the key features of the experience which they would wish to reflect on further on a later occasion. Many of the standard reflective techniques, such as diaries or critical incident analyses, require a while to complete. What is often needed is a simple cue which will aid recall later of more detail – a phrase or two jotted down or perhaps spoken into a dictaphone whilst moving from one place to another, or a mental association made (even the proverbial knotted handkerchief).

Phase 4 – Outcome

The outcome of reflection will vary according to the reflective processes undertaken and their effectiveness. If the emphasis has been on reflection on feelings it is likely the student will feel differently about the experience. Evaluative reflection may result in a change of values either locally about effective practice or more fundamentally in an awareness of the inadequacy of previous assumptions, what Mezirow (1981) calls 'critical consciousness'. The more cognitive processes of analysis and synthesis, however, will lead to a change of understanding or meaning.

It is the cognitive changes which are most emphasised in the literature. Atkins and Murphy (1993) write of forming new perspectives and Boyd and Fales (1983) refer similarly to 'Eureka' moments. However, much reflection is of a less wide-reaching or profound nature and leads to only slight shifts of understanding. Indeed, reflection can lead to a confirmation of previous understandings as well as new ones. This can still be considered a change, however, since it can increase the student's confidence in what they had previously thought. Burrows (1995) is concerned that reflection can sometimes lead to increased uncertainty. This is not necessarily a disadvantage, since for many aspects of practice there are no right answers. A progression from a false certainty to a realistic uncertainty is generally helpful learning.

Boud et al. (1985) suggest that progression from new understandings to action is not always straightforward. One of the considerable strengths of live supervision (see Chapter 6) is that reflective outcomes arrived at during practice are likely to be implemented, since the practice teacher is present to help the student implement them and there have been little or no changes to the circumstances since the reflection.

There are, however, other ways of seeking to ensure that new understandings result in appropriate action. Effective reflection can culminate in action planning in which future actions are planned: 'This is what happened, so what shall we do about it next time?' These plans are likely to be effective if they are specific, progressing from an abstract idea to a concrete action. The action is more likely to fit the future scenario if some thorough reflection-before-the-experience has taken place. Actions are also more likely to take place as planned, if there is an emotional commitment to the new way. Boyd and Fales (1983) usefully identify the emotional satisfaction which can accompany new ideas. This feeling can be helpfully translated into a commitment for the future. Their term 'resolution' interestingly also has an implication of a felt determination to implement the outcome.

Methods for encouraging reflection

Critical Incident Analysis There are a number of standard methods which have been found useful in helping students reflect on their practice experience. One of the most commonly used is the critical incident analysis. Brookfield (1987) suggests that the technique has been in use in the social sciences and education since the early 1950s. At its simplest, it invites the student to reflect on a particular incident which they have found in some way critical, that is particularly demanding, challenging or rewarding, although Benner (1984) also suggests using the technique for typical and routine events. Several writers (Benner 1984; Butler and Elliott 1985) and some professional educational programmes have produced formats, usually in question form, which the student can use to guide their reflection. Questions usually correspond to the various reflective processes described above and could include the following:

- Description: Where and when was the incident? What exactly happened in the incident? What people were involved? What were their actions, including your own?
- Analysis: Why was the incident critical? What did you find demanding, challenging, rewarding?
- Evaluating: What do think you did well? What do you think you could have done better? What else might you have done?
- Feeling: How did you feel during and after the incident?
- Synthesis: What is your main learning from the incident? How would you summarise the incident?

Some educational programmes have added other questions more specific to the students' learning and assessment at that stage in their learning, for example:

- What theories do you think help explain the incident?
- Which competences/assessment criteria did you demonstrate during the incident?

An interest in learning what triggers reflection and in fundamental critical evaluation in a student might also lead to further questions:

- What made you recognise this incident was critical?
- What fundamental assumptions, if any, have been challenged by the incident?

This method is of particular value in practice contexts where the student's practice is not easily separated into discrete parts, for example, in residential or group care settings where the student proceeds through a flow of activity throughout the day, often finding it difficult to distil the essence of their professional tasks from that flow. In community settings, on the other hand, the student often makes time-limited visits to clients' homes, which are relatively easy to isolate and reflect upon.

The reflective diary/journal/log Several writers (Else 1992; Shields 1994; Honey 1994; Palmer et al. 1994) urge the value of students' keeping a regular diary in which they record their reflections over a period of time, sometimes a whole placement or entire course. It has become quite a common reflective method on many nursing, social work and counselling courses. Both critical incident analyses and reflective diaries share the value which derives from the struggle to put vague thoughts and feelings into words – the process of conceptualising. Reflective diaries have a particular value in their continuity through a number of experiences, which can be reviewed periodically. This process of review, whether with the practice teacher or by themselves, can often indicate to students how their understanding is changing through time. The critical incident analysis, on the other hand, is a snapshot at one point in time.

Sometimes the student is encouraged to record in their reflective diary whatever they find significant about their experiences: sometimes a structure is suggested to them. Else (1992) and Honey (1994) both suggest three main components closely related to the model above: an account of what happened, conclusions drawn from the experience and a plan of action for the next occasion. Palmer et al. offer some more detailed guidelines:

1. Use an A4 notebook.
2. Split each page.
3. Write up diary on left-hand page.
4. Use right-hand side for further reflections/analysis notes.
5. Write up experience same day if possible.
6. Use actual dialogue wherever possible to capture the situation.
7. Make a habit of writing up at least one experience per day.
8. Balance problematic experiences with satisfying experience.

9. Challenge yourself at least once a day about something you normally do without thought or take for granted: ask yourself 'why do I do that?', that is, make the normal problematic.
10. Always endeavour to be honest and open with yourself – find the authentic 'you' to do the writing. (Palmer et al. 1994: 123)

Reflective diary-writing is not without its drawbacks: Else (1992) lists 15. Perhaps the most common are finding the time and keeping to the routine. These are particularly the case in settings which are very busy and rather devoid of routines around which the diary can be planned. Most of my own practice teaching experience has been in community settings which require continuous recording for the agency and on concurrent college/placement courses which entail the students' writing college assignments whilst on placement. For these reasons I have tended not to encourage an additional writing load on students. Else (1992) suggests some tips to overcome these difficulties, including building up the process slowly and the practice teachers keeping a diary themselves in order to understand the students' difficulties more easily.

Another difficulty concerns with whom the student shares the diary and for what purposes. One student working in a group care setting recorded in their diary some highly critical thoughts about the practice in that setting. The diary was read by a member of the setting, not at the invitation of the student and within a short time the placement had broken down. Putting aside the ethics of the practitioner and the carelessness of the student, this episode graphically illustrated the importance of agreeing within the placement the purpose and readership of the diary. The main issue is not so much whether the diary is read by the practice teacher or not, regularly or spasmodically, assessed or unassessed – it is the agreement between student and practice teacher which is paramount.

The SWOT analysis The SWOT (strengths, weaknesses, opportunities, threats) analysis is another framework which can be usefully used for reflecting about a situation and is recommended in the literature (Thompson and Bates 1996; Richardson and Stewart 1997). This method is particularly useful when reflecting on a broader area and at one point in time, for example how the practice agency may respond to a significant change in circumstances. One student was on placement in a residential home when the home was required to change location. This change became a major feature of the student's learning. A SWOT analysis could have contributed considerably to this learning, by focusing on the existing strengths and weaknesses in the staff/resident group and the possibilities that the change creates, both positive and negative. The framework focuses particularly on the processes of analysis and evaluation and on present and future times.

These methods are all in some sense 'off the peg', either in the range of experiences for which they are most relevant, or in the detailed areas they focus on. However, the most effective reflective processes are 'tailor-made' usually through the medium of effective questioning. Dillon (1990) suggests that questions involve three main elements - the assumptions, the question, the answer - all of which require consideration. The rather global assumption made by many in the caring professions - that open questions are always best - is misleading since in many contexts the practice teacher will need to direct the student's reflections to a particular aspect of the experience, for example, 'was there any sign of injury or neglect on the child?'

In teaching and learning contexts, much of the questioning is by the teacher but of equal importance is the student's questioning. The Socratic method, for example, emphasised asking questions as much as answering them (Dillon 1990). These questions can be asked of the practice teacher or anyone else, particularly in a culture where questions are encouraged and the students do not see themselves as being unnecessarily burdensome. I have found it helpful to ask students to think what it is they want to get out of a reflective dialogue on a particular piece of practice. This encourages myself as teacher and other peer group members to start where the student is at, and not to plunge in on any aspect of interest to us. It also helps the student to develop 'reflective hooks' when they present their practice. It is easy to present practice as a complete, inviolable entity, without inviting the listener in to consider aspects which may not yet be totally completed. 'Reflective hooks' give permission, as it were, for others to analyse and evaluate our own practice. By learning to ask questions of other people, it is hoped that students can learn to ask similar questions of themselves and develop self-reflective techniques.

4 Relating Theory and Practice

The injunction to 'relate theory and practice' is one to which many people involved in professional education, both students and teachers, experience some difficulties in responding effectively. A number of studies in different caring professions attest to these difficulties (Carew 1979; Waterhouse 1987; Eraut et al. 1995). It would seem helpful, therefore, to explore how these difficulties arise, including the many pressures to adopt an orthodox position which stresses both the considerable importance and the apparent simplicity of the processes involved in relating theory and practice. It would also seem helpful to develop strategies which can assist students in maximising this important 'learning to learn' skill. Four key questions can help to elucidate this area:

1. How do students and practice teachers subjectively respond to the injunction to 'relate theory and practice'?
2. What does 'relating theory and practice' mean?
3. Who determines the relationship between theory and practice?
4. How can the practice teacher help relate theory and practice?

How do students and practice teachers subjectively respond to the injunction to 'relate theory and practice'?

People respond to this injunction to 'relate theory and practice' in a wide variety of ways. Not only do they vary in how they think about it, in their understanding of what theory means and of its relationship to practice, but also in their more subjective responses – how they feel about it, how they value it.

In attempting to help both students and teachers, particularly practice teachers, relate theory and practice over a number of years, I have been struck by how apparently crucial these subjective responses are in shaping their whole performance in this area. For this reason I shall start this section with the affective responses, before turning later to the cognitive. It is, moreover, congruent with the overall aim of this book, stressing the caring processes of certain professions, to raise the profile of the emotional in a topic which usually emphasises the rational.

One emotion students often mention is 'distrust'. Sometimes it is as strong as fear, at other times it is at a level of scepticism. The fear may well be connected to the 'mystique' which Thompson (1995) suggests shrouds theory and which both practitioners and academics have a vested interest in perpetuating. 'Mystique' at least suggests that theory might become approachable, if the shroud were lifted. For many students and practitioners, accustomed to responding to the immediate and tangible world of practice, the abstract world of theory can seem positively alien. Moreover, their fear may also be linked to earlier experiences of formal education, particularly schooling, in which they may have been castigated for 'getting it wrong' or at least witnessed the impact of others 'getting it wrong'. Practice, on the other hand, is rarely right or wrong in quite the same cut-and-dried way and hence does not elicit the same worry.

Students' scepticism stems from their perception that theory often seems somewhat irrelevant. This response is borne out in the consumer research. In her small-scale follow-up study of qualified social work students, Waterhouse (1987) found that they could discern little relevance of theory to their practice. A much larger scale and more recent evaluation of Project 2000 courses for nurses (Macleod Clark et al. 1996) found a high level of student dissatisfaction with the lack of practical skills taught on the course, which increased at follow-up; apparently a similar concern over relevance.

One possible explanation of the perceived lack of relevance in theory rests in the large disparity between, on the one hand, the concrete, individualised need as presented in practice by clients and the rather abstract, generalised ideas offered, on the other hand, by theory. Whilst the theory may say that a given practice situation is *usually* caused by certain factors and can be remedied by certain courses of action, the student is still left in doubt as to whether it applies to this *particular* situation. Could this be the exception which proves the rule?

Practice teachers can often experience similar feelings. Walker et al. (1995) indicated from their large-scale survey that considerable doubt was expressed by social work practice teachers about applying theory to practice, citing as an example of this position: 'I am not a great believer in great social work theories, because at the end of the day no one case fits any one theory ... in depth knowledge of every theory under the sun actually doesn't work ...' (1995: 21).

Doel (1993) also alludes to an uncertainty which stems from a feeling of rustiness. Not only can practice teachers feel very remote from the theoretical base they acquired when they themselves qualified, but also may be quite uninformed about recent theoretical developments, which they assume the students will have fully assimilated and which will therefore place them at a disadvantage. In the face of theory, practice teachers can doubt their authority, which is none the less real, although often based on other sources. The effect of these doubts can be totally to discourage the practice teacher from engaging in the processes of seeking to relate theory and practice.

While these feelings are likely to deter students from seeking to relate theory and practice, others may encourage them, most notably the confidence and security which theory can give. This security is imbedded in Schon's well-known metaphor:

> In the varied topography of professional practice, there is a high hard ground overlooking a swamp. On the high ground, manageable problems lend themselves to solution through the application of research-based theory and technique. In the swampy lowland, messy, confusing problems defy technical solution. (Schon 1987: 3)

The rock-like security of the high ground derives from the external authority and assumed expertise of theory which can assuage the anxious uncertainty of personal decision-making. It is this security, in part, which leads to the curriculum organisation of 'front-loading', that is, starting the professional programme with theory before proceeding to practice. Williams suggests in her study of 27 students from four initial teacher training courses that some students valued the time in university before going out to schools: 'I think I would have gone in with absolutely no experience whatsoever and there'd be nowhere to draw from. I think that would have been extremely difficult' (1994b: 103).

The question begged somewhat by Schon's metaphor is whether that security is illusory or not. Gardiner (1989) suggests that learning based on the external authority of theory is the lowest of three levels, to be superseded by other processes including experience. Hunter (1996a) is highly critical of the misleading illusion of certainty, engendered by the current emphasis on evidence-based practice. It is also likely that some theory is more uncertain than other. Howe (1996) echoes Bateson (1973) in suggesting, for example, that there is some doubt about the certainty of much social science theory.

Another subjective response to theory and practice derives from the value which people place on theory. As Reed and Proctor (1993) suggest, theory is generally accorded a high value in our culture, for reasons which will be explored further below. Indeed language and the ability to conceptualise comprise a significantly human activity which distinguishes humans from animals; some would claim raises humans above animals. In a different generation, for example, Ryle suggested that 'it was in the capacity for rigorous theory that lay the superiority of men over animals' (1949: 27).

The particular value accorded to theory in professional education is of 'making sense of' or 'creating order in' the bewildering complexity of practice (Howe 1996; Thompson 1995). This high value may be a further contributory reason for 'front-loading' theory in professional education curriculum design, because the more important aspects must come first. Thompson (1995) places a further value on the way in which a conscious awareness of the theoretical and ideological basis of our practice makes us less susceptible to the oppressive actions which less conscious, more intuitive practice is prone.

However, there are those who place a lower value on theory, including many students and practice teachers. It is clear from several studies (Davies 1984; Coulshed 1986; Faiers 1987) that social work students indicate a preference for learning on placement rather than in a higher education institution. Even when in a higher education institution, they can prefer visiting practitioner lecturers to academic lecturers. Similarly in Project 2000 nurse education, Macleod Clark et al. (1996) and Eraut et al. (1995) found that while some students spoke favourably of some theory they had been taught, there was an overall sense of the theory having little impact and of the balance shifting too far from practice.

It would also seem to be the case that many practice teachers appear not to value theory highly. Walker et al.'s (1995) broad survey indicated that social work practice teachers made little use of theory, a finding which was borne out in Brodie's (1993) content analysis of practice teaching sessions. He found that the frequency of 'references to theory' by his admittedly small sample of six practice teachers amounted to only 0.35 per cent of all techniques used, compared for example to 33.75 per cent for 'offering opinions'. Moreover, he discovered that this behaviour on the part of the practice teachers correlated with their attitudes towards theory. Macleod Clark et al. (1996) discovered a similar tendency for nurse practice teachers to wish to concentrate on practical skills while academic teachers preferred to use their academic expertise. It is interesting to note that CCETSW (1996a) have not included a requirement to relate theory and practice in the revised competences necessary to achieve their Practice Teaching Award.

The lack of value attributed to theory by many students and practice teachers can be seen as one facet of a 'practitioner culture' which contrasts with an 'academic culture', within which theory is accorded a higher value. This differentiation would appear constant across social work (Sheldon 1978; Richards 1984), nursing (Davies et al. 1996) and teaching (Taylor 1969). Thompson (1995) suggests that it stems from an anti-intellectualism which has also been perceived in initial teacher education (Williams 1994d; McIntyre and Hagger 1993) and which can conceal a suspicion of potentially radical ideas emanating from academic institutions (Hill 1997b). However, this explanation imputes a somewhat negative and reactionary response to theory and rather ignores the more positive value which, within the practitioner culture, is being attributed elsewhere, namely to the personal experience of practice. Most of us place a high level of trust in our own experience, informed no doubt by the strong sense of subjective truth as indicated by Ayer (1956): 'I know it is true because I experienced it'. It is this trust which would seem, in large part, to account for the strength of the experiential learning tradition outlined above (see Chapter 3).

The capacity of theory to make sense of the messy complexity of practice, perceived by several academic writers (Howe 1987, 1996; Thompson 1995) as a strength can also be seen as a weakness. Undoubtedly, humans' capacity to conceptualise helps to create an order in a potentially disordered world. However, the danger remains that the order can be inappropriately imposed. Thomas (1997) summarises the view of postmodern and other writers that theory can become a strait-jacket which constrains thinking, particularly of a more imaginative and responsive nature. It is crucial that practitioners should remain open to the unique details of their clients, without becoming blinkered by some generalised understanding. Anyone who has experienced difficulty in fitting the details of a particular client's needs into the headings of a form, which are often derived from some form of theory, will be aware of this danger.

The differing perspectives of practice teachers and academic teachers towards theory and its relevance to practice can become confusing for students, particularly since they move between the two cultures during their professional education programme and need to satisfy both in order to achieve qualification. During the ten years of two joint appointments, I often taught the same students in both academic and practice settings, sometimes in the same week. These students would sometimes ascribe quite different values to theory in discussion with me according to the particular setting, forgetting that I was a common denominator and that my own position about theory was likely to be internally consistent.

A further difficulty posed by these differences in perspective stems from a tendency to polarise – theory is 'extremely useful' as opposed to 'not at all useful'. If academic teachers raise high expectations in students that theory will be very useful in informing most or all of their practice, there is a possibility that theory may be totally dismissed when it fails to fulfil these high expectations. Benner's theory of career progression in nursing suggests that nurses develop through five stages of performance and skills acquisition. The expert nurse, she suggests, 'no longer relies on an analytic principle (rule, guideline, maxim) ...' (1984: 31) but has a more intuitive grasp of the situation. Social work research in the late 1970s also revealed a similar lack of concern for theory on the part of experienced practitioners (DHSS 1978; Carew 1979). This diminishing reliance on theory after qualification may be associated, in part, with unfulfilled expectations of this sort. The practice teacher's tendency to minimise the value of theory, on the other hand, may dissuade students from attempting to discover its value for themselves in the first place.

It is likely that people's differing subjective responses to theory and its relationship to practice are related to their differing learning styles. (Chapter 6 contains a more detailed discussion of learning style.) In brief, theorists, according to Kolb and his associates (Kolb 1984) are more likely to espouse theory in their learning than pragmatists. Gardiner (1989) similarly suggests that what he calls 'level 1 learners' are more likely to learn from theory and external authorities than 'level 2 learners' who learn more experientially. Witkin et al. (1977) identify that 'field independent' learners are more likely to prefer context-free conceptual learning. Research by Kolb and his associates (Kolb 1984) suggests that most workers in the caring professions are likely not to be theorists but to learn mainly from practical (concrete) experience. This finding is largely corroborated by Witkin et al. (1977).

It is not clear how learning styles relate to approaches to theory: whether they are different ways of describing the same phenomena, whether the one causes the other, or whether the one reinforces the other. It would seem a reasonable hypothesis, none the less, that the minority of 'theorists' in the caring professions are attracted to academic teaching where their interest in theory becomes reinforced, while practical learners, including most students, are attracted to practice settings where their preferred style is also reinforced. There would, therefore, appear to be some danger that a minority of academic theorists generalise and enforce their own preferred mode of learning on the majority.

My own approach to the subjective responses of both students and practice teachers to relating theory and practice has become threefold over recent years. First, I attempt to encourage a dialogue about these responses. This can occur in the one-to-one situations of most practice learning and some academic tutorials, as well as in learner groups. The latter has the particular advantage of allowing discussion between learners' peers, which not only offers support to learners who currently experience relating theory and practice as problematical but also creates the possibility of other students explaining to them why, for them, theory and its relationship to practice is less problematical. Second, I seek to understand and legitimate learners' emotional responses, by encouraging their self-awareness and acceptance of the sources of these feelings. Finally, I attempt to encourage a realistic expectation of the role theory is likely to play in the learners' professional career, partly through discussions such as the above and partly through specific examples of experienced practitioners' use of theory, including my own. These discussions seek to stress the future value of theory *after* its role in socialising a new practitioner and to adopt a medial position, wherein theory is neither all-important nor insignificant.

What does 'relating theory and practice' mean?

Before considering the nature of the relationship between theory and practice, it is helpful to explore the meaning of its component parts. Of the two component parts, 'practice' would seem to have the clearer meaning. In the context of education for the caring professions, it is often prefixed by words such as 'fieldwork', 'clinical' or 'teaching' and refers to the actual professional performance within a practice agency and not to some rehearsal of that performance, for example through simulation, which could occur in either academic or practice settings. The range of that performance includes actions indirectly on behalf of the client as well as actions directly with the client. Thus, phone conversations and review meetings are considered as much part of practice as the face-to-face contact with the client.

'Theory', according to the literature (Thompson 1995; Thomas 1997), has a variety of meanings, including the everyday as well as the more specialist. Thompson succinctly gives a definition of theory as 'a set of ideas linked together to help us make sense of a particular issue or set of issues' (1995: 20). This definition highlights three aspects of theory: that a theory contains more than one idea, that the ideas are interrelated and that the theory offers an explanation as well as a description of the phenomena. Howe (1987) also reminds his readers of a stronger meaning of theory, particularly in the physical sciences, whereby it enables people not just to explain phenomena, but also to predict and even control them. This stronger meaning of theory has perhaps less relevance in the caring professions, which draw on the social as well as the physical sciences and have developed their own intrinsic bodies of theory.

Even when understood as a set of interrelated, explanatory ideas, theory does not refer to a totally homogeneous set of abstractions. Theories can be more or less abstract: so-called 'grand' theory or less abstract 'middle-range' theory (Loewenberg 1984; Thompson 1995). The strength of grand theory, such as Marxism or psychoanalysis, lies in its explanatory power – it can seek to explain a wide range of phenomena. However, it has come under considerable attack from postmodern writers. Middle-range theories, such as theories of professional practice methods, seek to explain a much more limited range of phenomena. Howe's (1987) taxonomy of social work theories indicates how middle-range theories can be clustered along two major ideological axes: subjective/objective, and radical change/regulation. It is possible to compare these different levels of abstraction with the view from an aircraft. On the runway, the passengers can see any number of details around them. As the plane takes off, the view becomes increasingly more distant and the patterns observed more simplified. From considerable height, the passengers can discern broad patterns over the whole countryside, but have lost the capacity to distinguish detail in any objects on the ground, or even discern some of the objects.

Some writers (Payne 1991; Sibeon 1991) also distinguish different *types* of theory, for example, theories about the nature and position of the different caring professions within society, theories about the particular methods and techniques of the professions and theories drawn from other disciplines which inform the practices of a given profession. This latter type of theory provides some explanation of possible differences in the credence given to theory by different professions. Medicine and radiography, for example, draw heavily on the physical sciences while social work and teaching draw more on the social sciences which offer less certainty (Bateson 1973; Howe 1996).

Theory, as an explanatory set of ideas, is contrasted in the literature (Howe 1987; Thompson 1995; Shardlow and Doel 1996) with other forms of abstraction, particularly 'models', which describe and aid understanding through simplification and analogy but do not offer any explanation. Research offers abstractions which can describe and explain as well as help predict and control phenomena. However, it is my view that many practitioners, including students and practice teachers, tend to use the term 'theory' in a broad way to encompass this whole range of 'abstract ideas emanating from remote other people', which contrasts with the more practically orientated ideas they might receive and value from trusted colleagues. Eraut (1994) contrasts the public knowledge, largely of published theory and research, with the personal knowledge of individual workers. It would seem to me that many practitioners would include under that which is 'personally known' the knowledge of those trusted colleagues with whom they have a personal relationship.

It has been my experience as a practice teacher trainer and academic tutor that many students first accept a theoretical framework, when it has been espoused by their own practice teacher and validated by the effectiveness of that practice teacher's practice. One very experienced student, for example, who was highly sceptical of theory, adopted with enthusiasm the transactional analysis which she could see her practice teacher using in her practice. Another student with a strong sense of the present nevertheless recognised the effective use his practice teacher was making of psychoanalytical ideas and began to incorporate them in his own practice.

Theory and practice, thus described, represent a variant, particular to professional education, of the duality between mind and body, the physical world and the world of ideas, which has been a consistent thread of Western thought from the Greeks through Descartes to the present day (Allmark 1995). Ostensibly, they are recognised as two different entities in professional education referred to, for example, as the 'twin pillars' (Evans 1987a; Walker et al. 1995). Furthermore, regulatory bodies such as CCETSW, the English National Board and the Teacher Training Agency seek to ensure that their separate identities are protected through periods in both academic and practice settings and through two forms of assessment between which there is no compensation. Thompson (1995) draws on this tradition when he characterises theory and practice as, respectively, 'thinking' and 'doing'.

When people seek, therefore, to relate theory and practice, are they attempting to bring together two essentially different and irreconcilable entities? The humour of one of Gulliver's lesser-known travels, in which the natives carry actual objects around in a knapsack for communication rather than use nouns, rests in a certain irreconcilability between the worlds of objects and of concepts. Likewise, Plato's ideal world in which there exists an idea of a table to which all actual tables approximate fails to capture the difference between physical objects and concepts. Allmark (1995) offers an argument against the possibility of connecting theory and practice, based on etymological difference between the original Greek words.

In direct opposition to the view that theory and practice are essentially irreconcilable is the view that they are essentially interconnected. Pilalis (1986) argues that the injunction to relate theory and practice is a paradoxical one since theory is already inherent in practice and vice versa. Thompson's (1995) 'thinking' and 'doing' duality is also susceptible to a similar analysis, since in purposive practice there is 'thinking' as well as 'doing'. Indeed, in practice which depends heavily on the conceptualisations of language rather than physical actions, such as most social work, much teaching and some nursing, the 'doing' is 'thinking'.

Howe would also seem to minimise the difference between theory and practice when he claims, 'The join between theory and practice is a seamless one' (1996: 170). If this is indeed the case, the difficulty experienced by many practitioners and students is hard to explain. It is tempting to suggest that, for a respected academic of many years standing, the inherent difficulties of the interface have somewhat receded.

A third position, which I espouse myself, is that it is possible to connect theory and practice but that the connection is problematical. At a relatively simple level, the relationship can be seen to proceed in one of two directions: from theory to practice, or what is commonly known as 'deductive' learning, or from practice to theory, or 'inductive' learning (see Figure 4.1).

Theory ⟶ Practice = deductive

Practice ⟶ Theory = inductive

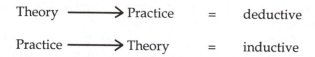

Figure 4.1 Deductive and inductive learning

The deductive relationship has undoubtedly been given greatest prominence in professional education. Often, this is indicated in expressions such as 'relate theory *to* practice' or 'apply theory *to* practice', commonly used by educators and educational regulatory bodies. It is also evident in the common curriculum design of 'front-loading', discussed above, whereby theory is learned before students practise, the assumptions presumably being that the students will subsequently put the theory into practice and that the practice would be less effective or impossible without the theory.

Inductive learning can take place in two main ways. Student and teacher can begin with a focus on the particulars of a practice event, probably the student's but potentially anyone's, and then seek to make connections with theoretical ideas. This can be for the purpose of simply identifying relevance, what might be called 'signposting', and is commonly employed in activities such as writing case study-based assignments. An alternative and, in my view, much more useful purpose is to consider in some detail how the identified theoretical ideas could inform the next stage of that particular practice or some subsequent similar practice. The problem-based learning methods (Birch 1986; Burgess and Jackson 1990) being developed in a number of professions would seem to employ similar processes although the starting point is more usually a simulated case study or scenario rather than an authentic practice event, experienced by the student in a practice setting.

Inductive learning can also take place as the students begin to generate their own abstractions from the accumulated experience of repeated practice events. This starts the career-long process of developing what is often called 'practice wisdom' (Curnock and Hardiker 1979; Lauder 1994) which can be conceived of as 'particularised theory', embodying what an individual practitioner with an individual style and unique set of strengths and weaknesses has found effective with particular clients in particular settings.

Deductive learning tends to predominate over inductive in academic settings, although an increasing emphasis on reflective learning in professional education (Elliott 1997a) offers the opportunity to redress this balance. It has its strengths in practice settings, too, especially when a student is about to undertake some practice for which they have had no previous relevant experience, or for which a given theoretical idea provides a secure and appropriate way of proceeding. Inductive learning is often the mode of choice in practice settings, where its main weakness occurs when major issues of accountability or risk require that full learning takes place prior to the practice and that the practice cannot be conceived of largely as an opportunity for subsequent learning.

Characterising the relationship between theory and practice as either of these two pure processes would seem, however, to be an over-simplification. It is likely that the difficulties experienced in relating theory and practice stem from complexity rather than simplicity. It is interesting that Bloom (1956) would seem to simplify 'application' by assigning it to a lower position in his taxonomy of cognitive processes than 'analysis', 'synthesis' or 'evaluation', all of which would seem essential components within the process of relating theory and practice. Curzon (1985), in contrast, cites other taxonomies which place aspects of relating theory and practice at what would seem to be appropriately higher levels of complexity.

One way of understanding the complexity of this relationship is to move from conceiving it as a simple dyad. Evans and Kearney (1996) argue that a third position inevitably introduces a complexity qualitatively beyond that of two positions, hence the expression 'merely two-dimensional'. The third position in this case is one which in some way mediates between the two. Eraut et al. (1995) emphasise the importance of mediating theory and practice in curriculum delivery and indicate a number of ways in which it can occur. By far the most common mediating process advocated in the literature (Kolb 1984; Bogo and Vayda 1987; Conway 1994; Thompson 1995) is that of reflection (see Chapter 3). Kolb (1984) suggests that, within the learning cycle, reflection is an intermediate process between concrete experience and abstract conceptualisation, as part of a generally inductive process. Bogo and Vayda (1987) elaborate this process in practice teaching through their ITP (Integrating Theory and Practice) loop, particularly by suggesting that theory is accessed during the process of abstract conceptualisation. The question begged by this model, however as already discussed, is how much are our reflective processes responsive to the uniqueness of the concrete

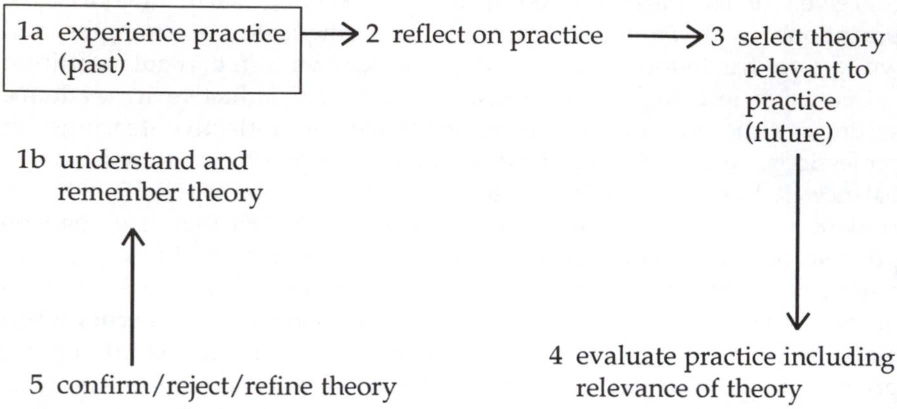

Figure 4.2 Relating theory and practice

experience and how much are they determined by prior abstract conceptualisations?

Kim (1993) introduces further complexity with a fourth process, apparently by subdividing the reflective phase. My own model proposes six discrete phases (see Figure 4.2). In this model, the process can begin inductively with an experience of practice (1a), or deductively with the understanding of a theory (1b), according to learning style and circumstances. However, one difficulty in starting with the theory can be the loss of memory if there is a considerable time lapse before the subsequent processes. For this reason it can be useful for Phase 1a to occur at or at least be reinforced after Phase 3. Another difficulty is the 'scatter-gun' effect of having to learn a huge preliminary range of theories not knowing which ones will actually be required in specific practice. None the less, some students report how the subsequent experience of practice can assist with the process of understanding theory which has been learned prior to the practice.

Phase 2 of reflecting on the practice concentrates on analysing key factors which are likely to be addressed by relevant theory. It is this analysis which extrapolates abstract features from the concrete practice. The reflection itself will be shaped but not constrained by theory. In Phase 3, a theory is selected which is perceived to be relevant to factors abstracted from the practice by analysis, a process of matching or mapping. A further period of practice is then evaluated (Phase 4), including the actual relevance of the theory. The relevance of the theory (Phase 5) is then confirmed, rejected or refined. The cycle is completed with a new understanding of theory and a further experience of practice.

This more complex model of the relationship of theory and practice includes both inductive and deductive processes and proceeds through all four of Kolb's (1984) learning cycle phases, including active experimentation. It would seem to be just one of the possible attempts to delineate a number of different processes within 'relating theory and practice'. Eraut et al. (1995), for example, offer an alternative model which delineates a number of discrete phases and stresses equally a detailed understanding of both the practice and the theory entailed. Both models emphasise the complexity inherent in relating theory and practice, and account in some degree for the difficulty which many people experience in implementing the relationship. Models themselves involve a process of simplification and it is therefore likely that the processes of relating theory and practice are yet more complex.

What the model does not address, however, is the question 'how much *does* professional practice actually entail this kind of process?' It is likely that it is more common in professions with a strong physical science base, such as medicine and radiography, for which the move towards evidence-based practice seeks to access appropriate theory at the point of use – at Phase 3 in the model. Even in these professions, however, there are areas of practice which entail more subjective knowledge and skills, including professional behaviour, communication, interrelating and team work, and which are given terms such as 'doctoring', 'lawyering' and 'pastoralia' (in the Church). These are areas which are sometimes described as the 'art' of the professions rather than the 'science' (Schon 1987; England 1986; Conway 1994) and for which a more reflective learning process (see Chapter 3) may often be more appropriate.

The model certainly does not address another related question – 'how much *should* professional practice entail this form of process?' – which is the focus of the next section.

Who determines the relationship between theory and practice?

It was noted above that different people place different values on theory. It would seem, moreover, that some people have the power to ensure that their value predominates. It would seem useful, therefore, not only for students and practice teachers who often feel relatively powerless in professional education, but for all those engaged in professional education to have some analysis of power in this particular area, in order to mitigate its worst effects.

Theory and its relationship with practice are inevitably key battlegrounds in professional education. The general relationship between knowledge and power has been well charted (Habermas 1968; Foucault 1980) and within the professions, knowledge is clearly a key factor in the bid which occupations make for professional power (Johnson 1972; Hugman 1991). Most commentators (Hugman 1991; Eraut 1994; Thompson 1995) agree that a distinctive knowledge base is one of the more compelling claims which an occupation can put forward for societal recognition as a profession. Whilst Eraut (1994) recognises that professional knowledge includes a range of capacities, it would seem to be the propositional knowledge – 'knowing that' – of which theory is comprised which has greatest value. Eraut characterises the professional knowledge base as:

- carrying the aura of certainty associated with established scientific disciplines (or if that is unconvincing, establishing strong links with university-based social and behavioural sciences);
- sufficiently erudite to justify a long period of training, preferably to degree level for all with specialist postgraduate training beyond that for some; and
- different from that of other occupations. (Eraut 1994: 14)

Payne (1991) suggests that some people doubt whether social work can lay a strong claim to the first of these characteristics. The second characteristic is one of the ways in which professions can manifestly demonstrate their accountability to society to produce effective practitioners, by guaranteeing they all will possess a given, substantial body of knowledge. Thompson (1995) argues that the issue of differentiation is of particular importance for nursing, given its proximity to medicine.

It is likely, therefore, that any occupation wishing to be seen as a profession would have little difficulty in achieving some form of consensus about the importance of its theoretical knowledge base. This particular consensus would be likely to cover professionals in practice as well as academic settings, and students as aspiring professionals as well as qualified staff.

The regulatory bodies of professional education in emphasising the theoretical basis of their educational programmes, seek to reinforce the professional status of their occupation not only in response to these varied constituencies, as well as central government, but also as part of their own wish. In first position within the nursing standard for the programme assessment strategy, for example, is the requirement that it 'examines research- and evidence-based knowledge ...' (English National Board 1997: 25), while the requirements which focus on practice are at lower positions in the list. Likewise, the standards for the award of Qualified Teacher Status

(DfEE 1997) are headed by a group entitled 'Knowledge and Understanding', with various skills and competences relegated to later groups. While the CCETSW, in association with the Care Sector Consortium of the NCVQ, have now developed a competence-based programme for qualification in social work, they take pains to emphasise at the outset that 'Competence in social work is the product of knowledge, skills and values' (CCETSW 1995: 17), thus retaining the traditional first place for knowledge within that threesome. Moreover, they elaborate the knowledge base of social work under 86 headings *before* proceeding to elaborate the competence base.

The increasing movement of the caring professions towards higher education institutions (HEIs) over many years (see Chapter 1) has undoubtedly sought to enhance the theoretical basis of these professions, by achieving the first two of Eraut's (1994) three characteristics, scientific certainty and degree level qualification. The apparently rising profile of caring professions within HEIs through discrete departments, chairs, journals and research output would seem to indicate the success of that policy. This policy itself has presumably enjoyed a consensus within the respective professions. Moreover, the financial pressures of recent years have compelled HEIs to generate income through increased research activity and theory-generation, thus reinforcing the theoretical orientation of caring professionals within the academic community.

This increasing emphasis on research and theory-generation in HEIs has, in my view, had two unfortunate side-effects. First, it has reinforced the strong territoriality whereby professionals in HEIs concentrate on their expertise in theory to the neglect of their expertise as practitioners, despite the attempts of regulatory bodies such as the English National Board (1997) to keep them in touch with practice. This territoriality is underpinned by the structural division in professional education between HEIs and practice agencies and reinforced by the recognition of opposing academic and practitioner cultures. The territorial claim of academics complements a similar one on the part of practitioners:

> The nurse teachers, managers and practitioners all concluded that the ultimate responsibility to impart clinical skills lay with those considered to have the relevant expertise – the practitioners themselves. The nurse teachers were seen to make their greatest contribution towards socialising the student into their professional role by using their 'academic' expertise rather than competing for clinical credibility. (Macleod Clark et al. 1996: 180)

The use of the word 'competing' would seem to confirm a sense of territoriality.

Second, academics from the caring professions tend to promote the importance of theory within the entire educational programme, including the territory of practice. The considerable literature on 'relating theory and practice' does not, to the best of my knowledge, include any contributions from professionals employed in practice settings. It would seem to be clearly in the interest of academics to persuade both practitioners and students of the value of their predominant activity (Evans 1987a). Moreover, academics tend to encourage the use of theory in the practice setting, not only through their formal and informal meetings with practitioners but also in publications such as Lishman's (1991) *Handbook of Theory for Practice Teachers in Social Work*. Undoubtedly, this book has been a valuable source for some practice teachers, particularly those worried about their theoretical grasp. However, it is the greater power of academics within the educational enterprise, I would argue (see Chapter 1), which makes the influence generally from the academic to the practice setting rather than the reverse. I have been unaware of practitioners advocating with equal force, frequency or apparent legitimacy that academics should acquaint themselves more with the details of practice. Nor have I heard of an eminent practitioner promoting their territory to a body of academics, presumably by inviting them to observe and discuss their practice.

The rise of evidence-based practice in the caring professions, particularly medicine (Sackett and Haynes 1995) and nursing, but also social work (Thompson 1998; Roberts 1998), would seem to indicate a new potential for academics to reinforce the powerful position of research-based theory in the professional domain (Elliott 1997b). Its origins, however, would appear to be more broadly based than this one aim. Eraut (1997) suggests the important impact of litigation in medicine as one source, while Hunter (1996b) sees the vital role evidence-based practice will play in rationing the limited resources of the National Health Service. Whilst evidence-based practice initiatives will undoubtedly make a wide range of evidence – selected from an ever-growing body of knowledge – available for busy practitioners to use, they have been criticised for their spurious claim to certainty and their devaluing of complexity in professional decision making (Carr-Hill 1995; Polychronis et al. 1996; Hunter 1996a). Moreover, Hunter (1996a) suggests that evidence-based practice initiatives promote a new hierarchy within research, namely that which conforms to a rather narrow, positivist view of science. From this perspective it can be seen as a bid for increased power not only by the academic community but also by one section within that community.

Some academic writers place less emphasis on the dominance of theory in professional competence. Schon (1987) and Benner (1984) both emphasise the more artistic and creative capacities which professionals employ in their work. Eraut also suggests the value of academics' moving out of their traditional territory not simply to promote their own wares but also to foster strengths within the territory of practice: 'Hence higher education needs to develop an additional role to that of creator and transmitter of generalizable knowledge – that of enhancing the knowledge creation capacity of individuals and professional communities' (Eraut 1994: 20). However, it is unlikely that this is a typical view within academic communities, particularly given the increasing demands being made within the academic setting and the increasing operation of the market place.

Academic communities within education for the caring professions comprise a dominant group, albeit of relatively limited scope. However, there are broader influences within society which would similarly seem to emphasise the importance of theory. Thompson suggests that 'theory is predominantly generated by dominant groups in society' (1995: 14). I would go further and suggest that dominant groups also generate an interest in the theory they generate.

Since the ancient Greeks, Western culture has placed great emphasis on rationality and science in learning (Ryle 1949; Chaiklin 1993). There is a clear continuity which links Plato's philosopher-king, the period of Enlightenment (Berlin 1956) and our current reliance on medical science, despite a postmodern scepticism of science in general (Lyon 1994). However, it would seem that Eastern cultures do not share this emphasis. The traditional Brahmin way of learning, for example, emphasised observation and reflection: theoretical instruction only gained prominence with the introduction in the nineteenth century of the Western Macaulay system of education (Narayanaraja 1996). Likewise, Buddhism stresses the experience of the 'master', with whom the learner has a personal relationship, and the learner's own meditative processes (Wegerif 1997). Maori culture would seem to place great value on the holistic integration of the spiritual, the emotional and the conceptual without according predominance to the theoretical (Harre-Hindmarsh 1997). Sacco questions the relevance of Western science to the native culture of South Africa which asserts 'I belong therefore I am' (1996: 36), rather than Descartes' '*Cogito ergo sum*' and therefore proposes professional action grounded in the stories and meanings of the clients rather than in science. Whilst 'enlightenment' in the West is suggestive of science and the rational, in the East it would seem to evoke the experiential and the spiritual.

The whole issue of gender difference is at best a controversial one (Durkin 1995), given the impact of stereotyping from an early age. However, there would appear to be some evidence that the preference for theorising is male. Williams and Best's (1994) study of gender stereotyping revealed a high level of agreement over thirty countries that an epithet such as 'rational' was more associated with males than females, whereas 'emotional' and 'imaginative' were more associated with females. Tennant (1997) cites evidence that women generally construct knowledge in different ways to men, relying more heavily, for example, on subjectivity and dialogue, and that current institutional structures tend to disempower them and promote 'androcentricity'.

Class is likewise a complex and somewhat problematic conceptualisation. None the less, there is some evidence from Bernstein's work on linguistic codes (Haralambos and Holborn 1990) that members of the working classes are limited to restricted codes which are particularised and contextualised while members of the middle classes can use both restricted and elaborated codes, which are more generalised. It may be therefore that theory is more readily acceptable to the middle than the working classes.

What, then, are practice teachers to make of the powerful forces constructing the relationship between theory and practice? It is interesting that in Brodie's study, full-time social work practice teachers 'made significantly more frequent, more explicit and more expansive references to theory than did the singleton teachers' (1993: 82). While Brodie does not appear to explain this finding, it could possibly be construed as evidence of the ways in which full-time practice teachers can tend to be drawn to such educational posts because of an interest in theory and, once in them, become further acculturalised through their increased contact with academic teachers. 'Singleton' practice teachers who remain more firmly within the practitioner culture are perhaps less open to influence in this way.

None the less, many practice teachers do indicate – in support groups, on training courses and in informal conversations with academic teachers – their concern about their ability to relate theory and practice. This has been heightened particularly in social work education since CCETSW (1995) required academic and practice teachers to mark an assignment jointly. My response in all these circumstances is usually to encourage practice teachers in their own authority. The whole purpose of practice placements is that students are helped to learn by people immersed in the details of practice. Likewise, that is the perspective most required of practice teachers in any joint marking. The total community of the different caring professions requires, in my view, that a healthy tension between the academic and practitioner sub-communities is sustained in order to achieve a helpful balance between the theoretical and the idealistic on the one hand and the practical and the pragmatic on the other.

Only after such validation would it seem useful to encourage some further exploration of theory and its relationship to practice. While it would seem desirable for practice teachers to increase the order of frequency of 'references to theory' beyond the 0.35 per cent reported in Brodie's study (1993), it would seem that the unpredictability and complexity of practice

(Papell 1996; Schon 1987) will often render 'off-the-peg' theory less helpful than other ideas. Paley (1987) suggests that it is appropriate for practitioners to be more interested in a question such as 'what ideas will help me in my practice?' rather than 'how do theory and practice interrelate?' Above all else, in the practice setting a student needs to be helped to learn how to respond to particular circumstances: theory can only be one means to that end, not the end itself.

How can the practice teacher help relate theory and practice?

Some writers indicate that practice teachers are well placed to help students relate theory and practice (England 1997; Eraut et al. 1995). Not only are they in a good position to help the understanding of practice and the application of theory to practice which the above models would seem to imply, but they are also strategically positioned to harness a major source of motivation to learn – the desire to help particular people in need – a source accounting for much of the strategic importance of practice learning in professional education (see Chapter 1). At the point of determining how to help a particular service user, the student may well be optimally open to learning from any source including theory. Students speak, for example, of how they can make sense of theory when confronted with practice: 'It's [theory's] all gobbledegook until you're on the clinic and you can actually relate to someone to see what's going on' (Eraut et al. 1995: 83). In this way the proximity to practice can count for more in the students' eyes than the proximity to theory which academic teachers experience and develop.

Despite this recognition of the opportunity practice teachers have to help students relate theory and practice, there are few practical suggestions in the literature about how they might proceed. Even Doel (1993) in a document which is full of valuable practical advice and accessible exercises has little to offer in this area beyond the more abstract understanding of what 'relating theory and practice' means. It would seem that there are three main points from which practice teachers can start – the student, themselves and the practice.

Students come to placements with a wide range of attitudes to theory, sometimes positive often negative; sometimes of recent origin, often of long-standing. It would seem an appropriate part of the initial introductory processes of a placement to seek to discover them, preferably within a mutual exploration which allows the possibility of difference. This could occur as part of a broader discussion about learning style, for example stemming from the completion of Kolb's (1985) or Honey and Mumford's (1986) learning style inventories.

Students also come to placements with their own orientation towards practice. This may be, in broad terms, a given style (Heron 1975) or a commitment to certain values, which can be either embryonic or well developed through personal maturity and work experience. As the practice teacher begins to appreciate this broad orientation, they may find themselves in a position to refer the student to theoretical ideas which can help the student develop it. A facilitative style, for example, may be enhanced by increased acquaintance with Rogers's (1974) humanistic approach. Several social work students have been interested in combating oppression in its various forms and have been interested to pursue some of the literature on empowerment.

Sometimes, the student has already developed an interest in particular theoretical ideas, including ideas espoused in earlier practice contexts. In such circumstances, it can be helpful for the practice teacher to focus on these ideas and discuss their relevance in this particular practice context. This form of discussion can target two learning-to-learn skills: transfer of learning, as well as relating theory and practice. Sometimes the practice teacher is quite unfamiliar with the student's espoused theories and may need to become more familiar with them in order to have such discussions. One student, for example, was firmly committed to the theories of Myers-Briggs about different personality types. In seeking to understand these hitherto totally unfamiliar ideas, I was able to some degree not only to focus on the relevance of those ideas to her practice on the placement but also to address issues of power differentials between us.

Student groups on placement (see Chapter 5) offer a particularly effective forum for addressing the relationship between theory and practice. There is some evidence (Evans 1987a) that the trust generated in such contexts can help students share the detail of practice, while students' attempts to understand each others' practice inevitably entails a level of abstraction and distancing which can lead easily into an identification and discussion of relevant theory. Some students are also more inclined to accept the testimony of another student about the relevance of theory than that of a teacher.

In a similar fashion, the trust which usually develops between student and practice teacher on a placement can also be the source of a growing appreciation of the value of certain theoretical ideas. As indicated above, students will often recognise the validity of their practice teacher's theoretical ideas as they discover the effectiveness of their practice, particularly when the practice teacher facilitates ready access to both aspects of their professional competence. This can often be a powerful motivation subsequently to try out the practice teacher's espoused theoretical ideas for themselves. While academic teachers may articulate the theory with considerable clarity, the practice teacher can demonstrate its effectiveness: the proof of the pudding is in the eating!

This process has a number of prerequisites. It is useful if the practice teacher has first achieved a reasonably balanced approach to theory, avoiding the polarisation discussed above. One way for a practice teacher who is generally opposed to theory to achieve this is to reflect on the positive impact, however slight, theory has on their own practice. For an experienced practitioner, it can take some effort to delineate the many different theoretical influences which have become subsumed and often obscured within their total professional competence. Some practitioners acknowledge a significant theoretical debt in much of their practice while others are less conscious of any theoretical influence. Thompson (1995) suggests that the notion of 'theory-less' practice is a fallacious one: a sustained attempt to unearth underpinning theoretical ideas is bound to succeed. Whilst this position would appear to be towards one end of a polarity greatly valuing theory, it would seem likely that practitioners who have progressed through an extended period of qualifying education at the very least, probably with additional time spent in continuing professional development, will have assimilated some theory.

In identifying their store of espoused theory, it may be helpful if practice teachers do not burden themselves with high expectations of discovering theories for most or all of their practice. Such expectations might well deter them from undertaking the exercise. One of the main aims in this aspect of learning on the placement is to help the student learn how to learn: to recognise the potential value theory can have for their practice. This can be achieved just as effectively with one theory clearly recognised as relevant as with a large number. Moreover, the learning is more likely to be effective if the practice teacher concentrates on a theory which they understand well and use reasonably frequently than a number about which they feel less confident or committed. A further development of this identification exercise can be to add the main theoretical ideas they espouse to the written profile of their characteristics as a practice teacher, which can be available for students as part of the matching and contracting processes (Preston-Shoot 1989) which take place before or in the early stages of the placement.

If self-reflection fails to reveal a store of espoused theory, practice teachers could discover the ways in which theory has influenced the practice of colleagues they respect. A genuinely open discussion with a colleague which is free from the established positions of the 'practitioner culture' may well reveal that the colleague values certain theoretical ideas in their practice.

All the above processes are prefaced on a willingness to move beyond the territory of practice into the territory of theory. This can develop further if the practice teacher is willing to work in partnership with the higher education institution in attempting to help the student relate theory and practice. Many programmes seek to inform practice teachers of the theoretical content which students are taught in the HEI, usually through programme handbooks and other handouts. Often these handbooks are inaccessible to busy practice teachers. Moreover, it is misleading to assume that teaching equals learning. For these reasons, it is often more useful to ask the student what they are learning or have learned in the HEI which they are struggling to find relevant to their practice in this placement. Some programmes go so far as to request the practice teacher to reinforce learning in particular theoretical areas. In the late 1970s, for example, systems theory was especially popular on social work courses and some practice teachers were asked to familiarise themselves, through course workshops and their own reading, with this body of theory in order to help students learn more about it, including how to apply it, on placement.

Partnership with the HEI takes on a more interpersonal aspect when the practice teacher meets an academic teacher from that institution, sometimes in a three-way meeting with the student. These meetings can, in my experience as both a practice teacher and a tutor, provide a fruitful forum for relating theory and practice, although there are usually many other pressing tasks to perform. Sometimes it is possible for either the practice teacher or the academic teacher to identify relating theory and practice as a particular learning objective for that student and to add it to the agenda for their meeting. Discussion on this topic is most effective when the practice and academic teachers have identified theoretical interests in common and are prepared to discuss them from positions of equality. It is also likely to be more effective when a relationship of mutual respect has developed between the practice and the academic teachers. As a full-time practice teacher and initially as a tutor, I had a particular interest in theories of family work, including family therapy, which was sometimes shared by the other partner in the student's placement and which could lead to highly productive discussion and student learning.

Whether the interaction between the practice teacher and the HEI is mediated by documentation or by the personal appearance of an academic teacher, it is likely that the practice teacher will need to feel confident about their own authority in order to engage in a productive exchange about theory. For some practice teachers, this only develops as the placement progresses and they recognise the student's growing respect for their practice and teaching or even as a succession of students are on placement with them. For this reason, it is sometimes helpful if three-way discussions seeking to relate theory and practice occur at meetings in the middle or towards the end of the placement, rather than at the beginning.

It is congruent with the learning style of most students and practice teachers (Kolb 1984) if both these three-way discussions and other discussions between just the practice teacher and the student start with the student's practice during the placement. The focus on practice can be, as Thompson (1995) suggests, through critical incidents (see Chapter 3) or through a consideration of the student's total work on behalf of a particular service user. It might even generalise into a discussion of a range of practice performed on the current placement and in past or future practice settings for which the same theoretical ideas are relevant, thus reinforcing the student's ability to transfer learning.

Some practice teachers prefer to teach theory in sessions which are separated from other teaching and supervision of practice. Usually they will have made a clear connection with practice on one occasion but consider, with the student's agreement, that more time is needed for theoretical discussion than is then available, often because of pressing issues of accountability. My own preference, however, has been not to separate theory and practice teaching in this way. Not only does it seem to accentuate inappropriately the value of theoretical as opposed to other ideas in learning how to practice, it also begins to erode the considerable advantage of *proximity* when seeking to relate theory and practice. It is at the time when the discussion about practice clearly demonstrates the relevance of certain theoretical ideas that the learning would seem most to occur. Moreover, the discussion will need to flick between practice and theory for relevance to be fully established. For similar reasons of proximity, it is helpful for practice teachers to have any theoretical literature that they have found useful close to hand so that they can either delve into it themselves or lend it to the student at the critical time.

PART III

Practice teaching

5 A Model of Practice Teaching

The practice teacher has a central role in the student's experience of practice learning. There is strong evidence within social work (Walker et al. 1995; Fernandez 1998) and nursing (Macleod Clarke et al. 1996) that students are already particularly appreciative of this role. The growing literature on mentoring (Wilkin 1992; Fish 1995; Brooks and Sikes 1997) suggests that the movement towards more school-based learning is also enhancing that role in initial teacher education. Most of the professional regulatory bodies clearly recognise the practice teacher's importance (see Chapter 1), although, significantly, whereas the Central Council for Education and Training in Social Work (CCETSW 1995) and the English National Board (ENB 1997) make clear requirements of the practice teacher, no such requirements are made in teacher education at the time of writing (DfEE 1997).

It is difficult to identify the origins of this key role in professional education. The early apprenticeship phase of professional education identified by Bines (1992) implies that the student would initially have been attached to an experienced practitioner for much of their learning, though not one with any specific claim to being an educator. The continuation of this arrangement may well have been influenced by the marginal position of practice learning in professional education, since the higher education institutions are predominantly concerned with scholarship and the practice agencies with service delivery. A minimalist perspective would suggest that the HEIs need to have easy access to the learning in the practice setting, preferably via one person, and the practice agencies need to ensure a minimum allocation of responsibility commensurate with ensuring that the student delivers an adequate service whilst in the setting.

Several models exist in the literature for what the practice teacher does. 'Model' implies a generalised description which distils certain key aspects in order to help others shape their thinking and practice. Wijnberg and Schwartz (1977) outline three models of practice teaching: apprenticeship, growth and role systems. Bogo and Vayda (1987) augment these with four additional models: academic, articulated, competency-based and their own 'loop' model, which is based on an adaption of Kolb's (1984) learning cycle. Shardlow and Doel (1996), likewise, augment Bogo and Vayda's list with two others: the managerial and their own 'structured learning' model, in which the notion of a planned curriculum is a prominent feature. Brooks and Sikes's (1997) list includes some of those already mentioned and some additional ones, including mentor as reflective coach, as critical friend and as co-inquirer.

These models are rooted in their contexts, both historical and professional. The apprenticeship model, as has been suggested, stems from an earlier phase in the development of professional education. The growth and role systems models have developed from the seminal thinking of, respectively, Freud and Parsons. Competency-based, the 'loop', reflective coach and critical friend all owe their origins to broader developments in educational theory and practice, while the managerial model probably stems from the growth of managerialism in the welfare sector. 'Structured learning' reinforces a developing emphasis on teaching as the primary task of the practice teacher and away from the managerial supervision emphasised at an earlier period. Co-inquirer draws on the considerable tradition of action research in teacher development.

The model presented in this chapter (see Figure 5.1) can be termed the Function/Phase/Partnership model (FPP) and was first briefly outlined elsewhere (Evans 1993). It is similarly born out of a context, particularly in social work education during the 1990s. Much of the literature on practice teaching in social work (Ford and Jones 1987; Thompson et al. 1990; Sawdon and Sawdon 1987; Shardlow and Doel 1996) identifies functions, often drawn from the general literature on supervision in social work (Kadushin 1976; Pettes 1979). CCETSW (1996a) has, moreover, recently undertaken a functional analysis of practice teaching. The 1990s has also seen a considerable interest in partnership, not only in professional education but also in other sectors such as health, welfare and industry. The focus on the chronological process of the placement, through divisions into phases, stems partly from the social work practice teaching literature, partly the delineation of a similar process within most of the caring professions (Evans and Kearney 1996) and partly from the experience of training practice teachers.

Models, however, are only one way of seeking to understand practice teaching. The literature reveals a number of other perspectives. Several writers (Secker 1992; Walker et al. 1995; Brooks and Sikes 1997; Fernandez

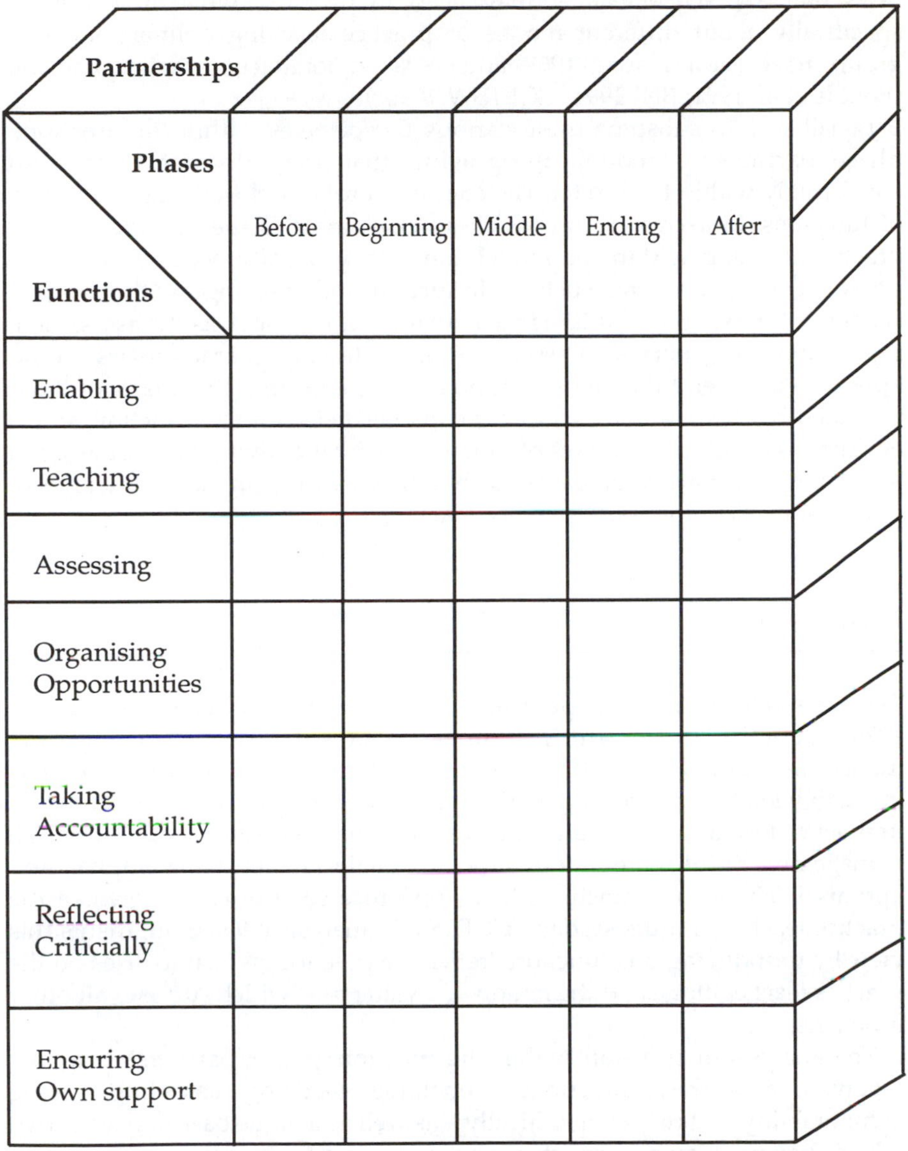

Figure 5.1 The function/phase/partnership model of practice teaching

1998) identify the characteristics of the effective/ineffective practice teacher. Some (Steinaker and Bell 1979; Tomlinson 1995) delineate a number of roles that the practice teacher can play. Most writers identify the various practical tasks that a practice teacher may need to perform, while a few write specifically about different modes of practice teaching delivery such as group supervision (Harper 1969) and so-called 'long-arm' practice teaching (Foulds et al. 1991; Bell 1991; CCETSW 1996c).

I shall seek to subsume these various perspectives within the function/phase/partnership model, recognising that they do not always sit comfortably within the model. The concept of roles is closely aligned to that of functions. Moreover, it is possible to chart most of the specific tasks of practice teaching within the model, since they usually occur at a certain phase in the placement, such as induction and meetings with personal academic tutors, or are fulfilling particular functions, such as the assessment report and the supervision session. Practice teacher characteristics would appear to transcend the model, although it is interesting that many of those indicated by the research literature are associated with one function only – enabling. The different modes of practice teaching delivery have developed in response to particular contexts, but they usually involve a degree of partnership, as in long-arm practice teaching.

Functions

The general literature on supervision in social work (Kadushin 1976; Pettes 1979) identifies three principal functions of supporting, teaching and managing staff. The particular context of professional education has inevitably led to the recognition of assessment as an additional key function in practice teaching (Jarvis and Gibson 1985; Ford and Jones 1987), although management of full-time staff in the 1990s entails an increasing emphasis on appraisal. These four functions focus on processes primarily between the practice teacher and the student. CCETSW's analysis (1996a) augments this view by introducing one function, 'reflective practice', which focuses on the practice teacher alone and the notion of a value base which suffuses all other functions.

The analysis of function within the function/phase/partnership model retains five of these functions – enabling, teaching, assessing, taking accountability and reflecting critically – as well as a value base and adds two others. Ensuring own support is a second function focusing primarily on the practice teacher. Organising placement opportunities is somewhat subsumed within CCETSW's (1996a) management function but gives the function greater prominence and moves beyond practice teacher/student activities within the one setting to include other people and settings.

Enabling

This term is used by Brown and Bourne to describe the function of helping people 'to work to the best of their ability, implying a person-centred caring function' (1996: 10). This function is central to all the activities of the caring professions and as such incorporates a value which is central to practice teaching in the caring professions. It is particularly crucial if the practice teacher's practice towards the student is to be congruent with how they encourage the student to behave towards their clients. It is also essential if the practice teacher's other functions such as teaching and assessment are to be effective: few students will be receptive to learning or able to perform at their optimal level, if they have not been enabled within a strange setting.

It is for this reason that the enabling function is invariably important at the start of a placement. I usually suggest to students that a primary aim in the first few days of a placement is to become comfortable and that they can seek my support in achieving that. Other aims about learning and assessment can wait. I have known of several early placement breakdowns which have primarily occurred due to practice teachers, and sometimes students, rushing precipitately into other functions. This is particularly the case with assessment, for example, when there has been a pre-existing assessment concern, which is making one or both of the participants too anxious to attend to the initial need for the student to become comfortable. However, enabling will also be a theme running through the placement, taking on different guises: as the student needs extra support when faced with difficulties on placement, in the HEI setting or at home, or when the student needs to become more autonomous as a worker.

Enabling can be seen to entail two allied processes, supporting and empowering. Practice teachers can support students by helping them to secure a comfortable, relatively stress-free environment within which they can feel confident and valued. Bond and Holland (1998) indicate a number of ways in which to support a student; these include basic punctuality and reliability, acceptance and encouragement. Anderson and Shannon (cited in Brooks and Sikes 1997) also refer to encouragement and include protecting and befriending. Several studies indicate how important this process is for students. Secker (1992) uses words such as 'warm' and 'reassuring' to describe the preferred style of social work practice teachers, while Fernandez (1998) refers to 'approachability' which is akin to the lower-key 'availability' noted by Walker et al. (1995). Rosenblatt and Mayer (1975) identified 'being unsupportive' as one of four unhelpful characteristics in a practice teacher. Earnshaw (1995) indicates how support is similarly valued by nurse students.

Bond and Holland (1998) and Gardiner (1989) recognise the potential danger of support developing into counselling, particularly when it entails responding to students' feelings. Whilst accepting the appropriateness of the student's feelings, allowing them to continue feeling them and helping the student resolve them somewhat through discharge or understanding, it is necessary to maintain a boundary which prevents that process developing into a more thoroughgoing counselling process. My first job as a full-time practice teacher directly followed a period primarily as a family therapist and I had to learn quickly that an appropriate response to the various stresses students experienced within their families whilst on placement was to be sympathetic and understanding, but not to embark upon therapy.

Empowerment is recognised as a valued process in the supervision of both nursing (Bond and Holland 1998) and social work (Brown and Bourne 1996) staff. Collins' (1998) analysis of empowerment suggests two strands. One is encapsulated in Adams' definition: 'The process by which individuals, groups and/or communities become able to take control of their circumstances and achieve their goals, thereby being able to work towards maximising the quality of their lives' (1990: 43).

In the context of practice learning, this occurs when a student is enabled to shape the placement to their own learning needs, often when these do not easily match what the practice teacher or the placement setting have to offer. One student had experienced a short period working in a residential setting in the midst of a predominantly fieldwork placement. They wished to pursue this learning opportunity with the same practice teacher in a second placement. As the practice teacher, I had to advocate on the student's behalf both with the HEI and the practice setting in order to achieve this unusual outcome.

The second strand in Collins' (1998) analysis is helping the student to confront oppression, of themselves or of other disadvantaged groups. One black student in a day care setting had become aware how the staff were tending to segregate and marginalise the small number of black clients attending the agency. The student felt vulnerable in bringing this to the attention of the manager, who was involved in their assessment. As a long-arm practice teacher not working in that setting, I was able to help the student develop appropriate strategies for raising the issue and achieving some change, without incurring any redress. The literature (Humphries et al. 1993; Burgess et al. 1992) also includes the value of black support groups and consultants in empowering black students within oppressive settings. Other students can be disadvantaged within different settings, partly because of their structural position in terms of gender, sexual orientation, physical abilities, or religious beliefs. One study (Evans 1990a) suggested that social work students on placement were most discriminated against in the assessment process on grounds of disability. In other settings students may be vulnerable to particular power relationships, for example, male students in early years placements.

Teaching

This function is being increasingly emphasised as the learning potential of the practice setting becomes more fully recognised within education for the caring professions: it is not simply a place to put into practice learning which has been acquired in the academic setting. The replacement of the earlier term 'student supervisor' with the current 'practice teacher' in social work education (Sawdon and Sawdon 1987) is symptomatic of this development. The role of the practice teacher in helping students to learn is the topic of much of this book, particularly in Parts II and III. There are, however, four points which can be usefully made in this section.

First, a useful distinction can be made between teaching as a transitive verb, 'doing something' to the student, and as a causative verb, helping the student 'do something', also made above (see Chapter 2). In the first usage, it is appropriate at times to inform, confirm, disconfirm and prescribe (Anderson and Shannon, cited in Brooks and Sikes 1997), particularly when students do not know or are unsure of something and when their learning style emphasises external authority. This process is congruent with Heron's (1975) authoritative modes of intervention and Gardiner's (1989) first level of learning.

In the second usage, it is appropriate at other times to encourage the student to learn for themselves, by organising appropriate practice opportunities, by questioning, modelling and giving feedback on their practice, particularly when they have some relevant experience to draw on and when their learning style favours internal authority. This process is more congruent with Heron's (1975) facilitative modes of intervention and Gardiner's (1989) second level of learning. Secker's (1992) study suggests that some social work students prefer the latter mode and Kolb's (1984) studies suggest this may be more widespread within the caring professions. The considerable advantage of choosing the latter mode, particularly when either is possible, is that it helps the student develop learning-to-learn skills which will be with them in future contexts when there is no practice teacher to tell them what to do.

Doel (1987) has made a major contribution to the practice teacher's teaching function by promoting the notion of the practice curriculum, whereby a degree of order or structure is introduced to the learning process within the practice setting. Shardlow and Doel's (1996) structured learning model continues this idea and they propose eight steps towards the development of the practice curriculum in a given practice context:

1. Defining aims
2. Identifying teaching content
3. Sequencing
4. Devising methods and strategies
5. Using examination methods
6. Publication
7. Review and evaluation
8. Summary

The considerable value of this contribution would seem to lie in awakening in every practice teacher an awareness that they can be more or less pro-active in influencing the student's learning whilst on placement. It has had a major impact in social work education, not only in placements but also in academic settings which can now more easily assign academic credit to learning in the practice curriculum.

The weakness in this conceptualisation, however, would seem to be in encouraging the practice teacher to consider that they will have the main role in structuring the student's learning on placement, when there are other important considerations. Competence-based professional education, as now exists in social work and initial teacher education, encourages an assessment-driven curriculum: students would be significantly disadvantaged if they were not able to learn how to perform satisfactorily all the required competences in order to pass their placement. Academic personal tutors may also be aware of learning that students need to acquire, either from past placement performance or from performance in the higher education institution. The model of practice learning proposed here in Chapter 2 also suggests that the student and the clients should have a major influence over the student's learning: the student will know what they are motivated to learn in terms of past gaps and future aspirations; the clients' needs should determine the practice and from the practice comes much of the student's learning.

It would seem more useful if the practice teacher considers what can be learned from the setting: from their own experience and understanding and from other learning opportunities in the placement, including the staff and work available. They would then take that thinking into the formulation of a placement learning agreement, which would comprise a synthesis of all the other perspectives as well as the practice teacher's.

Some writers (Fisher 1990; ENB 1996; Shardlow and Doel 1996) suggest that simulation has a role to play in practice teaching. There are undoubtedly some situations in practice when the student could benefit from rehearsal with the practice teacher and/or student peers before the actual practice performance, particularly when they are anxious about some unfamiliar practice or some possible risk to themselves or clients. Clearly the clients can benefit, too. However, Shardlow and Doel (1996) also suggest rehearsal for dangerous situations which are unlikely to occur on placement. If the purpose of placements is to promote learning for and from practice, it would seem more appropriate for this important learning to take place in the higher education institution.

Gardiner's (1989) study suggests that practice teachers' confidence in their teaching derives significantly from their confidence as a practitioner. Many students might well echo this view, recognising when the validity of the practice teacher's teaching is demonstrable in their practice. This raises the issue of which occupational context for practice teaching is most suitable. There are broadly three variants throughout the caring professions: predominantly practitioner with some teaching, predominantly teacher with some practice, and half and half practitioner/teacher. The first two develop one area of competence rather to the detriment of the other. Only in the 50/50 mode is the practice teacher/practitioner likely to develop and sustain competence in both areas. Whilst this combination is advocated for nurse education (Davies et al. 1996) and some part-time freelance practice teachers in social work are also part-time practitioners, there would appear to be little significant development of such arrangements in any caring profession nor any research to support current models.

Assessing

The general literature on practice teaching (Jarvis and Gibson 1985; Ford and Jones 1987; Bogo and Vayda 1987; Shardlow and Doel 1996; Brooks and Sikes 1997) fully recognises the importance of this function. Both CCETSW and the English National Board have for some time required that a member of staff in the practice setting contributes directly to student assessment. Since 1992 (DfEE 1992), this has increasingly been a feature of initial teacher education, although the latest requirements at the time of writing (DfEE 1997), do not specify a role for the practice teacher in assessment. This emphasis on practice assessment is firmly rooted in the political context of education for the caring professions, not only in guaranteeing a quality outcome of the educational process, but also seeking to ensure a qualified workforce which is economically effective (Skilbeck et al. 1994). The particular aims and practices of this function are elaborated in Part IV.

Taking accountability

The function of taking accountability within the practice agency for the student's service to their clients is one strand of the dual accountability the practice teacher exercises: the other is to the educational programme for the student's learning and assessment.

The importance of this function stems from the fact that the primary orientation of the practice agency is towards service delivery and not towards student learning. Ultimately, it will be the agency which will be accountable – to its clients, the public and the law – if a student not in their employment has acted against clients' interests. It is perhaps surprising that agency shortcomings due to student involvement do not reach the media more often. The agency will wish, therefore, that the designated practice teacher plays some role in ensuring that the student fulfils certain requirements of the agency, be they local policies or derived from national statutes. The practice teacher may not fulfil this function alone: often the line manager for the team in which the student is placed will contribute to its fulfilment.

The practice teacher will often discharge this function in the selection of work for the student, again often in conjunction with the line manager. They will need to balance the learning needs of the student against the level of service which should be available to agency clients. Excessive concern to protect clients against a diminished service can lead to the notion of 'student work', which usually inhibits the student's learning. The function extends further into the process of service delivery. If the practice teacher or manager are concerned about the quality of the service, they may decide to monitor the student more carefully, to work closely with the student or even to re-allocate the work to someone else. These decisions all involve balancing student learning, not only of the practice skills and knowledge but also of taking responsibility for their own practice, against client needs. Some of the reflective apprenticeship processes outlined in Chapter 6 allow a sensitive appraisal of this balance.

The extreme exercising of this accountability can result in the termination of a placement. One student was withdrawn from a placement because of sexual impropriety with a client, for example, while another was failing to perform a major service of the agency to an adequate level. In such circumstances, it is unlikely that the practice teacher will act alone, but they will probably contribute to the decision. CCETSW (1995) usefully require all social work qualifying programmes to plan for this contingency.

Not all practice teachers find it equally easy to fulfil this function. Being responsible for a student can be a professional rite of passage: it may be the first time that a practitioner is responsible for someone else's work. Some practitioners respond to this new responsibility by keeping too close a rein on the student's quality of service, others do not keep it close enough. Moreover, the relationship between the practice teacher and the line manager may further complicate the exercising of accountability. If the practice teacher is keeping the accountability function largely to themselves without adequately consulting with the manager, the manager may not allow the student certain practice opportunities. In one of my full-time practice teacher posts, I was also the students' line manager, thus eliminating one complication in the exercise of accountability. However, in the other I was not and needed to negotiate carefully with the students' different line managers over the delicate line between learning needs and service delivery.

Whilst this function is clearly crucial for the continued availability of practice placements in professional education, it has received different emphasis at different times and in different professions. The increasing emphasis on learning in social work practice teaching (Thompson et al. 1990; Shardlow and Doel 1996) has led to less focus on managerial supervision than is found in earlier literature (Pettes 1979; Ford and Jones 1987). Moreover, it may be that the strong traditions of accountability within local government has affected social work in ways that the traditions of professional autonomy in health and education have not. There is little recognition of the importance of this practice teacher function in either the nursing literature (Jarvis and Gibson 1985; Hinchliff 1992) or the initial teacher education literature (Fish 1995; Brooks and Sikes 1997). None the less, the growing climate of public scrutiny, quality control and litigation throughout the human services sector suggests that this function will increase rather than decrease in importance.

Organising placement opportunities

The preceding four functions focus particularly on processes between the practice teacher and the student. However, this fifth function recognises the fact that placements involve far more than the one designated practice teacher and sometimes more than the one practice setting. In order that the four preceding functions can be satisfactorily fulfilled, the practice teacher will need to work with other people, sometimes their peers sometimes their managers, so that their contribution to the student's placement can be planned and delivered. This function is in effect concerned with indirect work on the student's behalf rather than the direct delivery of a service to the student.

Its importance is recognised in the nursing (Jarvis and Gibson 1985) and social work (Shardlow and Doel 1996) literature. However, it would seem to attract special emphasis in the literature of initial teacher education (Hill et al. 1992; Hurst and Wilkin 1992; Mountford 1993), possibly due to the intermediate size of many schools as practice settings and the consequent designation of 'professional mentors' with a school-wide coordinating role.

Social services departments and hospitals, on the other hand, are generally large organisations, with restricted opportunities to coordinate the details of student placements at an organisational level.

The importance of organising other people to fulfil the enabling function with the student arises particularly if the practice teacher is not physically available to the student, being either in another part of the building or in another building altogether, as is the case with long-arm practice teaching (see below) or simply absent through leave or illness. In one of my full-time practice teaching posts, I was located in a central office and students were placed in different team rooms throughout a large building. We developed in the agency a system whereby one team member would usually undertake to be the student's immediate source of support, since they were more immediately available than I. Support may also need to be organised from another source at other times, for example if the student resents the practice teacher's assessment of them or if the structural difference between practice teacher and student is felt to be unhelpful.

The practice teacher will invariably need to organise different opportunities for meeting the student's learning needs on the placement. Chapter 2 provides a detailed exploration of placement learning opportunities beyond the practice teacher, all of which will require organisation by the practice teacher. Sometimes, however, the student's learning needs cannot be fully met within the one agency setting. This is more likely to be the case in educational programmes with fewer placements, such as social work and teaching, than with a greater range of placements, such as medicine and nursing. Social work education has developed the practice of setting up placements with more than one setting involved, sometimes called 'integrated' (Davis and Walker 1985; Johnson and Shabbaz 1989), 'complex' (Burger and Greenwell 1989) or 'network' (Boutland and Batchelor 1993) placements. These placements can be fairly evenly split between two settings or predominantly in one, according to learning needs.

From a study of these placements in one area, Boutland and Batchelor (1993) report two main advantages for student learning: a broader perspective on client need and an opportunity for transfer of learning within the one placement. The main disadvantages reported were the possibilities for confusion, given the number of people involved, and the time spent in organisation both of which, they suggest, diminish with experience. My own experience has been very similar. In one post, I organised a number of placements spanning a Social Services Department community child care team and a hospital-based child and family guidance clinic. Students were able to gain two very different approaches to working with children and their families, to understand their similarities and dissimilarities and to try out techniques in one setting which they had learned in the other. The organisational difficulties diminished and, I suspect, the learning increased, as the practice teacher in the other setting and I became more accustomed to our different practices, in much the same way as Davis and Walker (1985).

The growth of competence-based professional education has also placed extra demands on the practice teacher for organising opportunities to assess competences which cannot readily be assessed through the work which is routinely available to the student. This may involve the practice teacher in seeking work opportunities elsewhere within their practice setting or even outside it in another practice setting. The organisational task would not only involve finding the relevant work but also, frequently, arranging for someone to supervise and assess it. The need to organise with the line manager the exercising of accountability has already been discussed.

Reflecting critically

This phrase refers to the function of reflecting critically on performance as a practice teacher in particular. All caring professions expect their practitioners to be reflective in order to benefit their work with clients: students have a similar need for practice teachers to think carefully how best to deliver an educational service to them. It is tempting for practice teachers to spend what limited time and energy for reflection on their clients rather than their students. However, it is a salutary reminder that a failure to maximise a student's learning or to assess them adequately may rebound on generations of subsequent clients throughout that one student's career. A good practice teacher will, as Brooks and Sikes (1997) suggest, be generally reflective, about their practice as well as their teaching and England (1997) goes as far as to suggest that social work practice teachers have particular strengths within the profession as reflective thinkers.

CCETSW give full recognition to this function in their requirements for the Practice Teaching Award and indicate two aspects of reflection:

> Critically evaluate own performance as a practice teacher and the quality of the learning opportunities and assessment provided.
>
> Consider and discuss research, policies and developments with respect to practice teaching. (CCETSW 1996: 14)

These two aspects are discussed in detail above in Chapter 3, along with many other broader facets of reflection. Within practice teaching, there are particular advantages in including the student, as the 'consumer' of the practice teaching service, in the reflective process. If the practice teacher is seeking to help the student to learn the value of involving the client in evaluating the student's practice, for example, the practice teacher can effectively model that process in the practice teaching relationship. Moreover, if the student is involved in evaluating the practice teacher's effectiveness, particularly if this contributes to a formal process such as staff appraisal or assessment for a practice teaching award, this can contribute realistically to some equalising of the power differential between practice teacher and student which is inherent in the practice teacher's assessment function.

Ensuring own support

The importance of support is recognised throughout the caring professions due to the emotional, physical and intellectual stresses inherent in responding to client need, often in unresponsive organisations. Practice teaching also has its sources of stress, most notably when assessing a marginal or failing student (Williamson et al. 1989; Evans 1990a) but also when enabling a challenging student or when relationship conflicts emerge between the student and the practice teacher. Juggling the conflicting demands of practice and practice teaching can of itself be stressful.

It is likely that the support system to which the practice teacher turns at such times may not be the same as the one they turn to with the stresses of their practice with clients. Their peer professionals or managers may have little to offer over difficulties specific to practice teaching. Some agencies organise peer support groups for the practice teachers within the agency. Clapton (1989) reports the working of one such group in a social services department, while Brooks and Sikes (1997) explore the role of the mentor team within a large school. In some agencies, too, the presence of someone with a designated role in practice learning – such as the clinical teacher in radiography, the social work practice learning coordinator or the professional mentor in initial teacher education – can provide support on an individual basis.

Sometimes, however, the practice teacher will need to be more pro-active to secure relevant support. If no peer group exists within the agency, a practice teacher might invest the time in convening one, knowing they would benefit from it themselves as well as the other people involved. Alternatively the practice teacher may need to go beyond their own agency for support. Higher education institutions often convene meetings for the practice teachers working for their programmes which can provide some support, although these meetings often have other functions such as induction, information-giving or training. In some professions, support groups are organised at local and regional levels. Some community practice teachers in district nursing and health visiting, for example, meet together for mutual support and encouragement. The National Organisation for Practice Teaching (see Appendix) has some affiliated local groups in different places in England. Although these currently cater for social work practice teachers, the growth of inter-professional practice teacher training (Bartholomew et al. 1996) may lead to more inter-professional support groups.

This function has been described using the term 'ensuring' for good reason. The marginal position of practice teaching in both the practice agency and the HEI makes it likely that many practice teachers will not have adequate support as of right, but will need to organise it for themselves. Even the need for proper workload adjustment to allow sufficient time for practice teaching will not automatically be granted, as the literature for different caring professions suggests (Thompson and Marsh 1991; Hallett et al. 1993; Davies et al. 1995) but will need to be negotiated with colleagues and managers. CCETSW (1991, 1996b) have sought to ensure that all social work agencies approved by them as practice learning agencies provide adequate support for their practice teachers, but no published monitoring data indicates the effectiveness of this strategy.

Phases

Before the placement

A reflective approach to the responsibility of practice teaching will entail some preparation before the student arrives at the practice agency. Preparation can focus mainly on three areas: the practice teachers themselves, the student and the practice setting.

Practice teachers can prepare themselves for the task of practice teaching in a number of ways. One way is to reflect on what they bring to the activity, as a practitioner, a learner, and a teacher, but above all as a person. Preston-Shoot suggests several dimensions including:

1. Professional background
2. Training undertaken
3. Experience as a practice teacher
4. Learning from these experiences
5. Other experience of being supervised
6. How these might influence approach to practice teaching
7. Value base and preferred style of working

8. Special interests
9. Theoretical orientation(s)
10. Preferred methods of intervention
11. Knowledge about practice teaching
12. Attitude to practice teaching
13. Learning opportunities on offer
14. Expectations of students
15. Strengths and weaknesses
16. Expectations of and approach to supervision
17. Style of supervision. (Preston-Shoot 1989: 8)

Although lengthy, this list is not exhaustive. The practice teacher might also wish to reflect on their own experience as a student and their fundamental views on how learning takes place. The aim of this reflection is to begin to access many ideas and values, about learning and professional practice, which the student will undoubtedly touch on during the course of the placement. A first encounter with a student is more likely to entail such reflection, just as early encounters with clients also require some fundamental positioning. For a first-time practice teacher, this reflection will sometimes take place during a practice teacher training course. Preston-Shoot (1989) also helpfully suggests that the student could be sent the fruit of this preparation in advance as a practice teacher profile, in order to assess their compatibility.

The matching of the student, the practice teacher and the practice agency is also a task which can involve the practice teacher before the placement begins. This can occur not only in an exchange of profiles, preferably from the student and the agency as well as the practice teacher, but also in a meeting between the practice teacher and the student. This meeting, sometimes called the 'placement-making' meeting, is best timed after preliminary information has been exchanged between student and practice teacher, usually via intermediaries, but before the placement commences. Its purpose is to reach a decision whether the student can have their learning needs sufficiently met in that setting with that practice teacher, whether the practice teacher and student will be able to form a constructive working relationship and whether the agency's requirements for their workforce can be met – a sort of three-way vetting.

At its best, this meeting can have an important empowering role, particularly for the student (Walker et al. 1995) but also for the practice teacher and the agency, either of whom may at times feel somewhat put upon by the higher education institution. The shortage in placements throughout the caring professions, however, means that in reality people have little choice not to proceed with a placement following such a meeting.

Even without the possibility of choice, the meeting can be bring several benefits. It can reduce the student's anxiety at the start of the placement, since they will have some prior knowledge of both the agency and the practice teacher. It can, as Danbury (1986) suggests, provide a useful launch to the relationship between the student and the practice teacher. Moreover, the practice teacher will be more aware of the student's needs and hence be able to start their function of organising different opportunities for the student on the placement, including the possible workload and the role of colleagues and managers (see Chapter 2). This will be particularly important if the placement is a short one with less time to organise as it proceeds or if arrangements need to be made outside the practice teacher's setting.

Beginning of the placement

Beginnings are one of the twelve basic life situations outlined by Butler and Elliott: 'What is characteristic of a beginning? Not knowing what "it" will be like, excitement, apprehension, relief, fear, above all, the range of reactions to change' (1985: 32). However well the practice teacher has prepared before the placement, it is unlikely they will know how the student will be feeling on the first day of the placement. Hallett et al. (1996) describe the student's experience of this initial phase in a placement as 'encountering reality', particularly if the student has been in an academic setting for some time before coming on placement. Anxiety is a common emotion in the face of new experiences of such far-reaching consequences for a student's career. Students usually feel anxiety at an appropriate level, although some students can become somewhat paralysed by it and unable to act without guidance from the practice teacher. For this reason the practice teacher needs to attend particularly to the student's support at this time. I have always tried simply to be available as much as possible in the first two or three weeks of a placement, since the practice teacher is often the initial source of security, at least until the student has made other contacts within the agency.

Induction

One important process which can help the student allay some of their anxiety at the strangeness of the placement is an induction. Walker et al. (1995) indicate how important this process is for many social work students. The task of inducting students to a placement can involve three main principles. The first and most crucial is for the practice teacher to negotiate the induction process with the student concerned, as with all other aspects of learning on the placement. The learning needs and style of each student will determine a different pace and content of induction. One particular aspect of pacing concerns when the student begins to take on practice: some like to get settled for a while before taking on practice, others cannot wait to be like a 'real practitioner'. Another aspect for negotiation is how much of the induction programme is arranged by the practice teacher or the student. Some students, perhaps through anxiety, will be pleased for the practice teacher to arrange the entire process, others might feel somewhat patronised. The 'placement-making' meeting is often a convenient opportunity to agree the arrangements for induction.

Another principle concerns a process of gradually proceeding outwards, starting with the space the student will occupy (if there is one), to the other people in the room, to other people and resources in the building, to the welfare network beyond the agency. It is a common failing in induction programmes to send people far and wide from the start without allowing them time to become comfortable in their work base. Baldwin (1992) makes a similar distinction between the internal and the external in inducting students.

The third principle entails involving other people in the induction process – another organising function. This is mainly in order that the student can become acquainted with more people in a natural way. If, for example, there are already students in the practice agency, they will usually give an excellent 'student-eye' view of agency staff, resources and practices at the same time as beginning the process of peer support. There are many aspects of the agency which other staff are better placed than the practice teacher to introduce to the student. Administrative staff are often the best people to introduce administrative procedures, including health and safety matters. Management staff may be best placed to explain agency policies and resource allocation. Involving others can also reduce the student's dependence on the practice teacher. An induction pack (Brooks and Sikes 1997), particularly for an agency which frequently provides placements, has a similar effect.

Placement agreement

A second task which can contribute significantly to the student's orientation at the beginning of a placement and subsequently throughout the rest of the placement is the completion of a placement agreement or contract. Learning contracts are strongly advocated in educational theory and practice as a means of promoting student self-directed learning, particularly for adult students in contexts of some choice over the learning process (Knowles 1986; Anderson et al. 1998). They are of particular value in practice learning, partly because there is scope in placements for students' individual learning needs to be addressed in a way that is not usually possible among the large teaching groups of the higher education institution and partly because there are a range of different interests, including the student's, which need to be reconciled in planning a placement. The use of placement contracts is noted particularly in the social work literature (Collins 1985; Preston-Shoot 1989), perhaps because contracts are also frequently used in social work practice, and there is evidence that they are valued by the students (Walker et al. 1995). The English National Board (1996) also note their value for nurse placements, but they seem to receive little attention in initial teacher education.

Two main elements determine the effectiveness of placement agreements: the process and the content. The process of the agreement largely involves negotiation between the main interested parties. There are three main interests to be considered: the student's, the educational programme's and the agency's. Usually these three interests are brought together in a meeting, where they are often represented by, respectively, the students themselves, the academic tutor and the practice teacher. Sometimes it can also be valuable to include the line manager of the team in which the student is placed, since they often determine access to key resources for learning, especially clients. Increasing workload pressures in the higher education sector are reducing the presence of academic tutors at these meetings and risking the absence of a key interest. Although the meeting is a key point for negotiation, this process can begin before a meeting and proceed after it. Typically, the agreement is written down once negotiations are completed and signed by all parties, although it is best considered as a flexible guide which may need to be altered as the placement progresses.

Usually, the student is the least powerful of these parties and it is important to empower them in the negotiation process. One way of doing this is to encourage the student to reflect in detail on what they wish to learn during the placement and then to present these thoughts at the meeting. One student worked on their placement agreement for a period of two or three weeks, in the process refining their needs considerably, with the result that they contributed significantly to a highly detailed programme for the placement which the student was able to accomplish most successfully. Students can also, in my view, be empowered by the timing of the negotiation. If it occurs a short while into the placement, the student will be reasonably aware of the learning opportunities within the agency and will have developed some relationship with the practice teacher. Some educational programmes, however, seek to complete an agreement before the placement starts. Whilst this has some advantages in providing an immediate launch pad for shorter placements, the student can be highly dependent upon the practice teacher's and the tutor's view of what can be learned in that setting and not empowered to determine their own learning needs and strategies for meeting them.

Anderson et al. (1998) identify the four main items in the content of a learning contract as 'what is to be learnt, the resources and strategies available to assist in learning it, what will be produced as evidence of the learning having occurred and how that product will be assessed' (1998: 163). In the context of a placement agreement, these translate as: the student's individual learning objectives; the learning opportunities available to meet these – including the work available, supervision arrangements and other staff available – and the criteria and methods of assessment. Other areas for the agreement include arrangements for accountability for service delivery; support for all parties to the placement, particularly for the student if difficulties arise between the student and the practice teacher and links between the placement and the higher education institution, particularly if academic and practice learning run concurrently. All these items, particularly the learning objectives, are most helpful if they are detailed and specific. Placement agreements are more likely to be effective tools to guide the placement if they bear the individual mark of the student, the practice teacher and the practice agency, and are not simply some bureaucratic agreement produced in the standardised format of an educational programme.

Middle of the placement

Placements generally progress quickly beyond the beginning phase, since there are usually many new experiences to learn from and much that the practice teacher wishes the student to achieve. This rapid rate of progress makes it important to take stock before the end of the placement looms too near, in order to ensure that crucial aspects of learning and assessment are not neglected. Sometimes, however, particularly in placements of several months' duration, the first acceleration of learning and motivation can give way to a plateau with little further development. Erikson (1963) characterises the middle part of the human life-cycle as a tension between stagnation and creativity and a similar tension can occur on longer placements.

Interim placement review

A common strategy for dealing with both these possibilities is to review the placement. CCETSW (1995) usefully require this in all social work qualifying programmes. A well-constructed placement agreement can form the basis of a review, giving a focus for all aspects of the original agreement, particularly the student's learning and assessment. It is also helpful if the same participants are present for the review as were present for the original agreement: they alone are fully aware of what was achieved in the initial negotiations and can monitor its progress. Although academic tutors will be less in touch with the detailed placement activities, their very distance can be an advantage, partly in ensuring a broad view of the whole placement, including its aims, and partly in helping the student/practice teacher relationship progress, if for some reason it has become uncomfortable or inflexible. Likewise, the line manager may be helpful in suggesting new work opportunities which can assist the student's progression in the second half of the placement.

Usually the review has a retrospective and a prospective function. The retrospective function involves an evaluation of the placement experience (particularly by the student) and an evaluation of the student's performance (particularly by the practice teacher). These two evaluations introduce an element of reciprocity into the exchange: I usually encourage the student to give their perspective first in case it becomes swamped by other people's. It is usually helpful for the student if they can see their mid-way evaluation written down, even if it is not required by the educational programme. Positive feedback will be reassuring; negative feedback will make it clear what they need to address.

The prospective function usually focuses on learning methods which can help the student progress in the second half of the placement; the student may be in a better position to benefit from more reflective apprenticeship methods (see Chapter 6) or to be able to relate theory and practice better (see Chapter 4) now that they understand the practice a little more. This focus can help the strongest students as well as those who are struggling somewhat. Another prospective focus, especially for weaker students, is to clarify assessment targets which need to be met in order to pass the placement. As with the original placement objectives, the more specific these targets are the easier it will be for both the student and practice teacher to assess whether they are achieved or not.

Ending of the placement

Endings are another of the twelve basic life situations identified by Butler and Elliott (1985). Their analysis of ending focuses on the feelings of mourning which stem from loss. It is likely that both the student and the practice teacher will feel some degree of loss at the end of the placement, particularly if they have enjoyed a close and constructive working relationship (Clow 1998). Both student and practice teacher may experience some disappointment at not having been able to achieve all they would have wished. The student is also likely to miss the other staff and probably some clients in the placement. However, other emotions also pertain at an ending: pleasure at the achievements of the placement, relief after a period of extra work and anticipation of the next phase. The practice teacher can help the student express their feelings and further equalise the relationship by expressing their own feelings. Rituals are also helpful at such times and many practice teachers and students organise some social event, often involving other members of the team.

Final placement review

Another aspect of ending the placement is evaluation, usually through a review similar to the one conducted in the middle of the placement. The principal difference between the two reviews is the fact that the final review also has a mid-way process to look back at as well as the original placement agreement. The confidence generated by a positive mid-way review will sustain the final review. Likewise, if difficulties prevailed at the mid-way stage, they may well persist or re-emerge at the final stage, particularly if they have not been satisfactorily resolved in the intervening period. Usually, too, there is a greater emphasis on evaluating the student's performance (see Chapter 7), although care should be taken to equalise the process of evaluation: the practice teacher and the practice agency also need feedback. In my experience, some agency teams have considerably valued the student's more objective perspective on how they work and the experienced practice teacher is likely to learn more from student feedback than any general literature on practice teaching and learning. It is also tempting to adopt a solely retrospective focus at the final placement review. However, it is useful to focus on the future as well as the past: the student's learning needs in the next placement or in paid employment; the practice learning possibilities for future students in that practice agency.

Some of the final tasks concern the student's work with their clients. Just as much of the learning at the beginning of the placement will have focused on beginning work with clients – how to engage with clients and to assess new situations – so the learning at the end will focus on ending work with clients (Evans and Kearney 1996). Students will need to learn how to end working relationships, particularly when these relationships are of significance to either students or clients; they will need to learn any relevant administrative procedures for ending work. Often the future contact with the student's clients can become an issue. It can be tempting for the student's work to be transferred to another worker, since to terminate all contact may appear to give an unwelcome message that the student's work was of little consequence. Sometimes the practice teacher feels obliged to take on the student's clients rather than burden other team colleagues. Both these temptations can best be avoided, if inappropriate, by involving the line manager in making more objective decisions than the student or practice teacher may make.

After the placement

Once the student has left the practice agency, it is easy for the floodgates of practice demands to open and engulf the practice teacher once again. However, it is also useful to spend some time shortly after the placement ends and before the memory fades too much in reflecting on the placement. This can involve team colleagues and managers, for example, as a team meeting agenda item, or just the practice teacher. Useful pointers can be noted for future placements, including possible training needs for the practice teacher.

Partnerships

This third dimension emphasises the fact that the practice teacher does not work in isolation. This message of collaboration is an important one, particularly for practitioners contemplating their first experience of practice teaching and feeling somewhat daunted by the responsibility, and also for practice teachers who are encountering difficulties or whose own experience of being a student was with an isolated practice teacher. Moreover, there are pressures on the practice teacher from both the higher education institution and the practice agency to be seen as holding sole responsibility for the student's placement, due largely to the marginal position of practice learning in both organisations.

Partnership has been a familiar term in many aspects of the caring professions for the past decade and more, with an appeal based on its values of collectivity, cooperation and equality which contrast with prevailing values of individualism, competition and inequality. For the last decade it has played a prominent part in the implementation of professional education and has been enshrined in its regulatory frameworks (CCETSW 1989; DfE 1992; ENB 1993).

Despite its familiarity, partnership is at times a misleading term, since it vaguely celebrates communalities whilst minimising specific differences. Howe (1992) describes it as 'promiscuous' in its capacity to mean all things to all people. Two areas where differences often pertain are in the precise aims and degrees of power held by the different participants in a partnership. It is important that these differences are acknowledged and that attempts are made to resolve unhelpful differences. Howe (1992) suggests that more effective partnership arises through greater participation and choice for all concerned. Evans and Kearney suggest a number of steps towards establishing effective partnership:

- identifying common aims and values;
- listing the partners involved;
- recognising relevant differences in aims and values;
- recognising differences in resources and other powers between partners;
- allocating tasks and functions according to the different abilities of partners;
- delineating and allocating a lead role, when necessary;
- ensuring an essential, minimal flow of information between partners;
- identifying and establishing mechanisms for resolving differences. (Evans and Kearney 1996: 63)

Most of these processes will be relevant to four broad areas of partnership in practice teaching: with the student, experienced practice teachers, academic staff and practice agency staff and clients.

The student

The practice teacher and student will have a number of common aims and values derived from their common involvement in the same profession and the same educational endeavour. Resolving their differences will be a key process of their developing relationship throughout the placement, which is explored in detail below in Chapter 6.

The supervision session

One particular task through which their partnership is enacted is the supervision session. Shardlow and Doel (1996) prefer the term 'practice tutorial', thus emphasising the learning function and diminishing the accountability function. Whilst it has been historically and politically valuable to stress the learning which occurs in placements, it would seem, none the less, that accountability is still of paramount importance to the practice agency, since the protection of standards of service delivery will always be their primary interest. Moreover, supervision is gaining credence as a term and a concept throughout the caring professions. For these reasons, I retain the term 'supervision session'.

Supervision can take place in a number of modes: formal and informal, planned and unplanned, as suggested by Payne and Scott (1982). Chapter 6, entitled 'Reflective apprenticeship', explores in detail what they call informal supervision, since it occurs whilst practice continues. If formal has the meaning 'based on or observing conventional or prescribed forms and rules' (Longman 1984), the whole emphasis of that chapter is to suggest that reflective apprenticeship should be considered as part of the formal supervisory processes of a placement, since it functions best with agreed ground rules. In this section, the focus will be on specific sessions planned by the practice teacher and student to take place away from the demands of practice.

Planned supervision sessions in practice learning are usually either individual, between one practice teacher and one student, or in a group, between one practice teacher and a number of students. Payne and Scott (1982) and Shardlow and Doel (1996) allude to a number of other combinations which are occasionally employed, including pair supervision, when two students supervise each other and peer group supervision, a form of group supervision, when a number of practice teachers meet with a number of students.

Social work has a tradition of planned individual supervision sessions (Brown and Bourne 1996) and nursing is also developing this mode of learning (Bond and Holland 1998). However, other caring professions such as teaching and medicine would seem to have less experience to date, although they are aware of its value (Hinds 1998). Brown and Bourne define supervision as 'the primary means by which an agency-designated supervisor enables staff, individually and collectively; and ensures standards of practice' (1996: 9), which seems to emphasise the functions of enabling and accountability. Bond and Holland define supervision somewhat differently as 'regular, protected time for facilitated, in-depth reflection on clinical practice' (1998: 12), emphasising the learning function without reference to accountability, probably since the nursing tradition has been less management-orientated than social work. In practice teaching, supervision which is regular, planned and protected can underpin some of the 'availability' which students are reported to value highly (Walker et al. 1995; Fernandez 1998). In my view, a given supervision session may focus on any or all of the student-orientated functions (enabling, teaching, assessing, taking accountability, organising placement opportunities) and on reflective learning or relating theory and practice (see Chapters 3 and 4) according to circumstances. As Bond and Holland (1998) suggest, sessions are most useful when they are of sufficient length (more than one hour) to enable a more in-depth discussion than a passing conversation will allow. Moreover, their privacy ensures the possibility of confidentiality.

Students can be empowered in the supervision process if an agenda is negotiated between practice teachers and students at the start of the session and its items similarly prioritised if there are too many for the time available. Some practice teachers find it difficult to ensure that the student's items receive sufficient attention, while others neglect their own. It has been my practice to start with items which are important to the student, thus maintaining a student-centred learning process. Brief, clear recording of the sessions can also empower students by providing a reference point in the event of later disagreement, particularly if the content of recording and who writes it are also negotiated.

Individual supervision is often called one-to-one supervision, although Harre-Hindmarsh (1998) reports the growing use of the phrase 'one-*with*-one' in New Zealand, thus emphasising the reciprocal partnership in supervision. The main strengths of individual supervision sessions are the concentration on individual learning needs and a context in which most students feel confident to speak out. Its main disadvantage is that the power differential between practice teacher and student, not only derived from assessing and teaching functions but also at times grounded in structural differences, is undiluted.

Group supervision sessions, on the other hand, provide an excellent opportunity for peer learning and support and the possibility of empowering the students to oppose the practice teacher's position with less fear of reprisal. Group supervision is at its most effective when conducted in closed groups of no more than eight students. At such times, a knowledge of the principles of small group work which emphasise group functioning, group developmental processes and group leadership (Brown 1992) will probably contribute to effective supervision. However, group supervision can also accommodate a more open group in which students come and go, according to placement arrangements. The tradition of action learning sets (McGill and Beaty 1995) developed in management training has other insights to offer the practice teacher considering group supervision.

In placements with more than one student present, the practice teacher has three options for supervision: all individual, all group, or mixed. In my two student unit posts, there were invariably a number of students present and I developed the practice, particularly as I became more confident in group supervision and more convinced of its potential to empower, of encouraging students to choose between these options. Mainly they chose the mixed option, often alternating individual and group modes. Occasionally, they chose all group but never all individual, probably because of the empowerment and support potential of the group.

Experienced practice teachers

A practice teacher may wish to seek the assistance of another experienced practice teacher. Sometimes there are specialist posts within the practice agency which generate a bank of understanding and skill in practice teaching which other less experienced practice teachers can access, such as the clinical teachers in radiography, the practice learning coordinators in social work and the professional mentors in initial teacher education. In the absence of such posts, there are usually in any larger agency some members of staff who are known for their interest and experience in practice teaching and are usually willing to be consulted by other staff. Specialist post-holders and experienced practice teachers often convene the support groups which provide an alternative forum for assistance.

One common area for consultation is student assessment. A practice teacher who is not fully confident about expected standards will often find it reassuring to check their judgement with an experienced colleague. This may include organising an opportunity for the colleague to observe the student in practice. The CCETSW (1989) at one point made a requirement for the formal involvement of a 'second-opinion' practice teacher with all social work qualifying students who were either marginal or failing (see Chapter 7). Bogo and Vayda (1987) outline several other 'special situations' when the practice teacher may wish to seek advice from others with relevant experience and understanding, including when the student is exceptionally good or seen as 'resistant', is physically handicapped or sensorily impaired.

It is not just inexperienced practice teachers who can benefit from this form of consultation: every practice teacher can benefit from reflective dialogue with another. Sometimes practice teachers develop a process of co-consultation with one other particular practice teacher in their agency. In one of my student unit supervisor posts, I was fortunate to share similar employment conditions with another student unit supervisor and we frequently reflected on different aspects of the post together.

Academic staff

The increased emphasis on partnership in professional education has made it possible for the practice teacher to feel more entitled to approach any member of staff of the higher education institution with which the student is enrolled. However, the member of academic staff with whom the practice teacher is most likely to work during a placement is the placement liaison tutor. Sometimes this person is involved because they have a particular connection with the student for example as their personal tutor, sometimes their connection is with the practice agency and at other times it may be for a practical reason, such as the geographical spread of placements. It is useful to confirm the nature of this connection without making assumptions.

Three-way meetings

Most of the work is likely to occur at meetings during the placement, often called three-way meetings because of the three-way interests involved (the student, the agency and the educational programme), although in some circumstances more than three actual people may be involved, for example in long-arm practice teaching or when managers are present. There are advantages in three-way meetings occurring during the three main phases of the placement (beginning, middle and ending) so that all three interests can be represented in setting up, reviewing and rounding off the placement. However, the social work course investigated by Fernandez (1998) clearly expects only one such meeting, typically taken in the middle phase, while some programmes no longer have any such meetings.

The three-way meeting typically entails all three parties being able to work effectively together. It is possible to chart the development of the relationships between student, practice teacher and academic tutor throughout a placement (see Figure 5.2).

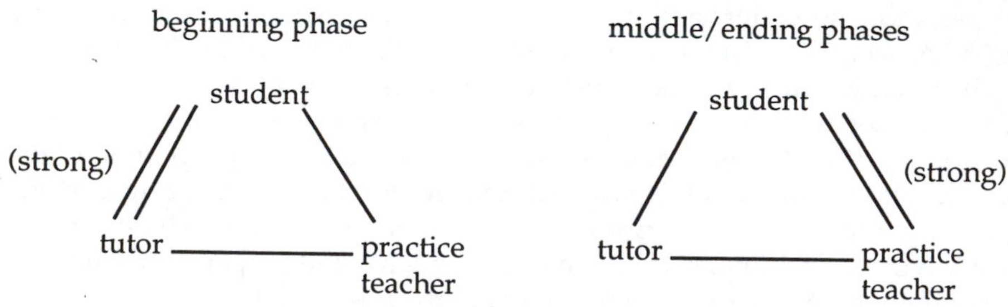

Figure 5.2 Relationship change during placement

At the beginning it is likely that the strongest relationship is between the tutor and the student, particularly when the student has been in the higher education institution for some time before this placement and the tutor and practice teacher have not yet met. However, by the middle and end phases of the placement, it is likely that the relationship between the student and the practice teacher will have considerably strengthened. The main implication of this change is the potential for collusion at different points in the placement which may need attention, for example, when the tutor can take a more objective role over assessment in the middle and at the end of the placement. The relationship which is least frequently strong, however, is the one between the practice teacher and the tutor. Sometimes, the attempts of the two more powerful participants in the meeting to work together can be made at the expense of the less powerful student, for example, as their conflicts are 'triangulated' (Evans and Kearney 1996) through the student. It is helpful if the practice teacher and the tutor can take some time to form a working relationship, either by phone before the three-way meeting or at the start of the meeting. A brief introduction to each other's professional histories, interests or values will usually suffice.

Both nursing and social work students seem to value these meetings (White et al. 1993; Davies et al. 1995, 1996; Fernandez 1998). Fernandez (1998) suggests that the most valued role of the academic tutor is in helping review the placement, which is probably related to the fact that most of the tutors on the course they studied visited placements in the middle phase. Another role valued by the students is the tutor's contribution to relating theory and practice. Students in this study did not generally find the academic tutors helpful in resolving difficulties, but the study neglects to report the precise nature of the relationship between students and academic tutors. It is my experience, both as a practice teacher and a tutor, that when the tutor is perceived, as potentially helpful by the student, for example, as their personal tutor, they can be helpful in allying with the student to resolve difficulties in the working relationship between the student and the practice teacher. It is useful if the practice teacher reflects before the meeting on how the presence of the tutor can be helpful to the progress of the placement.

Practice agency staff and clients

The different ways in which agency staff and clients can assist the practice teacher in the placement have been explored in some detail above in Chapter 2. One particular partnership which has not hitherto been explored, however, is the long-arm practice teaching arrangement.

Long-arm practice teaching

This term describes an arrangement whereby two people are involved in delivering the functions of practice teaching during the placement, one of them – the 'on-site supervisor' (CCETSW 1996c) – is within the accountability system of the placement agency, and the other is outside that system, usually working at a different location, and called the 'long-arm practice teacher'. This arrangement has developed in social work education

(Foulds et al. 1991), historically when students were educated through day release whilst in employment and someone other than the student's manager was needed to ensure the student's learning and assessment (CCETSW 1980, 1984) and more recently as appropriate practice teachers have become less available through workload pressures and the expense of training them. Often in this arrangement the long-arm practice teacher is experienced in the more usual arrangements for practice teaching and can be in a specialist post, freelance, or redeployed within a large agency. Lawson (1998) argues that long-arm practice teaching has provided a significant career pathway in social work. The on-site supervisor, on the other hand, can be either a practitioner, qualified or unqualified, or a manager in the setting.

One of the main purposes for this arrangement has been to maintain the quality of placements in the face of increasing shortages. However, there are other legitimate purposes, including: developing placements in the settings of other professions (Anderson et al. 1998), recruiting and developing staff in the responsibilities of practice teaching (Evans 1992) and developing placements in agencies which do not have an appropriate practice teacher (Evans 1992; CCETSW 1996c).

Bell (1991) describes a division of functions whereby the on-site supervisor takes accountability for the student's service delivery while the long-arm practice teacher is responsible for the student's learning. However, in my experience, the on-site supervisor can make a valuable contribution to the functions of enabling, teaching and assessing as well as accountability. It is usually the long-arm practice teacher who takes responsibility for organising the arrangement, sometimes after it has been initially set up by the educational programme. The *modus operandi* of long-arm practice teaching can entail the long-arm practice teacher meeting the student and the on-site supervisor separately, together or in a mixture of both methods. If the practice teacher is involved in a number of long-arm placements at the same time, they may also meet either the students or the on-site supervisors as a group. Choice between all these possibilities will depend largely on the particular purposes of the arrangement.

A number of difficulties in the arrangement are discussed in the literature. Marsh and Triseliotis (1996) report that the majority of students experiencing long-arm practice teaching in their study were critical of it. Bell (1991) suggests the possibility of confusion and feeling over-supervised, while Walker et al. (1995) report the opposite situation, with students feeling abandoned. A further difficulty encountered is that long-arm practice teachers find it difficult to locate themselves comfortably between the focus on practice of the on-site supervisor and the focus on relating theory and practice of the higher education institution.

None the less, Brewer and MacCowan (1992) advocate the strength of this form of practice teaching, particularly in its greater learning potential through the partnership between two different perspectives. This difference can include an informed and critical perspective on the practices of the practice agency and the consequent enhancement of learning-to-learn skills. Long-arm practice teaching can be effectively delivered through careful planning, a detailed delineation of functions which is incorporated in the placement agreement and clear communication throughout the placement.

Using the model

Any model provides a necessary simplification of reality. The three dimensions of this model do not stress other perspectives on practice teaching outlined above, such as the characteristics, tasks and roles of the practice teacher, although these have been somewhat subsumed within the analysis of this model.

Moreover, the somewhat static and inflexible delineation of different functions, phases and partnerships depicted diagrammatically in Figure 5.1 above does not accurately represent their complex interrelationship in the process of a placement. The different functions, for example, may overlap or conflict. The primary significance of feedback to the student during the placement is that it can contribute simultaneously to three key functions: enabling, teaching and assessment. On the other hand an overemphasis on monitoring all the student's service delivery may concentrate on accountability to the detriment of learning which is often best pursued by concentrating on particular aspects of their practice in depth. It is sometimes helpful to undertake periodic reviews of the student's total workload, whilst concentrating on key aspects of that workload for the majority of supervision time.

Two functions which can often conflict are enabling and assessing. On one occasion, I was the white, male practice teacher of a black, female student. At the beginning of the placement, the academic tutor stressed an emphasis on assessment for this placement since doubts about the student's performance in a previous placement had been raised by her white practice teacher in a rather unclear and informal way. However, the student was clearly highly anxious about these new developments and unsure of her position in this second placement, again with a white practice teacher. It seemed more important, therefore, to enable the student to establish herself in the new setting, becoming comfortable with new practices and staff, and involving a black consultant (Burgess et al. 1992; Anonymous 1994), before beginning to address assessment.

Likewise, the orderly progression through five phases suggested by the diagrammatic model is often far from the reality of placements. Studies of practice teaching in social work (Weinstein 1992; Walker et al. 1995) have revealed a significant tendency for placements to start late, which inevitably reduces or eliminates the pre-placement phase. Short placements such as the English National Board's (1997) minimum of 28 days allow very little development in the middle: they can be rather like a sandwich with no filling. At times, too, it becomes necessary for the placement process to take a backward step in order to regroup, for example, if difficulties arise between the practice teacher and the student, including issues about assessment. Placement breakdowns of the kind explored in Burgess et al. (1998) can often end abruptly with little or no opportunity to end properly.

Partnerships will ebb and flow throughout the placement, usually according to the student's changing learning needs and workload. At one point in the placement the team, for example, may have little role other than offering a degree of support, but later as the student comes to recognise similarities in values and approaches, they may have an increased role in the student's learning. Academic tutors may vary in the extent to which they aid the student's learning or their support during the placement. At times, too, partnerships which have hitherto proved fruitful may become counter-productive, for example, when a team member becomes overly allied to the student and begins to hinder the assessment process.

This model is offered as a general guide to the thinking of practice teachers and those who train and support them. However, it has also proved to have a more specific use as a review instrument in the support and training of practice teachers, whereby they can locate where they are in the placement process and systematically analyse and evaluate their current functions and partnerships and plan for those of the next phase.

6 Reflective Apprenticeship

Apprenticeship is an unexpected term to encounter in a book on aspects of professional education written at the end of the twentieth century. It has by now acquired many emotional connotations (Brooks and Sikes 1997), many of which are somewhat negative. The term is deliberately chosen, however, to provoke thought about the relevance of this long-standing mode of occupational learning to modern professional education.

Apprenticeship has been a common way of learning work practices since the time of the mediaeval craft guilds. According to Patrick and Geddie (1930), apprenticeship was regularised in Elizabethan England as a national scheme with six main components:

- a formally contracted arrangement
- between a learner and an expert practitioner (previously termed 'master')
- for the explicit purposes of the learning in the workplace
- of a craft or trade
- over a considerable period of time (as much as seven years)
- in the context of a close relationship (apprentices would typically live in the 'master's' house as one of the family).

Whilst the rigour of this national scheme was somewhat eroded in subsequent centuries, it persisted into the twentieth century. However, apprenticeship was heavily criticised in the early 1970s because of its emphasis on time-serving, with little focus on learning occupational competence (Torrance 1995).

Professional education has also placed a similar emphasis on apprenticeship in what Bines (1992) conceives of as the first of three phases in professional education wherein learning was 'largely on the job'. The pupil–teacher arrangement in teacher training (Taylor 1969) and the Nightingale nurse training (O'Brien and Watson 1993) are examples of this in the latter part of the nineteenth century.

Bines' main criticism of this form of professional education is, understandably from her position in an academic institution, the severe restriction to the academic institution's influence over the character and content of the training. Payne (1977) and Hislop et al. (1996) are also critical of apprenticeship in professional education on grounds of its potential conservatism when new ideas, for example from research, do not always penetrate the workplace. Jarvis and Gibson (1985) criticise the extent to which the excessive dependence of one learner on one experienced practitioner could be oppressive, when the learner is taught 'the only way' and is not enabled to develop their own style of practice. Brooks and Sikes (1997) are similarly concerned about an uncritical acceptance of one 'expert'.

While these are criticisms of substance, there are a number of strategies which can be employed to obviate them. In Chapters 1, 2 and 5, I have alluded to some of the processes whereby an academic institution can influence learning in the practice setting, although that is not a primary focus of this book. Moreover, an emphasis on reflective processes in the practice setting, as shall be seen later in this chapter, can obviate many of the dangers of conservatism, oppression and uncritical acceptance.

There are a number of important reasons for reappraising the value of apprenticeship in professional education. Most centrally, I believe that the growing role of higher education institutions in professional education has had the effect of shifting the focus of learning in the practice setting towards theory and away from practice performance. Macleod Clark et al. (1996) and Marsh and Tresiliotis (1996) report a deficit in skills learning in, respectively, Project 2000 nurse education and the Diploma in Social Work. Moreover, the practice curriculum advocated so influentially by Doel (1987a) and others (Phillipson et al. 1988) is modelled on the planned curricula of HEIs rather than the learning inherent in the unpredictability of practice.

While supporting a degree of theoretical and planned learning in the practice setting (see Chapters 2, 4 and 5), I would wish to reassert the central territory of practice learning, namely the effective conjunction of

practice performance* + *learner* + *teacher

which is also the essence of apprenticeship.

Another influence encouraging a reappraisal of apprenticeship is the increasing focus in assessment theory on validity rather than reliability (Brown and Knight 1994), which has found an echo in the workplace assessment schemes of the NVQ (Jessup 1991). Valid assessment methods ensure that the assessors have access to specified areas of professional competence, including practice performance. The English National Board (1997) now requires that assessors directly observe the practice of student nurses. Likewise, CCETSW have progressed from a strong but imprecise requirement for 'direct and systematic observation' of social work students' practice (CCETSW 1989) to a more precise requirement for three direct observations per practice placement (CCETSW 1995). GP trainees can be required to submit a video of up to ten consultations for their assessment (Anglia Regional General Practice Education Committee 1996). Requirements such as these produce a climate in which practice teacher/assessors are encouraged to increase their interaction with students during their practice performance, in other words

practice performance + assessee + assessor

At a broader level, the growing vocationalism in education discussed in Chapter 1 has been one factor contributing to a wider resurgence of apprenticeship in occupational learning. The 'Modern Apprenticeship' scheme promoted in the second half of the 1990s (Construction Industry Training Board 1995) has as a cornerstone the achievement of an NVQ award, thus rebutting the earlier criticism of time-serving without learning. Similarly, graduate apprenticeships are under consideration in higher education (DfEE 1998a; *Times Higher Education Supplement* 1998), not only seeking to ensure the vocational relevance of degrees but also addressing in part the growing disquiet over the funding of higher education.

Theoretical support for the processes of apprenticeship can be found in a number of sources. Social learning theory (Bandura 1977) emphasises the importance of observation and modelling in learning. The learner can learn to discriminate good and bad models and can be encouraged by the model to imitate their behaviours and values. Recent writers on initial teacher education have emphasised the value of these processes (Brooks and Sikes 1997), whilst its strength is also recognised by one of the nursing regulatory bodies (United Kingdom Central Council 1997).

It is possible to distinguish two types of modelling in professional education: unintentional and intentional. *Unintentional* modelling takes place, typically, in group care settings where a number of workers are working in the same physical space with a number of clients, for example, in a hospital ward or a residential home, and the student can observe the practice that is taking place around them and later integrate aspects of it into their own practice. *Intentional* modelling can occur when a student is invited to observe another worker with a view to modelling. This can occur without specifying the aspects of practice to be modelled, often called 'shadowing'. Intentional modelling can be more specific, for example, when a particular detail of technique is demonstrated to the student (Jarvis and Gibson 1985).

Kolb and associates' (Kolb 1984) extensive research into the learning styles of the professions has revealed that workers in the caring professions have considerable strength in learning from concrete experience and from active experimentation. When Kolb's learning cycle is expanded from a concentration on the individual learner to include the dimension of other people contributing to that learning (see above, Chapter 3), this strength indicates the potential learning, through modelling, from observing the concrete experience of other peoples' practice and from active experimentation in new practices with the help of an experienced practitioner.

Schon (1987) emphasises the role of coaching in developing reflective practice in professional education, a process which includes demonstration and imitation. Although much of his work concentrates on coaching in the controlled environments of the studio, 'master-class' or laboratory, the processes of coaching are clearly appropriate to a form of apprenticeship in the practice setting.

A model of reflective apprenticeship

The model of apprenticeship in professional education which is being advocated here is one with five key components:

- direct access to practice performance in the practice setting
- as part of a one-to-one relationship between student and practice teacher
- which is developed over time
- and moderated by mutual agreements
- and which encourages reflective learning about that performance.

It is noticeable that one major difference between this model and the sixteenth-century model outlined above is the addition of reflective learning processes. It is these processes, discussed in more general terms in Chapter 3, and, more specifically below, which mitigate against the potential conservatism, oppression and lack of critique which such a relationship could engender.

The other major difference is the shift from its application in Elizabethan crafts or trades to the modern caring professions. The well-developed knowledge and value bases of the modern caring professions clearly provide a significantly different context for learning. It is for this reason that the reflective apprenticeship I am advocating is far from the entirety of professional education. It is not even the entirety of the learning in the practice setting, However, it is, I would suggest, a central focus of learning in the practice setting which is in danger of being minimised rather than maximised. The impetus of practice teachers to define themselves as teachers as well as practitioners can lead them to gravitate to the well-known modes of teaching they have themselves encountered often for nearly two decades in academic settings, without developing the considerable learning potential of the practice setting.

A third significant difference between traditional apprenticeships and reflective apprenticeship within education for the caring professions is the status of the apprentice/student in the workplace. While the Elizabethan apprentice was a permanent member of the workforce, students in professional education are typically in a practice setting where they are supernumerary to the permanent workforce, and only for a fairly limited time-span. This arrangement ensures that the student's status as a learner is to a degree protected and makes a reflective learning approach more feasible. However, it also requires them to resolve the tension between being a worker and a student (see Chapter 2).

Schon's term 'reflective practicum' compares interestingly with 'reflective apprenticeship'. It is clear that Schon's 'practicum' is not the practice settings of professional workers:

> A practicum is a setting designed for the task of learning practice. In a context that approximates a practice world, students learn by doing, although their doing usually falls short of real-world work. They learn by undertaking projects that simulate and simplify practice; or they take on real-world projects under close supervision. (Schon 1987: 37)

The agency practice settings of education for the caring professions, however, are not specifically designed for learning practice but primarily for delivering services. This primary orientation often inhibits effective practice learning and the quality assurance processes of regulatory bodies for the caring professions often seek to ameliorate this effect (see Chapter 1). Schon's use of the term 'practicum', however, does not seem to accord with much of the more recent North American literature, in which it is synonymous with both the agency practice setting and the curriculum undertaken there (Doel and Shardlow 1996).

Direct access to practice performance

Direct access to practice performance can take place within three main contexts (see Figure 6.1).

1. student observes, practice teacher practises
2. student practises, practice teacher observes
3. student and practice teacher practise together

Figure 6.1 Reflective apprenticeship processes

Clearly these three are in some sense pure forms since different practice situations will indicate a need for interplay between them. Moreover, all three can occur either when the student and practice teacher are together in person or when their relationship is mediated by some form of technology, such as tape recordings or one-way screens. It is possible to consider these three basic contexts and the use of technology in terms of their advantages and disadvantages in facilitating student learning and also of strategies which can minimise the disadvantages. Their use in assessment will be considered more fully in Chapter 7.

Context 1 – student observes, practice teacher practises

Advantages This context, as with the other two, is most easily achieved in work settings where there is a 'culture of openness' (Walrond-Skinner 1974), that is, where both practitioners and clients are accustomed to the presence of other people during practice. Work settings with a major training function, such as teaching hospitals, social work practice learning centres and schools in School Centred Initial Teacher Training schemes are likely to have developed this mode of practice, as are residential and day care settings, where many practitioners and clients occupy the same physical space. However, many practices within the caring professions occur in a context of what Pithouse (1987) calls 'invisibility', for example, because of confidentiality or because the practice occurs in the client's own home. In such contexts, the practice teacher can offer to make their practice more visible and open to the student's scrutiny, given permission from the client. This in turn can encourage the student to do the same with their practice at a later stage.

By observing the practice teacher's practice, the student will be able to access one potential model. They will be able to understand better the practice teacher's orientation – their style, methods, models and values – and the ways in which their professional knowledge informs their practice. This is particularly the case when, as Schon (1987) and Benner (1984) suggest, the experienced practitioners are themselves not aware of all aspects of their practice. Some years ago I was invited to a specialist family therapy setting to observe a new form of therapy being practised. What I actually saw was therapy which bore a strong resemblance to how this setting had always practised, with only small amendments. Self-image can render even experienced practitioners' self-report unreliable.

As the student observes the practice teacher at work, it is likely that they will develop respect for their practice ability: this can add validity to the practice teacher's suggestions in other contexts, such as supervision sessions. An equally important effect can be that the practice teacher's practice is somewhat demystified (Fisher 1990). Even when removed from the practice learning setting as a long-arm practice teacher (see Chapter 5), I have usually sought to play tapes of my practice to students in order to achieve both these effects.

Both before and after the practice teacher's practice has been observed, the student and practice teacher can engage in a reflective dialogue about the practice – its aims, processes, outcomes, values and the feelings evoked in both the practitioner and the observing student. It is often difficult for the reflective dialogue to include constructive criticism of the practice teacher's practice, largely because of the power imbalance between the student and the practice teacher. However, the practice teacher can take steps to encourage critical reflection, principally by reassuring the student that it is totally welcome as part of developing the student's critical faculties and as an opportunity to learn from the student's more objective stance. Brooks and Sikes cite a mentor who espouses this latter view: 'The usual thing is to get them to look at how you talk to kids, who you talk to, things like that and you get some really interesting information back ... Because you don't always see it for yourself' (1997: 100).

The practice teacher can also encourage constructive criticism by taking a lead in indicating weaknesses in their own practice. This model of reflective dialogue focused on the *practice teacher's* practice can prepare the way for similar dialogue about the *student's* practice.

As Brooks and Sikes suggest: 'Observation has been and continues to be a central feature of most forms of Initial Teacher Education' (1997: 97). Much of the discussion within ITE (Haggar, et al. 1993; Fish 1995; Brooks and Sikes 1997) seems to support the value of a specific focus or structure to the student's observation. This is particularly understandable, given the wide-ranging activities of a classroom, but would also be of value within other professions. A student-centred approach to learning would suggest that at the very least the student should have a say in, if not determine, the focus for observing. From this perspective, there is a sense that there is no such thing as unstructured observation, since what the student observes will inevitably be influenced by their past learning about practice and their current preoccupations. The key issue becomes negotiating a structure between the student and the practice teacher.

In their book devoted to observation in a range of contexts including practice learning, Le Riche and Tanner (1998) emphasise the value of *pattern* in the process of observation. Whilst the pattern may at times be considered in observing the student for assessment purposes, for example at the beginning and the end of a practice placement in order to judge their progress, it is less likely to be considered when choosing opportunities for the student to observe the practice teacher for learning purposes. Observations could be chosen, for example, to give a sense of the range of work the practice teacher undertakes or to show progression in one given piece of work.

Disadvantages One disadvantage has already been mentioned, namely the possibility that the student may feel oppressed by a sense that the practice teacher's way is the only way. This can readily be avoided if the practice teacher encourages a reflective dialogue as outlined above. The dialogue could also include an invitation for the student to hypothesise about how they might have conducted that practice in their own style.

Practice teachers can at times feel insecure and exposed when being observed by a student. This may be with a very inexperienced student who has unrealistically high expectations of the practice teacher or a very experienced student who might be excessively critical of other people's practice. They may feel particularly insecure when practising in unfamiliar contexts or under the pressure of their own expectation to provide the best possible model for the student. I once took a very experienced student who had been used to supervising and training other staff to observe an interview with a delinquent child and his family, an area of practice in which I was generally confident. Immediately the interview ended the student offered a long list of rather destructive criticisms which made me somewhat defensive and cautious in our working relationship for some time.

Usually, it is sufficient for the practice teacher to choose very familiar areas of practice in order to retain confidence. Another helpful strategy in the above circumstances might have been to preface the observed interview with a discussion about giving constructive feedback (see Chapter 7). Such a discussion could also be related to the reverse situation of observing and commenting on the *student's* practice.

A common difficulty in observed practice concerns the ethics of opening out an encounter between one practitioner and client(s) to another practitioner. This is equally the case when the practice teacher observes the *student's* practice. The concern may be that the exchange between the practitioner and client is a confidential one, that the client is in some way being 'used' to further the student's education or that one client may feel 'outnumbered' and hence disempowered in the presence of two practitioners.

One strategy which can overcome these concerns is to explain clearly to the client the purpose of the observation and then to give them (informed) choice whether the other practitioner is present or not. The choice is maximised if given to the client in advance. It is difficult for them to say no if two people are standing in the rain outside their front door. The caricatured cinema image of James Robertson Justice arriving at a hospital bed pursued by a posse of medical students exemplifies this need.

Context 2 – student practises, practice teacher observes

Advantages In this process, in its pure form, it is the intention that the practice teacher will not join in the practice, although they are available if the student requires help because of issues such as risk, difficulty or accountability. As with the previous context, this can occur quite naturally in some practice settings. It has two major advantages. First, the student's autonomy as a practitioner is maximally preserved, given the presence of the practice teacher. Moreover, the student is fully aware of the restricted role that the practice teacher will play during the practice: the chances of unpredictable and potentially disruptive actions on the part of the practice teacher are slight.

The second major advantage is that the practice teacher gains a clear impression of the student's practice performance. Whilst this will often be for assessment purposes, it is equally useful in order to help the student learn: indeed, the two purposes overlap to a considerable degree (see Chapter 7). As a full-time practice teacher, I have always looked forward to the first time I could observe a student as an opportunity to see more clearly aspects of the student's practice which I had hitherto only inadequately perceived from their self-reports. Aspects such as style, sensitivity and warmth are difficult to convey through self report, no matter how well developed a student's self-awareness. In settings where practice is predominantly 'invisible' to others, self-report is often the accepted mode for accessing details of practice performance. It is easy for the practice teacher to adopt this accepted mode, without taking the initiative in developing a subculture of openness and thus losing important information from practice performance and, hence, opportunities for learning.

Disadvantages One of the main disadvantages of this context is that it can be perceived as rather unnatural for one person present at an interaction to play no part in it. Clients in their own homes would naturally expect to extend the same levels of hospitality to all the professionals visiting them. It can, moreover, feel somewhat persecutory to have a silent observer throughout an interaction: What are they thinking? Why exactly are they there? Will they change in some way what the student is doing?

This disadvantage can often be overcome by first including the practice teacher fully in the social stage of the interaction, such as the introductions and any small talk which seeks to set everyone at ease (Evans and Kearney 1996) and then by clarifying the practice teacher's role in the interaction and confirming the client's acceptance of this role. Usually it is better for the student to explain these roles since this establishes a pattern for the rest of the interaction. However, the student is sometimes taking over work with clients which was previously undertaken by the practice teacher. In such circumstances, it might be more appropriate for the practice teacher to explain their change of role, before handing over to the student.

Students sometimes describe how having a silent observer is in some ways more stressful than working together with the practice teacher, probably because the assessment function is more heightened. This stress is most likely to be reduced if the student has already received considerable reassurance on previous occasions about the standard of their practice. Moreover, the practice teacher can further reassure the student that on this occasion they will take into account the effect of this stress on their practice. It also sometimes helps students to be told that the feeling of stress usually diminishes as the interaction proceeds.

The very clarity of the respective roles in this context can at times become a disadvantage. The considerable potential of the practice teacher's presence to increase the student's learning at the time or to rescue them if in difficulty can remain unfulfilled if neither are willing to deviate from the rigid roles of observer and observed. For this reason, it can be useful in a discussion before the interaction to anticipate some of the circumstances in which both practice teacher and student agree to abandon the rigidity of pure observation.

Fish debates the pros and cons of both participant and non-participant observation in initial teacher education, particularly the extra understanding accruing from involvement set against the lack of interference with the 'natural sequence of events' (1995: 114). However, it is difficult to imagine the practice teacher's presence not having an impact on the student's practice, even when involving larger numbers of clients, such as a classroom full of pupils, let alone with only one or two. It would seem advisable to take that impact into account and work effectively with it.

Context 3 – Student and practice teacher practise together

It is possible to distinguish two main ways in which the student and the practice teacher can practise together: joint working and live supervision. I use the term 'joint working' in preference to 'co-working' since the latter suggests a degree of equality which is usually absent due to the power differential arising particularly from the assessment function. As Dowling (1979) suggests, it is often hitherto unrevealed differences and inequalities which can disrupt attempts at co-working.

In joint working, the roles of the student and the practice teacher are often not precisely defined. Indeed, they can sometimes be deliberately obscured in order to effect an appearance of equal *co*-work. Often the specific learner/teacher relationship is not made apparent to the client(s). Often, too, the main emphasis is on delivering the most effective service to the client(s) with correspondingly less emphasis on learning. Joint work takes place when a student becomes involved in the practice teacher's practice as well as vice versa, or the two share in some practice from the outset. The notion of 'sharing' can obscure to a degree who exactly is accountable for this particular practice. In initial teacher education, joint work is called 'collaborative teaching' (Burn 1992; McIntyre and Haggar 1993; Brooks and Sikes 1997) and comprises 'any lesson that is jointly planned and jointly taught by a mentor and a beginning teacher' (Burn 1992: 133).

Live supervision, on the other hand, occurs 'when a student's practice is influenced directly during its course by the practice teacher' (Evans 1987b: 13). The word 'directly' here implies that the specific purpose is to influence the student through teaching or coaching, as well as indicating the immediacy in time and place. While this is clearly a sub-category of joint working, the main emphasis is on student learning and the learner/teacher relationship is made apparent to the client(s). Invariably, the student has primary responsibility for practice in which the practice teacher becomes involved, usually by invitation. Live supervision contrasts with 'open supervision' (Branicki 1997) in which supervision takes place in the presence of clients but not during the practice itself.

Both joint working and live supervision have a number of advantages. The presence of two workers can help the client(s) receive a better service than one worker. This is usually through the practice teacher's greater practice ability and awareness of the requirements of the agency, but it can also arise when the student has greater practice ability in this particular area or brings a changed perspective to the practice teacher's practice. In both forms there is also good potential for student learning, particularly through modelling: what Schon (1987) terms 'demonstrating' and 'imitating' and Doel and Shardlow (1996) call 'modelling' and 'enactment'.

As with Context 1, the practice teacher is in a position to establish their credentials as a practitioner, sometimes more so since the student will also be experiencing for themselves the difficulties inherent in that particular practice situation. Likewise, the potential for the practice teacher to offer support, implicit in Context 2, is more explicit since the practice teacher is expected to play an active role.

One disadvantage which both these methods share is the pressure practice teachers can feel to know the answers when the student may feel stuck. Kingston and Smith (1983) describe the value of giving yourself permission, as the practice teacher, not to know all the answers.

Joint work

Advantages Joint work has a number of advantages and disadvantages of its own. One of its greatest advantages is that it can usefully attempt to address the power imbalance between student and practice teacher. In my view, this is most likely to occur in circumstances when student and practice teacher recognise that they both bring some strengths to a particular practice context. It is less likely to occur if either party do not have this view. It is also less likely to occur if the student takes on a role in the joint work which they are ill-equipped to perform.

Another advantage rests in the fact that joint work routinely occurs in many practice agencies, sometimes as a result of inter-professional working, sometimes because of the complexity or risk inherent in the work and sometimes due to the sheer numbers of clients involved in the practice. A third advantage is that joint work offers one opportunity to assess the student's ability to work with other people, albeit the practice teacher and student have another relationship as well as joint workers.

Disadvantages The greatest disadvantage in joint work is the potential for a lack of clarity over the respective roles of the student and the practice teacher. This lack of clarity can be felt by any one of the three participants – including the clients. The student can easily be overwhelmed and discounted by the practice teacher's greater power and at the end of the practice session be feeling de-skilled and disempowered. This can occur in any practice when the practice teacher can feel the need to 'take over' the practice. It is even more likely to occur when the student is invited to be involved in practice, for which the practice teacher was previously solely responsible. Under such circumstances, not only may the practice teacher be tempted to perpetuate their previous level of activity but also they may be encouraged to do so by client(s) who valued the service they previously received.

A further consequence of this potential lack of clarity is that the student and the practice teacher can begin to work in different directions, pursuing different purposes, which can reduce the effectiveness of the practice. One common example of this occurs when there is some conflict between a number of clients. The student might be engaging with one side of the conflict and so the other side might seek to engage the practice teacher, possibly inhibiting the student's attempts to engage both sides in resolving their differences.

Some discussion about respective roles is an obvious way of seeking to remedy this particular difficulty. This can include finding a well-delineated and achievable role for even the least experienced student. This can be accomplished quite easily when there is more than one client present: the agreement being that the student will interact more with some people and the practice teacher with others. Likewise, if the practice is likely to entail a number of reasonably discrete functions, it can be agreed that the student will take a lead on some of the functions. Often the practice teacher will engage the client(s) with the more pressing functions and the student the others, although the contrary positions may also be deliberately chosen.

Live supervision

Advantages The main reason I personally have tended to value live supervision above joint work is that the roles adopted during practice are explicitly those of learner and teacher, thus maintaining congruence with roles in other contexts of the placement. The stage is therefore set to maximise the learning potential of the practice situation. Evans (1987b) and Kearney (1989) both report glowing testimonials from students of this rich learning potential: 'It's a wonderful way to learn ... very powerful tool. It's hard to imagine how anyone gets trained without live supervision' (Kearney 1989: 45). Students seem to value the opportunity to observe a model, with the expectation that they will then take over: 'It is good when the supervisor is more active, when the student can sit back more, but pure observing is too passive' (Evans 1987b: 13).

There is also the opportunity for more traditional teaching as students seek and are given advice as to how to proceed – what Schon (1987) calls 'telling'. The strength of the teaching in this particular context is that it is not separated from the practice by time or space, and hence is prone to none of the distortions inherent in that gap (Whiffen and Byng-Hall 1982). If a major motivation to learn in the education of the caring professions is to increase the student's effectiveness in caring, there can be no better opportunity than when that caring is actually taking place.

Perhaps its greatest strength as a learning tool is that the student can be empowered in undertaking quite difficult practice for which they are feeling fully responsible but which might stretch them due its complexity, level of risk or simply its total unfamiliarity. Nevertheless, the student will be aware that the practice teacher is there to bail them out should the practice prove too difficult. It is therefore particularly appropriate for students who, it is agreed, need stretching or whose preferred style of learning is through active experimentation (Kolb 1984).

Disadvantages Neither Evans (1987b) nor Kearney (1989) disguise the fact that some students find disadvantages with live supervision. Their students described how they found it daunting and viewed it with apprehension, particularly initially. It is likely that these feelings stem from the combination of three main sources: being assessed, unfamiliarity with the roles, and the potential threat to their autonomy as workers in the powerful presence of their practice teacher. As described above, earlier positive feedback about their practice can help allay the first feeling. Greater familiarity can be achieved through prior preparation such as role-playing on placement and also through repeated practice. When the same group of three participants (student, practice teacher and client(s)) meet on more than one occasion the client(s) can also become more familiar and comfortable with the method. The third threat can best be addressed through prior discussion about who is in control during the practice and how that will be upheld, which is explored below.

Some students and practice teachers are concerned about how the client(s) might respond to this form of working together. My own experience over many years of using the method is that only rarely have they refused informed consent for live supervision. Moreover, some explicitly welcomed a service from two workers, particularly when the student was their regular worker and the practice teacher brought additional experience or a new perspective to bear.

A four-stage process

The three contexts of reflective apprenticeship described above are most effective when they operate within a four-stage process:

1. Discussion *before* the interaction with client(s)
2. Interaction with client(s)
3. Time-out
4. Discussion *after* the interaction with client(s).

Discussion before *the interaction with client(s)*

The learning potential of all three contexts detailed above will be considerably enhanced by discussion before the interaction with client(s) takes place. It is best if at least some discussion occurs reasonably close to the interaction, preferably immediately before it, because of memory loss and the changing nature of practice. In settings where home visits are common, such discussions can conveniently take place in the car on the way there.

It is useful for discussions at this time to focus on three main topics:

- Ground rules
- Practice aims
- Learning/assessment aims.

Ground rules seek to clarify how the student and the practice teacher will interact together when they later come into contact with clients. Practice aims are what the practitioner (or practitioners when student and practice teacher are working together) seeks to achieve during the practice. It is also possible for particular learning or assessment targets to be specified for the practice. Students can, for example, invite the practice teacher to a session in which they are wanting some support in trying out a given technique, with which they feel highly inexperienced. Sometimes it has been agreed that a student has yet to demonstrate a particular professional competence, which becomes an assessment target for the practice event.

The interaction between student and practice teacher which discussion of ground rules will need to cover includes their respective roles, their positioning and their communication pattern. Positioning may appear trivial but can often either reinforce or counteract agreed roles. If it has been agreed that the student will have a central role while the practice teacher is more peripheral, this will be facilitated if the student is physically positioned more centrally to the interaction with the client(s). This may require some negotiation with client(s), particularly if the contact takes place in their home.

The importance of a focus on ground rules stems from the unpredictability of practice: no matter how carefully the student and the practice teacher discuss how the contact with the client(s) will proceed, it may in fact turn out quite differently. In such circumstances, the two workers need to know how they will respond most effectively as a team.

There can be a tendency for both student and practice teacher to omit such discussion in favour of a focus on practice aims and learning/assessment aims, since discussions about these aims are more common in other contexts during the placement, such as ordinary supervision/learning sessions. Moreover, it can feel somewhat inward-looking to be discussing anything other than the needs of the client(s).

For all contexts of reflective apprenticeship, discussion on ground rules can usefully include not only the allocation of roles such as observer/

observed or when working together, but also how student and practice teacher can seek to reinforce those roles: by briefing the client(s) at the beginning of the contact and reminding them of the roles during the course of the contact. Reminders can be explicitly verbal or at times, if appropriate, more subtly non-verbal, when, for example, an observing practice teacher looks towards the student for an answer to a question inappropriately addressed to themselves by a client.

Another useful discussion includes ways in which roles may change during the interaction with the client(s). Students describe with some surprise and occasional irritation how an agreed observation session gradually develops into a form of joint work, in which the practice teacher takes an increasingly active role in what was mutually agreed would be a practice event for which the student would be solely responsible. Clearly, it must be understood by the student that the practice teacher reserves the right to intervene for reasons of accountability: if agency policies or the law are being unwittingly broken and if the student's practice entails too high a level of risk for the client(s). What is less useful, I believe, is if the practice teacher increasingly intervenes in the student's practice when it simply does not proceed as the practice teacher would have done it. My own rule of thumb for inhibiting such a tendency to interrupt is to consider whether I would think of taking action about some practice if the student reported it to me some days later, when physical proximity no longer makes the intervention easy.

On one occasion I had agreed with a student not to intervene in her contact with the clients. However, after a short while a young boy began to get rather boisterous while the student was concentrating on speaking with his mother. This escalated to the stage when the boy was opening a first-floor window and appeared to be on the point of getting out of it, at which point I had to intervene rapidly to ensure the child's safety.

Live supervision requires considerable discussion of how the student can retain control of a contact with client(s) for which they are the responsible worker. Some students like to establish control by conducting an initial period of the contact without interruption by the practice teacher. This may be a desirable aim, but is best approached flexibly for accountability reasons. On one occasion, I had agreed with a student not to intervene in her interaction with some clients for at least ten minutes. However, very early in the contact the conflict between the clients flared up and they were about to come to blows. I therefore had to stand up and seek to prevent the violence before the stage of the contact agreed previously with the student. Through both the above examples, I learned that while it is possible to make agreements to cover optimal circumstances, it is necessary always to allow flexibility for the unexpected.

Another aspect of control in live supervision concerns the communication patterns between the three participants: student, practice teacher and client(s). One way of maintaining the student's control in the interaction is for the practice teacher to influence the student's practice only by interacting directly with the student (see Figure 6.2).

Practice teacher ⟶ student ⟶ client(s)

Figure 6.2 Live supervision - process I

This is the traditional pattern of live supervision in family therapy (Whiffen and Byng-Hall 1982). However, it prevents an important source of learning through modelling, whereby the practice teacher interacts directly with the client(s) for a short while and then the student proceeds in a similar vein. One student was having considerable difficulty in obtaining information from a very anxious client who was speaking almost non-stop. I was able to model a form of communication which entailed a much greater degree of structure, including closed questions, which the student was able to imitate and adapt later in the contact.

Another disadvantage in this pattern whereby the practice teacher only addresses the student is apparent when the particular form of practice being used only comprises speech, as is often the case in social work. If the practice teacher asks the student to say something and all the student can do is repeat the practice teacher's words, the student can feel somewhat disempowered in merely parroting the practice teacher. This pattern is more likely to be helpful if the practice being employed involves actions, so that the student responds to the practice teacher's words with an action. It is also likely to be more helpful if the practice teacher merely indicates a broad area for further exploration, such as 'Can you find out when the difficulty first started?', rather than presenting the student with one specific question to ask.

It has been my preference to agree with the student to adopt a mixed pattern of communication, interacting with both the student and the client(s), thus maximising the potential for modelling as well as making suggestions (see Figure 6.3).

If it is agreed that the practice teacher will interact directly with the client as well as the student, it is helpful to clarify how the practice can move from student to practice teacher and back again to student, preferably under the student's control. The image of holding the reins, passing them over and then taking them back again seems to sum up what takes place. For these transitions to occur smoothly, both student and practice teacher must actively encourage them.

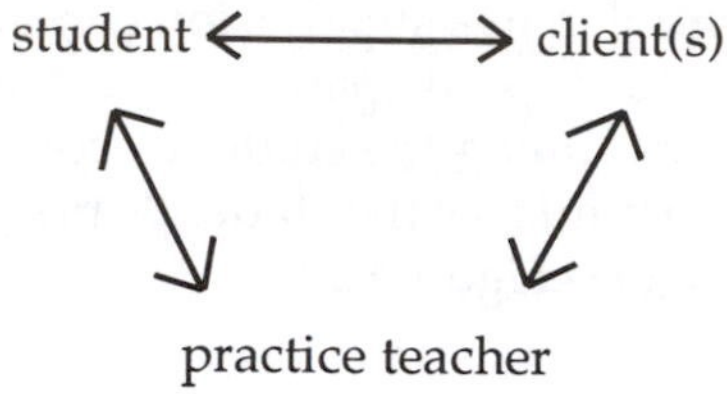

Figure 6.3 Live supervision - process II

The first transition is most effective if it is at the request of the student, thus retaining their control of the contact. Some students seem to think that it is an admission of failure and will reduce their status in the eyes of the client(s), if they request a direct intervention on the part of the practice teacher. However, they can often be reassured that a clear, firm request will sustain their authority in the interaction, particularly when they discover through experience that the client(s) do not then continue to ignore them. Sometimes, students seem to prefer it if the practice teacher gauges when the student would benefit from their intervention, often out of trust in the practice teacher's judgement. However, practice teachers do not know for certain when is the best time to intervene: the student may appear to be stuck but may in fact be just about to take the same course as the one the practice teacher interrupts with. I tend to prefer, once again, an agreement for a mixed mode of intervention, with an emphasis on the student's initiation but allowing for the possibility of practice teacher-initiated intervention if they are aware of a learning opportunity which the student is not.

The second transition, from the practice teacher back to the student, is more likely to be smooth if the practice teacher limits their intervention in time. The longer they continue, the harder it will probably be for the student to take over the practice again. Not only must the practice teacher be willing to give up 'the reins' but also the student must be prepared to accept them. This transition can also be requested explicitly by either participant.

Discussion about the various aims for the interaction will closely mirror that which occurs in other supervisory and teaching contexts during the placement. It is important for either participant to know what the other's purposes and intended methods are, partly so that they can understand what the other is doing more fully and partly so that they can intervene more usefully when working together in different ways.

Discussion about aims can also begin the reflective dialogue (see Chapter 3) which is necessary if the student is to transcend a conservative and oppressive adherence to one model of practice. The student needs to be empowered to debate the practice teacher's aims, including their defence of those aims. Likewise, the student may be challenged by the practice teacher over their choice of aims and will need encouragement to debate their relative strengths and weaknesses.

It is possible that the period before a practice performance may allow the opportunity to broaden the discussion into the origins of given practice aims – in theory, in the individual's practice wisdom or in knowledge transferred from some past experience. Usually, however, such broader debates can only be registered immediately before a contact with service users and then pursued in more depth on another learning occasion, such as a planned supervision session.

Interaction with client(s)

Following the preparation outlined above, the interaction with the client(s) will seek to implement the agreed mode of operation. Early in the interaction, it will be necessary for clear differences in role to be explained to the client(s) and for informed consent to be obtained from them for that way of working. Most clients are well aware of the need for students to learn and to be assessed and, in my experience, are generally willing to agree to any sensible arrangement which facilitates those processes. The interaction can then proceed as agreed, with flexible adjustment as required. On occasion, however, difficulties arise which cannot be easily responded to, whilst still interacting with the clients. Such occasions are often an opportunity to take 'time-out'.

Time-out

Time-out occurs when student and practice teacher disengage from the process of interacting with the client(s) and embark upon a more prolonged discussion between themselves. Sometimes it is precipitated by a difficulty in the interaction with the client(s), such as an unexpected need or problem. Sometimes difficulties arise in how the student and practice teacher are working together: agreed roles may no longer be tenable and require renegotiation.

Some students and practice teachers express doubts about the process of dis-engaging from the client(s) in the middle of an interaction. However, it is my experience that client(s) readily understand the need for such discussions either to ensure that they receive the optimum service or to facilitate greater student learning. The possibility of time-out can, moreover, be agreed with the client(s) at the start of the interaction.

The principle of maximising the student's control can determine much of how time-out proceeds. It is, for example, useful if the student is encouraged to ask for time-out when they feel they need it, rather than wait for the practice teacher to determine an appropriate opportunity. It is also helpful to give the student the choice as to whether time-out takes place in the presence of the client(s) or not. Some students have strong feelings that they could not possibly discuss the client(s) behind their backs. Others feel it will be awkward searching for the right words when discussing the client(s) in their presence and with the additional risk that the client(s) will seek to continue the practice interaction before the student is ready.

As already indicated, both circumstances have their advantages and disadvantages. The presence of the client(s) empowers them to interrupt if the workers have misinterpreted something (Toussaint et al. 1989). It also discourages both workers from speaking in a judgemental way or using excessive jargon. On the other hand, some students feel embarrassed talking about the client(s) in front of them but not with them. It can also be harder to maintain a useful boundary between time-out and the interaction with the client(s) when they are present. Moreover, clients speak of the value of having some time by *themselves* in the middle of an interaction in order to collect their own thoughts. I usually encourage students to give the client(s) the choice, particularly if the interaction takes place in the client's own home.

Sometimes students and practice teachers are dubious about the logistics and ethics of taking time-out away from the client(s) when the interaction takes place in the client's own home. Strong social norms about proper behaviour as a guest on someone else's territory probably fuel these feelings. However, it is my experience that, once clients understand the reason for time-out, they will willingly consent to workers going to another room or to leaving the room themselves. If there is no other room, there is always the garden, the yard or the workers' car.

Time-out is particularly useful when student and practice teacher are working together and need some time to redirect the practice. To this end, time-out can have both a retrospective and a prospective function. In this way it encapsulates much of what Schon (1987) describes as 'reflection-in-action'. Time-out usually begins with a reflective dialogue about the preceding practice. It is often helpful for the practice teacher to ascertain where the student is 'at', particularly if time-out has been called because of a difficulty experienced by the student. At times, they may be bewildered or even upset by how the interaction has proceeded. Discussion can also increase the student's understanding of the preceding interaction. The focus will then often shift to planning for the next phase of the interaction, including how the student will round the interaction off.

On one occasion, a student was undertaking an apparently straight-forward assessment for an epileptic youth currently living in a different part of the country to receive day care on his return from residential school. The student was fairly quickly informed of a harrowing past history of sexual and physical abuse suffered by the youth and his sister. The student used a period of time-out to recover emotionally from this disclosure and to plan how to deal with it. On another occasion, a highly experienced student had been quite disorientated by the unexpected appearance of an estranged husband. As the practice teacher, I had to rescue her and conduct much of the first part of the interaction. Initially in time-out the student was able to express her embarrassment at having been so disorientated. We were then able to discuss how she would be able to take over the rest of the interaction.

It is not usual for there to be more than one or two times-out during an interaction with clients, since the whole process can start becoming too disjointed. Moreover, the delicate balance between delivering an effective service, on the one hand, and maximising the learning potential for the student, on the other, might become too skewed towards the latter. Clients might begin to feel they were guinea-pigs.

Discussion after *the interaction with client(s)*

Discussion at this stage is most useful if it can occur immediately after the interaction with the client(s), when both workers have their most complete recall of all its detail. Such immediacy can also help prevent the student retaining difficult feelings about the interaction for an unnecessary length of time or forestall the possibility of a growing misapprehension on the part of the student about aspects of the interaction. Although car journeys offer an opportunity in community-based practice, time pressures for either participant will sometimes not permit discussion immediately afterwards. In such circumstances it is helpful, as Brooks and Sikes (1997) suggest, for them to arrange another opportunity as soon as possible.

As with time-out, this discussion can also have both retrospective and prospective functions, although the primary focus is often on what has previously happened. First and foremost, it is a time for mutual feedback. If the student has been practising at all, it is most likely they will wish to know what the practice teacher thought of their performance. This will include evaluation of their achievement of the different aims for the practice performance – practice aims, learning aims or assessment aims. It may also include the need for some reassurance if the student felt the interaction had gone particularly badly.

It is also useful if the two participants can evaluate how the ground rules agreed for their own interaction have been implemented during the interaction with the client(s). As with the first stage, it is easy for both the student and the practice teacher to overlook the ground rules in favour of the practice with the client(s). Without some evaluation of the ground rules, however, it is highly likely that discomfort or lost learning opportunities will be replicated at a future time.

This focus on evaluation can considerably enhance the reflective dialogue between student and practice teacher. By encouraging the student to be both analytical and critical of what the practice teacher does, whether in interaction with the client(s) or with the student, the practice teacher invites acceptance of possibilities beyond the model of their actions. Similarly, in evaluating the student's actions, the practice teacher can encourage the student to be self-critical and to defend actions which the practice teacher has constructively criticised. Students are often well able to indicate how the practice teacher has misinterpreted their actions and, particularly, their intentions.

This important focus on evaluation is particularly reinforced by the immediacy of the events. However, it can also be easily distracted if an appropriate climate for reflective dialogue has not begun to be established. The principal distraction is often for the student and the practice teacher to join together in discussing a third party, namely aspects of the client's situation. This avoids the potential discomfort of conflicting in their evaluations of their own actions. In the family therapy literature, this form of conflict avoidance is known as triangulation (Burnham 1986; Evans and Kearney 1996).

As with discussion *before* the interaction with the client(s), this discussion *after* the event can also broaden out beyond that particular event. Such broader discussions can similarly make connections with theory and indicate ways in which learning from that event can be transferred to future practice. Usually, however, time pressures constrain such discussion at this time and topics will need to be identified for further exploration at a later date, for example in supervision sessions.

The use of technology

A range of technological equipment can be used to mediate the working relationship of student and practice teacher in reflective apprenticeship. Equipment such as one-way screens and ear bugs are confined largely to clinical settings with a strong learning orientation and can be difficult and expensive to install. The uses and abuses of such equipment are described elsewhere (Whiffen and Byng-Hall 1982; Kearney 1989; Doel and Shardlow 1996). In this section I shall concentrate on technology which can be used in any setting, both cheaply and easily – the tape recorder.

Advantages

Tape recordings have a number of advantages in reflective apprenticeship. Foremost is the fact that they make practice performance available at a different time and in a different place to when and where it initially occurred. This can be of great value to busy practice teachers who are unable to accompany their students at their practice as much as either party would wish. Students can develop the routine of taping their practice and then bring to the practice teacher those tapes which they consider afford greatest learning. Practice teachers can ask students to tape specific practice events for both learning and assessment purposes.

Separated from the practice event in time and space, the tape can become a focus for a more lengthy reflective dialogue than can often occur when student and practice teacher are together at the time of the practice. The practice can be analysed and evaluated in detail, including discussion of what the student might have done differently under the same circumstances. Moreover, the dialogue will be grounded in the actuality of what did occur rather than on the vicissitudes of memory. This can enable both student and practice teacher not only to focus on fine detail – what are sometimes called the micro-skills of practice – but also to resolve some clashes in perspective due to differential memory. Repeated playings of selected pieces of tape can assist in this process.

A further advantage that tapes can have over the practice teacher's presence in person is that taping, particularly audio taping, can be felt as less intrusive by either the client or the student.

As well as using tapes as the basis of discussion with their practice teacher, students can also learn from the tapes themselves. Students report how replaying tapes increases the accuracy of their self-awareness and improves their analysis of the detailed processes of practice (Evans and Langley 1996). Star (1979) similarly describes how tapes can improve the self-image of the worker. Some students suggest specific aspects of their practice, such as planning and communication skills, which tapes have helped to improve. Some also develop imaginative ways of integrating the process of taping into the caring process with the client(s). One describes linking the tape recording with the client's interest in photography while another replayed a video tape to help improve a severely disabled client's self-image (Evans and Langley 1996).

One useful variant on students' learning from tapes by themselves occurs when the practice teacher helps inform the student's reflections on their own practice, for example, by indicating specific aspects of practice to focus on, and yet the practice teacher is not actually present when the student reviews the tape. One practice teacher long since retired produced a useful checklist of key aspects of practice for students to use when replaying tapes. It would also be possible for student and practice teacher to generate between them a checklist for the student to use as a focus for meeting current learning needs at any given point in a placement.

Disadvantages

Possibly the greatest disadvantage of tapes as a practice learning tool is that they do not offer an opportunity for the practice teacher to influence a particular piece of practice prospectively. The focus on the particular practice is entirely retrospective: any prospective focus is on practice which is yet unplanned and possibly quite distant in time. For this reason student and practice teacher need to choose carefully whether the practice teacher's presence in person or taping for later perusal suits their purposes best.

The fact that tapes can be saved and stored can heighten issues of informed consent which may not arise when the practice teacher's access to practice is in person. Clients and students may be reluctant for the practice to be recorded in case the recording is put to unauthorised use, for example, beyond the student's learning or assessment. Some clients are aware of the legal implications of what they are saying and others can feel particularly paranoid. A written consent form, specifying the ways in which the tape can be used and when the tape will be deleted which is then signed by both the client(s) and the student, will often set both at ease. However, a small number of agencies particularly in drugs advice and mental health totally prohibit the use of tapes for these sorts of reasons.

It must be remembered that while tapes capture much of the practice performance with considerable accuracy, the record is essentially incomplete in a number of respects. Communication is a multi-channel process (Birdwhistell 1970) in which all five senses can play a part. Even video recording only captures two of these senses and important information in many settings, particularly through smell and touch, will be lost. Another way in which video recordings omit information is through the directionality of the camera. Only one angle will usually be available whereas the practice teacher can adjust their position, if present in person. A third area of lost information is the student's thoughts and feelings during the practice which are more likely to be accurately ascertained when the practice teacher is present in person, rather than relying on the student's memory at a later time.

Many students and practice teachers are accustomed to listening and watching radio, television and film programmes for sustained periods of time. This dominant mode of observing recorded material can be a disadvantage to learning from taped practice. It is tempting for student and practice teacher to be seduced into observing large chunks of practice at a time, thus losing a focus on detail. The message from initial teacher education about the need for structured observation in person is equally applicable when using tapes. One helpful strategy is to encourage the student to pre-select one or two short periods of practice within the whole practice event which in some way concern them most and will be the focus for reflective dialogue. Another strategy is to encourage the student (as well as the practice teacher) to use the pause button at any point of particular interest.

For some students, technology is a major barrier to be overcome and they shrink at the possibility of incurring an additional stress during their practice by attempting to operate a tape recorder. It can be helpful in such circumstances to allow the student ample opportunity to rehearse the use of the recorder, either on the placement or in the academic setting, until they are fully confident in its use. Sometimes they have familiar equipment of their own which is suitable for practice learning purposes.

Audio and video equipment have their respective strengths and weaknesses for learning. Video, of course, covers both sound and sight and this is particularly important when actions form a significant component of the practice and not just speech. However, when the practice is predominantly through the medium of speech, as with much social work, health visiting, community mental health nursing and teaching among others, it is easy to overstate the advantages of video. It is true that video captures non-verbal communication such as posture and gesture, while audio does not. None the less, the extra linguistic features of speech such as volume, rate and pitch usually convey similar and congruent information to non-verbal communication. We can learn much from how people speak as well as what they say. All this is adequately recorded on audio tape. One dramatic demonstration of the primacy of sound in human communication can come from inviting a student to chose whether to turn off the sound or the picture on a video and yet still discover what is being communicated.

Video is also particularly useful for identification purposes when more than one or two people are speaking during the practice, for example, in a family or group context. The extra cues provided by slight shifts in position as people prepare to speak or actually start speaking are often sufficient to identify exactly who spoke. Video is also essential when communication is largely not spoken, when working with clients who are profoundly deaf or severely learning disabled.

Audio has a number of advantages in recording predominantly spoken practice. Recording equipment is cheaper and easier to operate. It is also easily portable and generally inconspicuous. These are of particular advantage when working in clients' own homes. The whole process of erecting tripods and setting up the camera angle can be quite obtrusive, whereas an audio recorder can be quickly placed on a nearby table or chair and soon forgotten. It is unfortunate that the CCETSW has ignored these advantages in audio recording when setting out their latest requirements for observation (CCETSW 1995).

The context of reflective apprenticeship

Setting it up

The exposure of one person's practice to another person as described above can entail a high level of vulnerability, not only for the student when being formally assessed but also for both student and practice teacher at other times, since it can be of significance to them how something as important as their professional practice performance is perceived by another person. For this reason, reflective apprenticeship in all its forms requires a degree of sensitivity and forward planning.

On all placements it is helpful if expected levels of reflective apprenticeship are agreed on the placement learning agreement (see Chapter 5). In some instances the regulatory body requires a specific number of observations for assessment purposes, for example, social work and general medical practice (CCETSW 1995; Anglia Regional General Practice Education Committee 1996) which clearly must be specified on the agreement. However, any party to the placement agreement, particularly the student, the practice teacher and the academic tutor, may seek to encourage any of the contexts outlined above for learning purposes. It is advisable if their advantages can be established and disadvantages worked through in discussion at the beginning of the placement and if necessary enshrined in written agreements.

This early discussion is more likely to be profitable if all parties are aware of the potential of these methods. When training is available to practice teachers, it often focuses on teaching and learning methods which occur at a distance from practice performance and rather neglects methods which include the practice performance. Live supervision in particular would seem to require some opportunity to understand how it can work and to rehearse its detailed techniques prior to use with a student. Over a period of years, I have been asked to provide a number of workshops on live supervision for practice teachers who are experienced and trained in other methods of teaching, but as yet diffident about attempting this method.

Likewise, students can be prepared either in the academic setting or on the placement to maximise their use of these methods. An exploration of the student's preferred learning style (see below) and discussion of the different learning opportunities in both the academic and the practice settings which build on that style can include reflective apprenticeship methods. Similarly, in both settings, students can rehearse the experience of live supervision, particularly, in order to appreciate its learning potential and to overcome unfounded reservations.

In practice settings such as clinics, residential homes, day care centres and schools, practice teacher and student usually practise in the same place, whereas in community or fieldwork settings they are often practising in different clients' homes. The proximity of the former settings makes it much easier for student and practice teacher to find the time and opportunity to come together during practice. However, this same convenience can have the disadvantage of making private, autonomous practice less easy to protect. Brooks and Sikes (1997) advise against a practice teacher's 'dropping in on spec' to observe a student's practice, without giving them the opportunity to prepare for the event. Prior agreement will allow the student to prepare more thoroughly for the practice as well as the emotional impact of the practice teacher's presence.

Clients also need an opportunity to prepare themselves for the appearance of more than one practitioner in practice settings where one is the norm. This is best done in advance of the practice event particularly on domiciliary visits, when the unexpected arrival of two practitioners on the doorstep can make for some awkwardness in deciding whether one of them is admitted or not. The client, as host, may not wish to appear inhospitable: the practitioners may wish to avoid a wasted journey and, for both reasons, willing and informed consent may be jeopardised. At times when it has not been possible for clients to be informed in advance, it is helpful if the practitioners go with the expectation that one of them may not be admitted.

Progression in the use of reflective apprenticeship

Like any process of learning, reflective apprenticeship will have different relevance for different students at different points in an educational programme. McIntyre and Hagger (1993) suggest three levels of mentoring in initial teacher education, one dimension of which is the extent to which reflective apprenticeship, as outlined here, takes place. My own experience indicates that it is important to negotiate with each student at what points in the placement practice performance features prominently in the learning and assessment processes. Some of this negotiation can occur at the start of the placement but much of it takes place as the placement develops.

Many educational programmes in the caring professions emphasise the value for students of their observing other skilled practitioners at an early stage in the programme. Some nursing programmes have placements with a largely observational purpose early on, as did some social work courses when placement resourcing was less constrained. These placements gave highly inexperienced students an opportunity to observe models of good practice before embarking on practice themselves. However, growing resource constraints and concern about transferability from one setting to another has led to a decrease in such observational placements.

Currently, it is more likely that observation will form an early emphasis in a given placement, thus providing the student with one or more models of how practice occurs in this particular setting. The importance of the student having adequate opportunity to observe their own practice teacher during a period of induction can easily be overlooked in the practice teacher's desire to introduce the student to other aspects of the placement: colleagues, other resources within the setting and the relevant network of other settings. Moreover, it can feel somewhat conceited to invite the student to observe oneself in particular. None the less, it is essential for both learning and assessment purposes that the student begins to discover what the practice teacher means by good practice: seeing what they do is just as potent a way of determining their meaning as hearing what they say.

Observing the student early on in a placement also has some advantages. It can provide the practice teacher with a baseline picture of the student's strengths, weaknesses and preferred style of working. This can then inform the practice teacher in some of the important decisions they need to take, for example about the level of work which can be allocated to the student and the level of support they may need in performing it. Just as observation can help the student to understand the practice teacher's practice better, it can often give the practice teacher a more valid view of the student's. Some students can, intentionally or unintentionally, give quite a misleading account of their practice abilities, which early observation can rectify.

The value of observation is clearly not confined to the early stages of a placement. Another stage when it can be particularly valuable is when the student is moving on within the placement into new areas of practice. It can play an important role in keeping the placement moving forward with progressive learning objectives, particularly in the middle of the placement when the initial impetus is in danger of faltering (see Chapter 5). Its role towards the end of a placement, however, can often be for final assessment purposes. Contrasting the early baseline with an end point can give important information in forming a judgement about the student's ability to learn. With respect to additional learning towards the end of a placement, the student's observation of others can offer the opportunity to gain a slight and rapid understanding of areas of practice which the student has not been able to undertake themselves. It is likely, too, that for many students in most settings there will be areas of practice which are beyond their competence or kept from them for reasons of accountability and which they can only learn about through observation.

Working together in joint work or live supervision often develops once a placement is well under way. Dowling (1979) advises of the importance of choosing a partner for joint work, in order to achieve matching styles or methods. This is not possible for a student and their given practice teacher when thinking of working together. However, as the placement progresses, they will be more mutually aware of how compatible their ways of working are and how to overcome significant differences. Moreover, it is later in the placement that they are more likely to have developed the degree of mutual respect and trust which necessarily underpins the sharing entailed in working together.

Some students like to have reached the point of feeling reasonably confident in working by themselves before undertaking work with others. It is as if they first need to prove to themselves they can do it unaided. For others, however, working with others in the security of knowing that they have some support to hand can give the confidence necessary to embark on similar work alone. This degree of variability in students would suggest the value of negotiating when working together might take place. It has been my practice to discuss the possibility of working together with the student at frequent intervals during the placement, for example, when the student reported some difficulty they had encountered or when they were hovering on the brink of trying out an approach with which they were not yet fully confident. The student will usually be aware of when they feel confident to accept that offer.

Often it is the need for support over a particular difficulty which encourages the student to work together with the practice teacher. That aim can then itself sometimes develop into a more general desire to learn.

Some students have agreed with me to undertake a series of live supervision sessions with the same client(s), during which all parties usually become comfortable with and make best use of the work process. These agreements have usually occurred after a live supervision session with another client has proved helpful to the student.

Broadening out reflective apprenticeship

Thus far, discussion has centred on learning processes in which both student and practice teacher are present during a practice performance and the period of time immediately before and after that performance. It is possible, however, for the learning to broaden out from that context in two main ways: to encompass other learning processes and to include other practitioners.

The great advantage of discussing practice immediately before, during and immediately afterwards is in overcoming memory loss. One of the biggest constraints in these opportunities, however, is the amount of time available for developing the learning potential of the experience, particularly when student, practice teacher or both have other pressing work commitments before or after the practice event in question. It is often useful to identify during or after the practice one or two key issues which can then be explored in greater depth at a later practice learning session. In one live supervision session, for example, a student made good use of self-disclosure in reassuring a parent. The issue of self-disclosure became an agreed focus for critical analysis and evaluation at the next full supervision session, including relating to the literature on the subject.

There is also considerable value in encouraging students to observe and work with practitioners other than the practice teacher. Other practitioners can include students as well as experienced staff members and colleagues in other agencies and professions as well as the practice teacher's own. These practitioners will provide the student with a point of comparison with the practice teacher's way of working which can heighten the student's reflective powers of analysis and evaluation. The learning potential of such comparisons can be further enhanced if the practice teacher is able to discuss comparative strengths and weaknesses in a constructive way with the student. Such discussion can also help the student integrate the meaning of what might to them appear quite separate experiences.

One particularly effective placement structure for such comparative reflection is the split placement (see Chapter 5), where the student will have in effect a minimum of two practice teachers. When these two practice teachers mutually respect each other's work and are prepared to share their different strengths and weaknesses with the student, three-way discussions can help the student considerably in developing reflective learning skills.

The relationship between student and practice teacher

The relationship between the student and the practice teacher is the second major component of reflective apprenticeship. It is, however, an aspect of learning which would seem to receive insufficient discussion. Much educational debate focuses on the content of learning and assessment. The emphasis on national curricula in school teaching and national standards in occupational training has fuelled this focus, with an apparent assumption that if appropriate outcomes are selected and assessed, success is assured. A cursory review of two of the more competence-based caring professions suggests that initial teacher education (DfEE 1997) regulates student outcomes *seven times* more than the processes which achieve those outcomes, while approximately two-thirds of the CCETSW's (1995) regulatory framework specifies student outcomes. On the other hand, the recent regulations for nurse training (ENB 1997), which is not currently competence-based, focus largely on educational processes with clear but limited specification of outcomes in other documents. One of the strengths of the practice learning component of education for the caring professions, however, would seem to be its focus on the processes of learning and assessment. Central to those processes is the relationship between the student and the practice teacher.

The importance of relationship in learning

It is commonly accepted that relationships are of significance in helping children to learn. Meadows (1993) suggests the importance of peers and parents in the learning process. Piaget and Vygotsky (Crain 1992) both recognise the value of peers, while Winnicott (1971) emphasises the key role of the holding relationship between parent and child as a context for learning. Hirst and Peters suggest that relationship is also a major component of formal education: 'Education is not just a matter of the meeting of minds; it is a process of personal encounter' (Hirst and Peters 1970: 88).

When it comes to adult education, however, relationship is less often debated. The general assumption appears to be that the teacher needs to know their subject rather than their learner, an assumption which seems to begin in secondary school education, although the tutoring systems of secondary and tertiary education provide a mitigating factor. Carl Rogers (Rogers 1983; Kirschenbaum and Henderson 1990) is perhaps the best-known educator to emphasise the importance of the relationship between the learner and the person who facilitates that learning. He suggests that three key qualities in the facilitator assist learning: realness, or genuineness; prizing, acceptance and trust, and empathic understanding. These three are also essential, he suggests (Kirschenbaum and Henderson 1990), in other helping relationships such as therapy, hence indicating a congruence between working as a practitioner in the caring professions and as a practice teacher. Hinchliff's (1992) summary of research findings on the characteristics of an effective teacher includes these qualities. Other human characteristics indicated by Hinchliff (1992) include self-awareness, patience, emotional stability, maturity and enthusiasm for teaching. Boud and Miller (1996) have a similar, though perhaps less focused, interest in the role of relationships in the facilitation of adult experiential learning.

There is evidence that students and practice teachers are well aware of the importance of their relationship in practice learning. From their major study of practice learning in social work education, Walker et al. conclude that 'The relationship between practice teachers and students is clearly central to the learning process and it would seem that most practice teachers were much appreciated by their students' (Walker et al. 1995: 69). Bell and Webb (1992) suggested from their smaller scale study of practice teachers that establishing the relationship with the student was a crucial concern for them.

A similar picture is painted in other professions. Brooks and Sikes, drawing on research findings and practice teachers' accounts of their experience, suggest that one distinctive feature of practice teaching is 'its reliance on close, one-to-one relationships as a means of delivering education and training' (Brooks and Sikes 1997: 33). The finding that, of all the staff encountered in their education, nurse students appreciated particularly the practice agency staff (mentors and staff nurses) suggests that relationships are of similar significance in practice teaching in nursing (Macleod Clark et al. 1996).

In determining the significant dimensions of the student/practice teacher relationship, it seems helpful to delineate three major strands: a basic human relationship, a learning relationship and a power relationship.

A basic human relationship

Boe's study of residential social work placements in Norway identifies this aspect of the student/practice teacher relationship: 'It is important in practice that there are two human beings who match each other' (Boe 1996: 124). Both Walker et al.'s (1995) and Fernandez's (1998) findings in the UK and Australia support Rogers' (1983) analysis of basic human characteristics. Students seemed to value honesty, openness and sincerity (akin to Rogers' realness or genuineness) as well as acceptance and respect. Other aspects which they favour include a commitment and interest in them and their progress and a level of sharing. A sense of friendship is one strand of the relationship identified by Brooks and Sikes (1997).

These comments seem to indicate the importance of the practice teacher's allowing the genuine development of a relationship which goes beyond a concentration on the responsibilities of the job, as outlined in Chapter 5: a personal as well as professional encounter. This is not to suggest that student and practice teacher must become close friends, although such developments do occur and persist beyond the limits of the placement, or should strive too hard to achieve a personal relationship. However, it does seem important to recognise that the student has a personal life outside the placement, with other relationships, interests, pursuits and values. Hinchliff (1992) uses the term 'personalistic' to describe this broader interest. Sometimes, a student's personal life will manifest itself in the learning, as facets of the practice resonate with personal experiences. Sometimes, more personal information arises through the informal exchange that occurs. Throughout my own working life, I have had a tendency to keep strong professional boundaries. However, a full-time practice teaching colleague tried to teach me some important lessons early in my practice teaching career about relaxing those boundaries more, some of which I was able to learn, for example, being available to share lunch together from time to time, or seeing chatting not as an indulgence.

The literature (Burgess et al. 1998; Walker et al. 1995) seems to indicate that the collapse of this human relationship, often called a 'personality clash' can have a major impact on the placement, sometimes leading to its breakdown. Eysenck's and Cattell's theories of personality traits (Gross 1996) might offer some explanation for these clashes. Other key dimensions of relationships (Evans and Kearney 1996) include the extent to which people take up similar (symmetrical) positions or different but matching (complementary) ones and the level of closeness or distance with which people are comfortable. A failure to match in these fundamental aspects of relating can undermine the professional task to be performed.

Sexuality is also a major factor in human relationships which will impinge on the student/practice teacher relationship. A student may use sexual attractiveness to militate against the power of their practice teacher or conversely the practice teacher might harass the student. A student and practice teacher of the same gender but different sexual orientation may need to adjust to this difference, particularly if they have had no prior experience of this difference in working relationships.

The concept of transference can also help understand some of the complexities which arise in the human relationship. Rogers (Kirschenbaum and Henderson 1990) and other writers with a psycho-dynamic perspective (Salzberger-Wittenberg et al. 1983; Hinds 1998) recognise the importance of transference in the processes of learning wherein 'The tendency to repeat past patterns of relating is a universal phenomenon and recurs in any important relationship' (Salzberger-Wittenberg et al. 1983: 33). In the context of practice teaching, images of past relationships with school teachers, parents, and others associated with learning may well loom large in the current teaching/learning relationship.

A learning relationship

One of the key facets of the relationship between a student and a practice teacher is whether it fosters learning. Both student and practice teacher will have preferred styles of learning. Two major approaches to learning style have already been examined above in Chapter 1. Kolb's (1984) analysis focuses on the two axes, concrete/abstract and active/reflective, while Witkin et al.'s (1977) concept of 'field-dependency' emphasises the extent to which perception and understanding are influenced by context or occur in isolation.

However, Sparkes (1998) summarises a number of other differences in learning style. One important distinction (Entwistle 1988; Gardiner 1989) is between surface and deep learners, who are more concerned, respectively, to look for facts and remember them or to seek meaning and relate facts to a context. I am aware of a sense of irritation when students are seeking simple answers so that they can remember them and apply them rigidly, which I attribute to a difference in depth of learning style. Another distinction (Entwistle 1988) is between a 'serialist' step-by-step, sequential approach to learning and a 'holist' approach, which is more global and prone to anecdote. Some students find it difficult to progress beyond a chronological account of a practice event into a summary of its overall meaning, which would seem to arise from a more serialist approach.

The key issue for the student/practice teacher relationship concerns the extent to which their learning styles need to match. Smith (1984) indicates that prolonged or excessive mismatch between teacher and learner is generally undesirable, but a degree of difference can be creative. This position is also adopted by other writers (Bogo and Vayda 1987; Tennant 1997). Tsang (1993) recommends that practice teachers seek initially to accommodate to their students' learning styles and subsequently progress to helping them explore more unfamiliar styles. This approach would seem consistent with an overall student-centred approach to learning. Moreover, it would help to achieve a general approach towards encouraging a diversity and choice in the student's style of learning, which would equip them for a wider range of learning contexts. The use of the words such as 'challenge' and 'confront' (Walker et al. 1995; Fernandez 1998) suggests that some social work students welcome a degree of difference in learning approaches.

This fairly simple strategy, however, is somewhat complicated by the flexibility of learning styles. While Kolb (1984) suggests they can be reasonably stable characteristics in learners, he also indicates that they can change according to different contexts, including personality, educational specialisation, professional career, job role and specific task or problem. Using Kolb's (1984) analysis, Tsang (1993) similarly found that students' learning styles varied according not only to the demands of the particular stage in the social work programme with which they were faced – on placement or in the higher education institution – but also to the expectations of their teachers. It appears likely that student and practice teacher might tend to approximate towards each other during the course of the placement.

Another aspect of the learning relationship is the practice teacher's teaching style and how the student responds to it. Walker et al. report that 'nine out of ten students considered that the teaching style of practice teachers enabled them to learn during their placements' (Walker et al. 1995: 69), although they do not clarify exactly which dimensions of teaching style had this effect. The literature indicates a number of possible dimensions. One of these is the degree of formality/informality (Entwistle 1988). Although Entwistle is focusing particularly on schooling, there would seem to be some suggestion that this dimension is significant in practice learning, with social work students valuing a relaxed approach to learning (Walker et al. 1995), but without degenerating into amorphousness (Secker 1992). Closely related to this in terms of teacher control is the 'constrictive style' which Secker (1992) reports was disliked by students because of the teacher's attempts to persuade the student to 'do it my way'.

Another major dimension of teaching style would seem to be the extent to which the practice teacher is an authoritative leader. Jarvis and Gibson (1985) suggest that the practice teacher's preferred orientation towards an authoritarian, democratic or *laissez-faire* leadership style may be of significance in the learning relationship on placement. Heron's (1975) analysis of interventions into two main types – authoritative (not authoritarian) and facilitative – would suggest a similar emphasis on the practice teacher's approach to the exercising of their authority. Closely allied to this dimension is the indication that the practice teacher is more likely to be effective if they are knowledgeable (Hinchliff 1992). In Walker et al.'s (1995) and Fernandez's (1998) studies, students comment on the value of the practice teacher's knowledge and experience. This is not to say that practice teachers need considerable theoretical knowledge: they need to know the job, to be able to explain what it entails and to be confident in demonstrating these abilities.

Whilst the research findings and theoretical understandings outlined above can offer some general perspectives on learning relationships, the process of fitting together students' and practice teachers' learning and teaching styles will need to occur at an individual, specific level. The individual practice teacher will need to discuss these issues with their individual student, so that both of them can become aware of helpful and unhelpful approaches to learning as the placement evolves. It can be helpful to begin this discussion at the start of a placement, for example, by suggesting that both the student and the practice teacher complete one of the many learning style inventories (Smith 1984; Kolb 1985; Honey and Mumford 1995). This task can lead to a discovery of differences between the two and to a more detailed exploration of what styles and differences mean in terms of learning opportunities and teaching strategies during the placement. This form of dialogue helps the student not only to learn how to practice in this placement but also to learn how to learn to practice in the varying contexts of the rest of their career: to acquire learning-to-learn skills.

The power relationship

Brown and Bourne begin their excellent exploration of power in supervision with the following: 'Issues to do with power, and how it is managed, lie at the heart of supervision and the supervisory relationship' (Brown and Bourne 1996: 32). Bond and Holland (1998) strongly support this analysis and indicate its relevance to the supervisory relationship between nursing staff. Power would seem an even more significant aspect of the practice teaching/learning relationship, since students are not yet qualified and usually unemployed. If an employee is sacked, they do not necessarily lose their qualification/registration, whereas a student who is failed does not gain a qualification in the first place. Shardlow and Doel (1996), likewise, recognise the 'inescapable' role of power in practice learning.

Brown and Bourne summarise the many types of power within two major categories:

- the formal power that derives from the role and position of the supervisor vis-a-vis the supervisee
- the informal power of both the supervisor and supervisee that derives from personal and professional attributes, *and from the structurally determined identities and roles based on key characteristics like race, gender, class, age, sexual orientation and (dis)ability.* (Brown and Bourne 1996: 39, original emphasis)

The formal power of the practice teacher derives from the functions which are attributed to them by both the educational programme and the practice agency, as outlined above in Chapter 5. The teaching function rests on the power of expertise (Hasenfeld 1992), which it has already been suggested is generally valued by students. It must not be forgotten, however, that students will also often have such power, not formally through their position but through their past experience. The function of organising the placement can owe much to the practice teacher's positional power with a knowledge of how the practice agency operates and who to approach to meet the student's learning needs.

The aspect of formal power which is mentioned most in the practice teaching literature, however, stems from the assessment function. Shardlow and Doel (1996) draw attention to this source of power and so, too, do some of the students in Walker et al.'s (1995) and Fernandez's (1998) studies, although mainly indirectly through comments on constructive or destructive criticism. This power is double-edged - an ability to recommend a pass as well as a fail, although students are naturally concerned about the latter. The accountability function is also a source of significant power, felt most severely on the very few occasions when placements are terminated abruptly because of the student's harmful or dangerous practice, but also relevant to the practice teacher's ability to provide an appropriate workload for the student.

The informal power of the student as well as the practice teacher derives partly from what Kadushin (1992) calls personal attributes, such as size, force of personality, interpersonal skills, energy and partly from people's structural position in society, not only those listed above by Brown and Bourne (1996), but also others such as religious beliefs, cultural attitudes and language use. There is significant evidence of these structural factors influencing the progress of placements. Burgess et al. (1998) indicate their impact, particularly that of gender, on placement breakdowns, while others (de Souza 1991; Burgess et al. 1992; Humphries et al. 1993) report how black students have been discriminated against in their relationships with practice teachers and others on placement.

Formal and informal power can coalesce in complex patterns within particular student/practice teacher relationships. Brown and Bourne (1996) give a detailed exploration of the 16 variations in power difference when practice teacher and student are either male or female, black or white. They also note the possibility of an unexpected role reversal, whereby black people and women can abuse their formal power as practice teachers. This possibility is also reported by Evans (1990a), who observes how structural inequalities can compound the exercising of power through the process of assessment. In one placement, for example, a white, male practice teacher who was relatively new to supervising and a white, female student who had strong views about supervision, based on considerable experience as a manager, experienced some power struggles over the nature of supervision and the practice teaching task.

One important strategy to counter the abuse of power in the practice teacher/student relationship is to become aware of it, to recognise its significance and to discuss its ramifications in supervision sessions, what Taylor and Baldwin (1991) call 'acknowledging' and 'addressing.' Brown and Bourne (1996) make a significant contribution to these processes. Closely allied to this is the need to construe power appropriately. When properly acknowledged and used to the student's advantage, the practice teacher's power can be positive; when hidden and destructive, power will be negative. Kadushin's (1968) interesting article explores some of the hidden, and hence potentially harmful, games played by both students and practice teachers in supervision to covertly realign the power balance of the relationship.

Another strategy to redress unhelpful power differentials in the student/practice teacher relationship is to encourage a greater collective approach on behalf of the less powerful person, usually the student (Evans and Kearney 1996). The importance of peer support for students through group supervision or simply the contact with peers in the higher education institution by virtue of concurrent college/placement designs has been discussed in Chapter 2, as has the provision of support networks or consultancy for students who are structurally disadvantaged.

The whole emphasis on the human aspects of the student/practice teacher relationship, moreover, can help to neutralise unhelpful power differentials through a focus on mutual interests and reinforce an equal value as human beings. However, this may be ultimately insufficient to counter structural difference, since as Brown and Bourne suggest: 'the pervasive influence of institutional discrimination and oppression is a more intractable challenge than the personal relationship' (1996: 49).

PART IV

7 Practice Assessment

The context of practice assessment

Socio-political context

When practice teachers recommend to an educational programme that a student has passed or failed a placement, they are participating in a political act. Professions have been allowed certain powers and privileges in society on condition that they contribute to the regulation of those who attain and retain professional status (see Chapter 1). The individual practice teacher is thus near the end of a regulatory chain which proceeds from the general voting public through Government to professional regulatory bodies and educational programmes. Most practice teachers are only too aware of this broader context and approach their assessment function with a due sense of responsibility and apprehension. This introductory section seeks further to raise awareness about the broader contexts of practice assessment, although there is often little that the individual practice teacher can do to influence them.

The power of the caring professions in the regulation of its members, however, would seem to be diminishing. Becher (1994a) charts the rising clamour for the professions to be held publicly accountable, as does Eraut (1994), with an increasing tendency for the state to control aspects of professional education. As Torrance (1995) suggests, the outcome of education can easily be shaped to drive the entire curriculum. Hence, much of central government control has been focused on assessment. This is nowhere more evident than in initial teacher education, in which the current outcome standards for Qualified Teacher Status have been produced by central government (DfEE 1997), superseding others which were also the product of an earlier government department (DfE 1992). Social work education has also felt the hand of central government firmly on its shoulder, for example, when the revision of its value base responded to the government's attack on its 'political correctness' (Jones 1995). Together with the probation service (Williams 1996), these professions have been vulnerable to major government policy shifts in recent years and it is scarce wonder that their assessment systems have received considerable government interest. It remains to be seen how much other professions come under similar scrutiny.

An overriding interest of successive Conservative governments and now a Labour government has been in economic prosperity. Commentators (Hyland 1994; Wolf 1995) suggest that the government's economic imperative to compete with other major world economies gave rise to *A New Training Initiative* (DoE 1981), which led to the creation, in the mid-1980s, of the National Council for Vocational Qualifications (NCVQ), with a remit including the establishment of national standards of vocational competence throughout every occupational sector. This initiative has seen the development of competence-based assessment in the UK on a scale, which Wolf (1995) suggests is not matched in any other country. It has provided a backdrop to debate on assessment throughout the occupational sectors, including the caring professions, creating both avid proponents and fierce critics.

Moreover, it would appear that a competence-based approach is likely to influence assessment in the caring professions increasingly. Despite significant criticism of its form and substance by employers (Hyland 1994; Targett 1995) and a major review (Beaumont 1996), the National Vocational Qualifications (NVQ) (SVQ in Scotland) framework has shown little sign of disappearing. Following the review, the framework is currently being actively overhauled by the Qualifications and Curriculum Authority, successor to the NCVQ (Qualifications and Curriculum Authority 1998). Its support from Conservative administrations is unlikely to diminish under Prime Minister Tony Blair who appeared to be an advocate of the scheme when Shadow Employment Secretary. There are signs, too, that the framework is having an increasingly favourable reception in the higher education sector (Tysome 1995).

In 1989, the NVQ remit was extended to include the professions (NCVQ 1989). Moreover, although some people, for example, Brooks and Sikes (1997), have seen the framework as more appropriate for lower status (vocational) occupational groups, Wolf (1995) argues that the considerable costs entailed in the competence-based approach are more likely to be justified in the future for the higher status (professional) occupations.

During the second half of the 1990s, social work and initial teacher education have been significantly influenced by the framework; the latest nursing standards (ENB 1997) also show some influence, despite a generally sceptical position. In December 1996, a government consultation paper (DfEE 1996) indicated an interest in involving all professions within the framework, although that has yet to materialise.

Attitudes to assessment

Saltzberger-Wittenberg et al. (1983) suggests that one key role of the teacher is to be a judge and there is some evidence that this is one role which practice teachers are rather loath to play. Brooks and Sikes indicate that 'It is the summative element of the assessment process and the possibility of failing individual students which are the most onerous aspects ...' (Brooks and Sikes 1997: 122). Similarly, Williamson et al. (1989) found a general reluctance on the part of social work practice teachers to make definitive judgements about absolute standards, although willing to indicate progress. Both Walker et al. (1995) and Owens (1995) indicate how the growth of competence-based assessment has been received rather negatively by social work practice teachers. Walker et al. quote one extreme response 'I have never come across such a rigid and mechanistic approach to social work than the competence document. It is a NIGHTMARE and the sooner something is done about it, the better for all concerned...' (Walker et al. 1995: 108). Since the time of both these studies, CCETSW (1995) have further elaborated their competence-based system and the impression seems to be that practice teachers are adapting effectively.

Social work students generally seem to have a favourable view of practice assessment. Walker et al. (1995) report levels of satisfaction at around 80 per cent, while in Evans' study (1990a) only 12 per cent overall registered dissatisfaction. This compared favourably with the 20 per cent who expressed dissatisfaction over college-based assessment. As competence-based assessment has developed in social work education, students initially showed a mixed response, with a majority of negatives, particularly at a perceived distortion of the assessment process (Walker et al. 1995). It is difficult to know how their views have changed since the second stage of competence-based assessment (CCETSW 1995), but my impression as an internal and external assessor is that both academic and practice teaching staff have become increasingly familiar with the system and are more able to guide students effectively through it.

The dearth of strong evidence makes it similarly difficult to evaluate the response of academic staff to practice assessment. In the late 1970s and throughout the 1980s, a number of academic social work writers (Brandon and Davies 1979; Curnock and Prins 1982) indicated a number of deficiencies in practice assessment, including the lack of clear assessment criteria and a reluctance to fail students. Despite a reduction in many of these difficulties, it often appears that academic staff continue to find practice assessment problematic, as White et al. (1993) reported within nurse education. The cause of this anxiety may be found in a comparison between the norms of academic and practice assessment in professional education (Figure 7.1). It could be claimed that the two systems reflect the different ways in which judgements are reached in the respective domains of research and professional practice. Academic staff are thus generally in foreign territory when dealing with practice assessment. Two experienced academic staff were examining the largely practice-based assessment system of a course with which I was involved and seemed to find difficulty in determining how to start their examination, given its remoteness from traditional academic assessment systems.

	academic	practice
nature of student evidence	largely written	largely oral and behavioural
access to student evidence (internal assessors)	direct	often indirect through self-report
access to student evidence (external assessors)	direct	usually indirect through practice teacher's report
sampling method	structured and limited (ie essays)	largely unstructured and extensive
reliability	double, blind, quantitative marking	usually one qualitative opinion

Figure 7.1 A comparison between academic and practice assessment

Principles of assessment

The complex context of practice assessment, both within a socio-political climate and a mixture of attitudes on the part of its participants, would indicate the importance of clarifying fundamental principles. Fundamental principles have the value of being a source of guidance within complex and changing contexts. There would seem to be three of particular importance: clarity of purpose, clarity of process and student empowerment. Shardlow and Doel (1996) also stress the importance of a principled approach to assessment. However, their three principles are more properly related to one area of the assessment system only – the choice of assessment methods – and will be discussed below.

Clarity of purpose

The literature on assessment records a large number of different purposes or functions for assessment. Rowntree (1987) lists six while Brown and Knight (1994) include 13 and Yorke (1998) 14, several of them overlapping with Rowntree's. In the context of professional practice assessment, it would seem sufficient to highlight two broad purposes. One is the 'selection' of appropriate candidates for the specific profession, or perhaps more accurately the de-selection of inappropriate candidates. This is the purpose most overtly required by the public and the government in their efforts to render the professions more accountable. It is consequently often uppermost in the practice teacher's and the student's minds during much of the assessment activity on placement.

The second purpose could broadly be termed a 'learning' purpose, although it alludes to processes which lead both directly and indirectly to student learning. Assessment feedback from practice teacher to student, whether oral or written, can lead directly and often immediately to learning on the student's part. However, feedback can also give students confidence in their ability, which in turn may encourage them to make further strides in their learning: 'You're doing well at this, so why don't you have a go at that'. Moreover, by assessing the student, the practice teacher gains information about the student's current level of practice, which helps them shape their next teaching strategy or choose which work opportunities to organise next. These choices will subsequently influence the student's learning.

These two purposes do not always sit easily together. At one extreme, an appropriate insistence on the selection function by a practice teacher who considers a student is marginal or failing may render the student anxious, defensive and inhibited in their learning, possibly even leading to a breakdown in communication. At the other extreme, the tendency to prefer to support students in their progress rather than make objective judgements of standard noted by Williamson et al. (1989) may dissuade the practice teacher from failing a student who really should be failed. Discussions about assessment often polarise 'summative' and 'formative' assessment in terms of, respectively, the 'selection' and 'learning' purposes. However, this distinction, as Rowntree (1987) suggests, is often blurred, particularly in practice assessment when there is usually no final assessment event such as an essay or examination. Even a written report at the end of the last placement of a programme can significantly influence a student's learning for subsequent employment.

Moreover, the two purposes are not of equal weight. In any situation, where a student should be de-selected from the profession, accountability dictates that this should prevail over the learning purpose. However, the failure rate in professional education would seem generally to be rather low, perhaps due largely to rigorous admission processes. For the large majority of students, therefore, for whom de-selection is not an issue, it would seem appropriate to concentrate on the learning generated by the assessment process, rather than erecting a number of meaningless hurdles which students must jump.

The principle of clarity of purpose is thus both a reminder to practice teachers to be aware that selection is not the only function of assessment and also an indication of the value of reflecting over the precise purpose for a given assessment process in order to proceed in an appropriate manner. The major assessment events, for example, written placements reports, require careful consideration in order to maximise their learning potential.

Clarity of process

Evans (1990a) reported that a significant minority of social work students were unclear about aspects of practice assessment. Students need to know every aspect of the system: what is expected of them in terms of the dimensions and the processes of assessment, who will make the decisions about their practice standards and how they can legitimately influence those decisions. Sometimes these details are provided in writing by the educational programme, sometimes they are not. Often, for example, students are unaware that practice teachers' written reports are only a recommendation which requires confirmation by an assessment board and even by other people, such as the practice assessment panels required in social work education (CCETSW 1995). Even when information is written down, students' anxiety can often blind them to the implications.

However, it is not simply the students who need to be clear about the assessment system: so too do the practice teachers. Not only do they need clarity in order to fulfil their own assessment role satisfactorily, they may also be called upon by a student on placement to assist them in theirs. Written handbooks can offer practice teachers a useful guide. However, as busy practitioners, they often lack the time to sift through reams of material to find the guidance they seek. Moreover, handbooks usually emanate from academic staff who are aware of the constraints on assessment, such as modular systems of delivery and regulatory frameworks, but do not always recognise the need to clarify these contextual factors for practice teachers. For these reasons, it can be useful to include practice teachers in the drafting of such guidance.

Student empowerment

Syson and Baginsky, in their comprehensive study of assessment in social work some two decades ago, provide a graphic quotation from a student about the impact of power in practice assessment which could apply equally today in any profession: 'I wasn't going to argue, I was a student and she was the supervisor and when I did have discussions about it, I got it all hurled back at me in my placement report' (Syson and Baginsky 1981: 141). Whilst the reality of this power differential is indisputable, there are ways of empowering the student's position in the assessment process. Ensuring clarity of process is one such way, since the student becomes fully knowledgeable about the assessment process and is therefore well placed to present their case.

A second way to empower students is to give them choice where possible within the assessment system. In some of the caring professions, the criteria for practice assessment within an educational programme are still negotiable. In those professions where they are not, it may still be possible to negotiate individual learning objectives for the placement which can form some of the dimensions for assessment. Most of the regulatory bodies do not, however, specify assessment methods to any great detail, so these can be more readily negotiated with students. CCETSW make a potentially empowering requirement of all social work qualifying programmes, that they should consider 'evidence provided by the student and drawn from their practice' (CCETSW 1995: 53), thus leaving the choice of practice evidence to the student.

A third way of empowering students is to give them right of reply to assessment judgements. This is particularly crucial in practice assessment, since their practice performance and reflective thinking are not always as transparent as the understanding demonstrated in an academic essay. A prerequisite for this reply is that the practice teacher reveals the judgement in the first place as outlined in the processes of reflective apprenticeship (see

Chapter 6) and does not store it in their mind for a future formal report. Once the student hears the judgement, it is useful for a process of dialogue in which the student can present their own judgement and negotiation takes place, before the practice teacher reaches a more considered position.

A fourth empowerment strategy lies in the provision of support systems for the student, many of which were outlined in Chapter 2. This becomes particularly important when the student is seen to be failing (see below). The possibility of a discriminatory use of power in assessment is recorded in the literature. Ahmed et al. (1988) and de Souza (1992) are concerned about discrimination against black students, while Trotter and Gilchrist (1996) indicate how lesbian and gay students can be discriminated against in assessment. Evans' (1990a) study suggested that a significant proportion of students who felt they were vulnerable to discrimination thought they actually did experience it within the assessment process. The discrimination could be on the grounds of age, gender, class, disability and language use, as well as race and sexual orientation. As Ahmed et al. (1988) suggest, this discriminatory use of power in assessment can be combated by a number of strategies, including support from students and staff in the same position of structural disadvantage, practical assistance in areas of difficulty, such as physical or sensory disability, and choice of assessment methods which do not focus on those areas of difficulty.

The dimensions of practice assessment

This section seeks to explore the question 'what are practice teachers looking for when assessing practice?' The exploration is divided into three broad and related areas. First, it seems sensible to gain some broad perspective on the nature of what makes professional practitioners effective, since so much discussion of dimensions seems to focus immediately on the minutiae, and the broader picture, particularly of the interrelatedness between the detail, can easily get lost. The second section looks more closely at the detailed aspects of professional ability, while the third section discusses how we know when a student has achieved well enough in any one of these detailed aspects.

A model of professional competence

In this broad perspective, the phrase 'professional competence' is used advisedly, in recognition of the current, pervasive influence of the term 'competence' within occupational education and training in the UK.

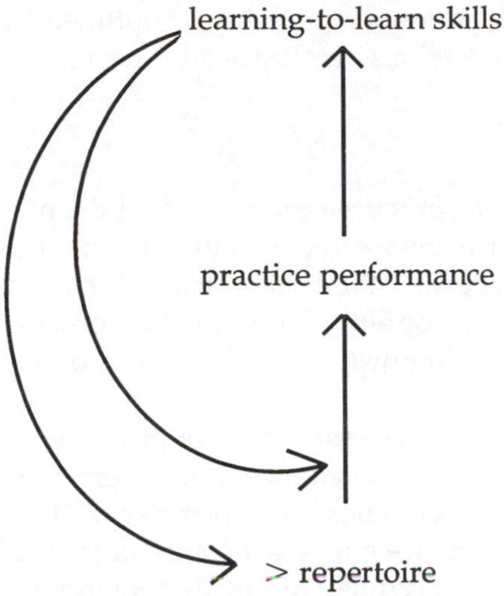

Figure 7.2 A model of professional competence

However, I use the phrase here not with the technical meaning of the NVQ/SVQ framework, but simply to refer to a broad sense of professional ability, as in Fish (1995). The model of professional competence depicted in Figure 7.2 delineates three different areas of professional ability: practice performance; a repertoire of knowledge, skills, values and personal qualities, and a set of higher-order learning-to-learn skills. It also seeks to explain the interrelationship between these three areas.

These three elements appear in varying ways in other models of professional competence. Schon (1983, 1987) and Winter (1992) emphasise two elements – practice performance and reflection, the latter of which in my view incorporates many of the learning-to-learn skills. Fish (1995) concentrates on a wide repertoire of abilities and some learning-to-learn skills. Despite the general impression of a narrow view of competence within the UK NVQ/SVQ framework, the definition offered by the Training Agency is in fact quite wide and incorporates some aspects of all three elements: 'Competence is a wide concept which embodies the ability to transfer skills and knowledge to new situations within the occupational area' (Training Agency 1988: 1).

Knowledge and skills are part of the repertoire, the ability to transfer is a learning-to-learn skill and practice performance is what occurs in specific occupational situations. The notion of capability as outlined by Eraut (1994) and Stephenson and Yorke (1998) also includes all three elements.

Practice performance

At the heart of this model is the practice performance of the practitioner. This includes both the work performed directly with the client as well as the indirect work performed on behalf of the client. It also includes all aspects of that performance: the internal cognitive and affective processes as well as the external behaviour, both linguistic and physical, for example, when performing practical tasks.

It is difficult to conceive of an understanding of professional competence which does not include practice performance. It is by practice performance that most clients judge the effectiveness or otherwise of their practitioner: unsatisfactory practice performance may elicit complaints or litigation. Most clients, however, remain generally unaware of the practitioner's repertoire of specific abilities or their learning-to-learn skills. Practice performance is of central importance in the NVQ/SVQ competence assessment framework, to the extent that it is often criticised for neglect of the other two elements (Hyland 1994). Whilst the notion of 'capability' propounds a broader, more forward-looking concept of professional ability than competence, for some people it still includes a place for practice performance. Stephenson (1998: 2), for example, includes the ability to 'take effective and appropriate action' within his explanation of capability. Moreover, professional regulatory bodies such as CCETSW (1995) and the English National Board (1997) insist upon the assessment of professional practice, while many of the standards articulated for initial teacher education (DfEE 1997) clearly cannot be assessed other than in practice performance.

The key determinant of practice performance is context, ranging from the widest aspects of the socio-political context to more specific aspects, such as the aims and ethos of the agency within which the practice occurs, the practitioner's work orientation, and the client and their individual need. In a given practice performance, the effective practitioner selects from their repertoire of abilities those which are appropriate to that particular context. The practitioner's competence lies partly in having a repertoire from which to choose and partly in recognising the contextual variables which guide that choice.

Repertoire

Every professional practitioner has a repertoire of abilities on which they can draw in any given practice context. The repertoire is therefore a potential which is far wider than the actual which is apparent in any given practice performance. Many models of competence, including the NVQ/SVQ framework, include four elements within the repertoire - knowledge, understanding, skills and values. All four elements are included within the outcomes of social work education (CCETSW 1995) and nurse education (HMSO 1992), although the recent standards for Qualified Teacher Status (DfEE 1997) appear to have little reference to values.

The notion of capability (Stephenson and Yorke 1998) includes an important fifth element within the repertoire: personal qualities. These qualities vary according to the profession but can include: creativity, stamina, patience, commitment, determination, intelligence and warmth. The importance of personal qualities rests partly in the nature of the caring professions, whereby the encounter between different human beings is a significant component of practice, and partly that qualities have a permanence within practitioners and their practice which specific behaviours do not: patient people occasionally lose their temper. Whilst qualities of this sort do not figure prominently in the outcomes of qualifying education, it is interesting to find a number within the standards for headteachers as specified by the Teacher Training Agency:

i. personal impact;
ii. resilience;
iii. adaptability to changing circumstances and new ideas;
iv. energy, vigour and perseverance;
v. self-confidence;
vi. reliability;
vii. enthusiasm;
viii. intellectual ability;
ix. integrity;
x. commitment. (Teacher Training Agency 1997: 4)

Current competence-based assessment systems make it difficult to assess legitimately qualities of this sort. My own response has been to seek to introduce personal qualities into the selection criteria for entry into educational programmes, which are not typically specified by regulatory bodies.

Learning-to-learn skills

Dearing (1997) suggests that learning how to learn is of particular importance among what he calls the four key skills, because of its capacity to facilitate lifelong learning. The growing emphasis on continuing professional development within the caring professions is a recognition of the extent to which all professionals will need to learn and change once they are qualified. It is particularly the learning-to-learn skills which will assist in this process. They are therefore crucial cognitive skills which, although potentially learned during qualifying education, will undoubtedly be of value throughout a career, while other skills learned at the same time may have a much more limited relevance. Smith (1984) lists 15 learning-to-learn skills for all adult learners. Within the caring professions, the main learning-to-learn skills would seem to include: self-awareness, reflective learning, transfer of learning, ability to relate theory and practice, and use of supervision and other in-service learning forums.

These are higher-order cognitive skills since they govern the use and development of other cognitive skills within the repertoire. They would seem to operate in two main ways: they help the practitioner choose which parts of the repertoire will be relevant to a particular practice context and they help the practitioner generate new aspects of repertoire (and discard old). In both uses they are generative: generating practice performances and generating repertoire. Eraut (1994) draws an interesting analogy with the distinction made by linguists from Saussure onwards between language performance (*'la parole'*, or actual speech) and language competence (*'la langue'*, or the potential to create speech). In the model of professional competence presented here a further distinction is made between two types of potential: the potential repertoire, some of which will be actualised in a particular context, and the cognitive skills which guide that choice from the repertoire and which extend the repertoire, akin to Chomsky's generative rules in language.

Benner's (1984) study of nursing practice suggests the further possibility of progression in the use of learning-to-learn skills throughout a practitioner's career. She suggests that novice nurses will have no experience to draw on and will generally seek to apply rules rather inflexibly to guide their actions. This suggests a rather rudimentary grasp of how to relate theory and practice and little reflective learning or transfer of learning. An expert, on the other hand, no longer relies on rules to guide their actions, and 'with an enormous background of experience, now has an intuitive grasp of each situation and zeroes in on the accurate region of the problem ...' (Benner 1984: 32).

Relating theory and practice has, thus, diminished as a key learning-to-learn skill and even the reflective learning typical of intervening stages has given way in many situations to more intuitive self-awareness. While the detail of this analysis may not hold for all professions, or even for those nurses who enter the profession with considerable relevant experience, the notion of progression within the learning-to-learn skills would seem generally helpful.

The significance of this model of professional competence to the practice teacher is primarily one of orientation. Most practice teachers are aware of the importance of assessing practice performance. Eraut (1994) reports a focus on this area for the three caring professions - nursing, social work and optometry - included in an Employment Department study. Moreover, CCETSW (1995) and the English National Board (1997) both require such an emphasis. Most practice teachers will also be aware of the need to assess aspects of the student's growing repertoire. However, it is the learning-to-learn skills which, in my experience, receive least attention. Any observation of practice performance needs, in my view, to be accompanied with a dialogue about the reasons for the students' choice of skills and knowledge for that particular situation and an exploration of the values intended to guide the behaviour. Of the learning-to-learn skills, practice teachers seem to be most attuned to the relating of theory and practice, largely due to pressure from regulatory bodies and academic partners. However, on the basis of reading many practice teachers' assessment reports, it would seem to me that students' transfer of learning skills, reflective learning skills and use of learning forums are infrequently commented on.

Criteria for assessment

This model of professional competence offers a broad perspective on what practice teachers are expected to assess. However, it does not answer the more specific question 'But what exactly do we look for when assessing?' One part of the answer to this question is provided by the criteria. Criteria indicate a desired outcome which students are expected to achieve and Rowntree (1987) explores the strong position criterion-referenced assessment has in education. For many of the caring professions, the criteria are devised by the professional regulatory body. Sometimes their criteria are then transmuted by a particular educational programme, which are then agreed through the process of validation. Some professions, including professions allied to medicine, allow the educational programme to determine criteria directly. The current criteria for assessment in nurse education, for example, include the following: 'an understanding of the requirements of legislation relevant to the practice of nursing', and 'the use of the appropriate channel of referral for matters not within her sphere of competence' (HMSO 1992: Rule 18a).

The first criterion is rather general and not likely to be fully observable in practice performance, while the second is more specific and observable. Criteria other than those set down by professional regulatory bodies or educational programmes will be explored below.

The competences devised within the NVQ/SVQ framework are, as Wolf (1995) suggests, simply one particular form of criterion. 'Competence' as defined within the NVQ framework is 'the ability to perform the activities within an occupation or function to the standards expected in employment' (Employment Department 1991: 1). Thus the ability to perform one specific activity is described in one specific competence. Jessup (1991) emphasises that the level of performance implied by 'competence' is one of effective achievement and not merely adequate, as is a common meaning of the word. Two examples of competences from social work education are

- Establish initial contact and the reason for contact with children, adults, families, carers and groups.
- Communicate effectively with children, adults, families, carers and groups. (CCETSW 1995: 25)

The particular linguistic form of a competence generally starts with an active verb in the simple present tense, thus emphasising performance, whereas the nursing criteria above are less precisely a call for action.

There has been much debate over the strengths and weaknesses of competence-based assessment. One strength would seem to be this focus on practice performance, providing that other major elements of professional competence are also assessed. This emphasis on performance offers an alternative possibility for measuring and predicting occupational ability than those currently offered by traditional academic systems. Wolf reviews the evidence against academic assessment in occupational education and training and concludes that 'The evidence on the link between academic measures and vocational performance is almost consistently damning' (1995: 45).

A second important strength is the delineation of clear, overt criteria for assessment. This clarity of process allows the possibility of fairness for students and a strategy to prevent oppression against students who are structurally disadvantaged (Evans 1990; Brown and Knight 1994). This possibility is most likely to be realised if the quality assurance of the assessment system seeks to ensure that assessors adhere to the criteria which have already been communicated to students. As an external assessor, for example, I consider it to be a key responsibility to attempt to ensure that practice teachers in very different settings are confining their judgements to the criteria which students have been required to meet.

A third strength in competence-based assessment is that it offers a nation-wide consistency in the criteria of assessment. This is important for professions wishing to assure the public that there is a consistency between its members. The claim of the NCVQ and its successor QCA would also include nationwide consistency of standards, but this claim will be refuted below.

There would seem to be four major criticisms of competences as the criteria for assessment. First, there is the emphasis on behaviour, which reveals a major influence from the behaviourist movement (Eraut 1994). This is in part a corollary of a focus on practice performance. However, behaviour is only part of practice performance and the A.S.S.E.T. scheme (Anglia Polytechnic University and Essex Social Services Department 1994) has demonstrated how the cognitive and affective aspects of practice can also be built into competences. None the less, behaviour is an inadequate indicator of learning-to-learn skills and of the extent of the repertoire of knowledge, understanding, values and personal qualities. Moreover, an emphasis on behaviour is likely to minimise the development of critical faculties which might challenge existing practices, and can therefore lead to the creation of a compliant workforce.

A second criticism centres on the process of functional analysis which generates the competences within the NVQ/SVQ framework (Eraut 1994; Wolf 1995). In this process, a number of people well acquainted with the occupational area are asked to define its main current functions. While it is claimed that this generates a useful consensus within the occupation, the process can be criticised for its inherent conservatism. Such an analysis is unlikely to consider major critical evaluations of current functions or the development of functions at the cutting edge of the occupation. Nor is it likely to include significant representation of minority views (Kemshall 1993). The process thus tends to produce from one generation some middle-of-the-road functions which the next generation of workers will be trained to perform.

Competences have also been criticised for their reductionism, in the tradition of scientific positivism (Gould 1996). The particular form of competences in the NVQ/SVQ framework involve three main levels of specificity, with units of competence as the most general, elements as more specific and performance indicators as the most specific (Wolf 1995; Hyland 1994; Eraut 1994). Wolf (1995: 55) suggests, however, that the tendency to create a 'never-ending spiral of specification' is shared by all criterion-referenced assessment systems, as increasing levels of clarity are sought for the students' outcomes.

The level of specificity entailed in performance indicators particularly, has three main effects. First, they make it difficult to synthesise rather than analyse: to make a more holistic judgement, for example, in answer to the question 'is this student overall a satisfactory practitioner?' The second effect is that the considerable number of criteria generated for assessment can become unmanageable. CCETSW (1995), for example, have devised 117 evidence indicators – their equivalent to performance indicators – for the assessment of social work students. There is some evidence that assessors can only manage a limited number of criteria when assessing. Bridges et al. (1995) report that practice teachers in initial teacher education tended to reduce the long list of specific competences to not more than six broader criteria. My own approach in seeking to help practice teachers manage the CCETSW competences has similarly been to emphasise the six more general criteria, to minimise the 26 which are more specific and required and to ignore the 117 which are most specific but are not required.

A further effect of such specificity is that it encourages a bureaucratic approach to the process of assessing: the tick-box approach. Such an approach can reduce the meaningful learning which students can gain from the process, largely through the reduction of useful feedback. However, provided that tick-boxes are accompanied by qualitative feedback which can be useful to students' learning, the exercise need not lose meaning. The danger is that the practice teacher will put more energy into the tick-box than the qualitative feedback, unless advised otherwise.

The CCETSW fully embraced a competence-based framework for social work before most other caring professions, although Wolf (1995) suggests that health visitor education has also operated a competence-based assessment system for several years. CCETSW's (1995) achievements in this process would seem considerable. Perhaps most significantly, they recognised the likelihood of the competence framework embracing many if not all of the caring professions. They accordingly worked in partnership with the Care Sector Consortium, the standard-setting body for the occupational sector at that time, thus ensuring a level of conformity compatible with exercising statutory control. They resisted the NVQ tendency to require a high level of specificity in competences. They also managed to introduce some competences which focused more on learning-to-learn skills as well as performance behaviour, a strategy which they have continued when designating 'reflective practice' as one of five units of competence for their Practice Teaching Award (CCETSW 1996a). They even did some preliminary work in mapping the knowledge base against the competences, thus offering some guidance as to how the knowledge component of the repertoire relates to practice performance.

Their achievement would have been greater, in my view, if they had concentrated on a more limited, manageable number of competences, for example, the six most general units of competence, offering greater specification for guidance only and not as requirements. They could also usefully have included other key learning-to-learn skills, such as transfer of learning, self-awareness as a learner and relating theory and practice, in the competence framework. A third area for development is determining the extent of the knowledge repertoire and its relationship with practice performance, for example, how much of the knowledge repertoire should be demonstrated in performance?

Whether competences or not, criteria devised by the professional regulatory body or the educational programme are not the only criteria which may shape a practice teacher's assessment judgement. The practice agency where the student is placed may have some clear criteria of good practice, sometimes written into policy or procedural documents, which the practice teacher and student will need to bear in mind as well as any criteria from the educational programme: criteria for accountability rather than criteria for assessment. The National Standards governing practice in the Probation Service have been an interesting example of this. Senior (1994) reports the generally favourable opinion of practice teachers towards these agency criteria for good practice, although there is no account of how they dovetailed with the assessment criteria of the educational programmes. It is possible that the practice teacher could help the student discover similarities and dissimilarities between the two sets of criteria or, failing that, to recognise the different reasons for seeking to fulfil the two sets of criteria.

As well as criteria set at an institutional level, some of the most powerful criteria influencing assessment are those developed at a more individual level, since it is ultimately individuals who make assessment decisions. The individual practice teacher is likely to have developed over the years a sense of what makes a good practitioner. These ideas are sometimes not consciously articulated as criteria. Nevertheless, they will clearly influence the judgements formed in the practice teacher's mind during the placement. When not consciously articulated, they are somewhat akin to the impressionistic 'connoisseurship' which Eisner (1985) advocates for assessment. Impressionistic judgements of this kind pose difficulty in accountability. It is important, therefore, to the student that the practice teacher makes these criteria overt, since they can then be debated and compared with the predetermined criteria of the educational programme. If they are then found to be incompatible with the programme's criteria, it would seem that the practice teacher should seek to limit their influence in the assessment process, on the grounds of fairness and consistency between placements. For many years as a practice teacher, I found the typology of intervention styles outlined by Heron (1975), a useful framework for assessing students, but reluctantly had to abandon it as detailed national criteria were introduced.

A fairer form of individual assessment criteria are those generated during the process of constructing an individual placement agreement, often called 'individual learning objectives' (see Chapter 5). This seems fairer since all students on a programme can be involved in the same process and the criteria are agreed and recorded. By virtue of the role of the practice teacher in the negotiating process, these criteria are likely to be consistent with the practice teacher's sense of good practice and also to be achievable in that practice setting. The student's role in the negotiation can, if suitably empowered, ensure a clear link between student-centred learning and assessment and, as Brown and Knight (1994) suggest, form an initial springboard for self-assessment. Moreover, if the academic tutor is also present in agreeing individual learning objectives, the likelihood of those objectives being consistent with the educational programme's general assessment criteria may be increased. Another advantage of more general criteria or competences, for example, CCETSW's (1995) 'assess and plan', is that it is then easier to agree for a particular placement which aspects of assessing and planning would advance a particular student's learning, conform with the agency's and the practice teacher's sense of good practice and be achievable in that placement.

Standards in assessment

The NVQ/SVQ language of competence is also the language of standards. When the National Council for Vocational Qualifications was set up for England and Wales, part of its remit was 'to secure standards of occupational competence and ensure that vocational qualifications are based on them' (NCVQ 1986).

The development of occupational standards for different occupational groups was achieved through the specification of competences at different levels. However, it was the most specific level - performance indicators - which purported to give a clear, unambiguous indication of the level required so that any assessor could apply them. However, several writers (Evans 1990; Winter 1992; Brooks and Sikes 1997) suggest that competences, even as specific as performance indicators, do not give a clear indication of the level required and that an additional judgement needs to be made by the assessor which is independent of the written criteria. This was one of the suggestions of a review of some pilot NVQs in social care (Jowett et al. 1989). Moreover, Paley (1987) makes a similar criticism on theoretical grounds, based upon Wittgenstein's notion of private language, suggesting that the only people who will understand what particular written criteria mean, including any attempted allusion to standard, will be the people who wrote them.

Taking one of the CCETSW evidence indicators cited above as an example, it seems clear that practice teachers will need to make an extra judgement of level, independent of the stated competence, about what constitutes 'effective' communication. Just in the area of listening, for example, should the student accurately hear and understand 100 per cent, 70 per cent or 40 per cent of what the client says? Should accurate understanding include the emotional significance of what is said or only its practical implications? Is it reasonable that a trained counsellor or therapist might expect a better understanding of emotional significance than another worker? It is the evaluative word 'effective' which still requires additional interpretation and judgement.

It can be reasonably claimed, therefore, that occupational standards do not actually give the standard, in the sense of the precise level of performance expected within that specified activity. Nor, moreover, do any other forms of criteria, particularly when they refer to the complicated activities undertaken in the caring professions. How, then, are practice teachers to judge the standard of their students' practice?

The standard-setting process

Practice teachers in training or otherwise new to the responsibility are often particularly concerned whether they will be able to make an accurate judgement of standard. The single most useful message would seem to be that they do not have to make this judgement alone. Moreover, there is a strong argument that they *should not* make the judgement alone. If nationally agreed criteria do not offer a perspective on standard, there is certainly no other single national yardstick of standard: no wise person sitting in a quiet backroom of the professional regulatory body, for example. Some writers (Gardiner 1985; Paley 1987) suggest that agreement about standards is achieved within the community of assessors, what the Higher Education Quality Council (1997: 8) call 'a shared assessment culture'.

This occurs, in my view, as different assessors make judgements about the same assessment event, discuss their judgements, and then seek to resolve any disagreements. One considerable strength of much academic assessment is that two internal assessors judge the same assignment and can seek resolution of differences. Subsequently, a further external opinion can be sought and discussion can then occur between the internal and the external opinions. Although this community of three is only a small subset of the total number of assessors for the profession, the complex network of external assessors ensures access to a wider community. The Quality Assurance Agency (1998) would seem to recognise this crucial role of the external assessor in their current review at the time of writing.

The transitory and private nature of much practice makes it difficult to replicate this particular strength of the academic system. However, the practice world operates similarly when reaching difficult judgements about service delivery, for example, when seeking the opinion of other team members and seeking a further skilled opinion from outside the team if necessary. Practice teachers can take steps to approximate towards this in two main ways: by inviting other members within the agency to form an opinion of the student's practice, and by making it possible for skilled practice assessors from outside the agency, particularly the programme's external assessor, to have access to the student's practice. The first way involves a choice of people, particularly which people within the team and whether clients should be included in the community of assessors. The second way entails particularly a consideration of method: how can people not working within an agency have access to practice within the agency? Both people and methods are discussed below.

Intrinsic factors

Before seeking to involve other people, the practice teacher will usually have begun to form their own judgement of standard. They can do this with reference to factors which are intrinsic and extrinsic to the student's practice. Intrinsic to the student's practice are three main factors: frequency, range and level. Frequency refers to the number of times a particular criterion should be met. In some assessment systems, such as NVQ and police training, only a small number of demonstrations are required for each criterion. One important issue concerns the counterweight of demonstrations that the criterion was definitely not met. Does one failure to fulfil a criterion balance out a number of occasions on which it is achieved?

Range is a concept of considerable importance in the NVQ/SVQ framework and it concerns the range of different situations in which the student should be expected to demonstrate satisfactory practice. Referring again to the CCETSW (1995) evidence indicator above, the immediate question to address is 'should the student communicate effectively with all of the five categories of people mentioned?' Moreover, each category offers a potential range, for example children: of all ages? Both sexes? Different ethnic origins? Different levels of ability, both intellectual and physical? With communication difficulties? The NVQ/SVQ framework clearly defines the range required, but professional statutory bodies do not currently. The choice of range rests with the practice teacher and in this as other aspects of assessment they do not need to choose alone.

Level is the factor most commonly considered when determining standards. It means the degree or quality of the student's practice with reference to a particular criterion: using the CCETSW (1995) example again, just how effective does the communication have to be? Rowntree (1987) suggests that some criteria can be fully achieved, while for others there is no limit to the extent to which a practitioner can improve. The latter would appear to be the case with 'effective communication' and most of the criteria in professional education. Since it is rarely a case of 'yes, the student did it' or 'no, they didn't', the question remains 'how well did they do it?'

Extrinsic factors

It is not possible to judge a student's practice simply by reference to one particular practice event: other factors extrinsic to that event will also be relevant. The reference to criteria has already been discussed. Two other forms of referencing are also discussed in the literature (Rowntree 1987; Brown and Knight 1994): norm-referencing and self-referencing.

Norm-referencing consists of comparing a student's practice with a sense of the generally accepted norms of practice, gained by reference to other people's practice. The issue for the practice teacher is which norm. There are two main norms which a practice teacher can easily access: those of the practice agency and their own practice norms. In most settings, practice teachers get to know about their colleagues' practice, certainly enough to acquire a sense of norm: the more 'visible' the practice (Pithouse 1987), the stronger the sense of norms. The difficulty in using agency norms, however, arises from the variable standards of practice agencies. The professional regulatory bodies are mainly aware of this and seek to regulate minimum standards in different ways (see Chapter 1). The success of these strategies is questionable, given the resource available for quality assurance of practice learning and the greater imperative to deliver a service for clients. Even if minimum standards were ensured, the difficulty would not be removed, since practice agencies will also vary over their maximum standards. Specialist agencies often have a higher practice norm in their specialist area of practice than other agencies. One example I have encountered was of the Probation Service, for whom much of the practice centres around the production of formal reports for the courts which seem generally to be of a higher quality than formal reports written in Social Services Departments, for whom report-writing is a less central activity. Often, academic tutors who have contact with a number of agencies can reassure practice teachers about the norms of their agency.

The practice norm with which the practice teacher is most familiar is their own: not their very best practice but not their worst. It could well be that this is the sense of norm which influences practice teachers most, since it is so deeply imbedded in the practice teacher's thinking. However, it can be a misleading norm since practice teachers are generally, in my experience, practitioners with a higher commitment to professional standards than many other qualified staff. It is this commitment which motivates them to become involved in helping maintain or improve standards for the next generation of practitioners. Although there appears to be no research evidence to support it, it is my impression that quite a high proportion of new practice teachers have initial concerns about whether the student placed with them is of a sufficiently high standard. These concerns seem to diminish as practice teachers become accustomed to the norms of students on placement.

This third norm, of students practising in the particular agency, is a particularly useful one in judging standards. This sense of norm develops as either the agency as a whole has a number of students placed within it, or as a particular practice teacher is involved in the assessment of a number of students. The experienced practice teacher, sometimes holding a specialist post within the agency, has a particularly valuable perspective on assessment standards. Academic tutors also usually have a clear sense of student norms, including for the different stages of the educational programme. Despite the restricted access many tutors have to the student's practice, it can be useful for the practice teacher to consult the tutor on issues of standard.

Norm-referencing can be criticised for the variability between the different norms available to different practice teachers in different settings and the consequent inequity of treatment any student may receive (Yorke 1998). Although criterion-referencing is often preferred for its avoidance of potential inequity by referring to one fixed point, the difference between the two is in fact blurred (Rowntree 1987; Wolf 1995; Yorke 1998). In attempting to use criteria for standard setting, the assessor is inevitably drawn to a sense of comparison with other students, since, as has been discussed, standard is not inherent in the criteria. The practice teacher can become more confident in the use of norms, partly by becoming more aware of which norms they are using and avoiding less helpful ones, and partly by reaching out beyond the norms of their own practice and their setting to access other norms – in other agencies and in the higher education setting.

Two other points of reference outside a particular piece of practice can be helpful in the judgement of standard. One of these is self-referencing, comparing the student's practice at one point in time to some earlier time. The disadvantage of this reference point is that it still begs the question whether the student's practice is good enough, even if it has improved or deteriorated. However, self-referencing has two considerable advantages. First, it can involve the adult student in the process of self-assessment, since who can know the student's practice in more detail than the student? This is particularly true at the beginning of a placement, when the student is clearly more aware of what they bring to a placement than a practice teacher can be. The other advantage is that self-referencing provides indirect evidence of learning, or a lack of it, and hence of the learning-to-learn skills which can be difficult to access directly. Williamson et al. (1989) seemed rather critical of social work practice teachers for being more concerned about improvement than absolute standards. However, whilst students must clearly reach the pass standard during their educational programme, evidence of learning and development is likely to be a good predictor of future practice standards.

Another point of reference is a model (Evans 1990; Brown and Knight 1994). Whereas norms are abstracted from a number of people's practice, a model, in this sense, is one actual example of practice. Students can easily be referred themselves to observe a particular piece of practice which is deemed to be of a certain standard. Practice teachers, too, can have models in mind when assessing. The models I have tended to use as a practice teacher in assessing students are models of poor practice: comparing a student with another student who had previously failed on the same criterion and asking myself 'is student A as bad in this area as student B?' Models themselves are generally selected with reference to norms: this is an example of good/adequate/poor practice.

Marginal and failing students

While it is clear that several writers (Thompson et al. 1990; Shardlow and Doel 1996; Brooks and Sikes 1997) recognise the considerable difficulty practice teachers can experience in deciding whether or not to recommend that a student fails, there would appear to be little guidance on this difficult area. Burgess et al. (1998) in their interim report of research in Scotland covering, among other areas, social work student failure make no reference to any prior research on the topic. There would seem to be three key areas for exploration: the main areas for failure, the difficulties practice teachers' experience in reaching their judgements, and the possible strategies to adopt.

Reasons for student failure will undoubtedly vary according to the particular caring profession. A number of studies of social work students, however, indicate some criteria which could well be generalised to other professions. Burgess et al. (1998) indicated the importance of power differences, particularly on grounds of gender and dyslexia. Coulson (1993) also found gender to be significant, although in her case female students suffered while in Burgess et al.'s (1998) study it appeared to be male students. Both Coulson (1993) and Pink (1991) indicate that ethnic minority students have been disproportionately failed. Syson and Baginsky (1981) and Hughes and Heycox (1996) both note the importance of the student's interest and commitment to the job. Williamson et al. (1989) and Syson and

Baginsky (1981) suggest that personal qualities played a key role in failing. Several of these studies occurred before tighter criteria were produced in social work education. However, these reasons still serve as a caveat against the possible abuses of power and the halo effect of rather vague, 'hidden' criteria influencing the practice teacher's judgement.

Perhaps the greatest difficulty for practice teachers in the caring professions when considering the possibility of failing a student lies in the conflict between their enabling and assessing functions: of caring about them and their progress in the context of a human relationship, and yet assessing them in a way which apparently harms them, certainly in the short term. Hughes and Heycox (1996) conclude from their study that assessing marginal students is stressful for all parties and not just the student. It is sometimes helpful at such times to remind practice teachers of their responsibility to care for the future generations of clients which the student might harm if they were to pass when they should not. Some caring professions, such as health visiting and district nursing, have dealt with this difficulty by insisting that the person who assesses the student is different from the person who teaches and supports them, although this separation of functions has proved difficult to sustain.

Doel lists a number of other possible reasons for difficulty in assessing marginal or failing students, including:

- lack of confidence, in the absence of a general measure of 'good-enough' practice
- lack of confidence, for fear that your own judgement is culture-specific
- difficulties pinpointing the evidence to back up your concerns
- fear that the student's failure reflects on your own teaching abilities
- 'all-or-nothing' effect of a pass-or-fail choice. (Doel 1993: 215)

Hughes and Heycox (1996) also report that practice teachers can experience difficulty with the assessment criteria.

One response to these difficulties is to put the onus of decision making onto someone else. Sometimes that entails hoping that the student is also showing deficiencies in their academic assignments, although most assessment systems do not allow compensation between practice and theory. On early placements, it often entails the hope that a later placement will show up the same difficulties, only more starkly (Hughes and Heycox 1996). This latter is a particularly risky position, since the deficiencies indicated in one practice setting may not emerge in another very different context. Moreover, there would seem to be a tendency for the later placement to look back at the earlier one and think 'oh well, they passed this student, so why shouldn't I?'

There would seem to be three main strategies to assist the practice teacher who is struggling to make this difficult decision: increased rigour in assessment, increased support for the practice teacher, and increased support for the student.

The practice teacher can seek to increase rigour throughout the assessment system in a number of ways, including clarifying in detail, in writing and as early as possible those criteria in which the student is seen to be deficient; ensuring sufficiently robust and appropriate assessment processes to check the identified criteria, both in terms of the people involved and the methods used to gain evidence (see below), and intensifying their discussion with other people about standards.

Difficult decisions require confidence and practice teachers can gain confidence in their decision making through strong support. Some of this support will come from people who are knowledgeable in assessing students: people who have themselves been confident enough to fail a student, either in practice or college settings, or who have acquired a strong sense of the necessary standard. However, wider support systems can also be important at such times, in their capacity to uphold the practice teacher's values and more general decision-making powers.

Students are likely, as Burgess et al. (1998) report, to feel particularly powerless when at the receiving end of a difficult assessment decision. Beaton (1989) describes his own experience that the final judgement simply confirmed the earlier subjective views of the assessors, without genuinely weighing up the evidence. It is important, therefore, that the practice teacher considers how the student can be empowered in this process. In order to achieve this, I have suggested elsewhere that the student should:

- be clearly informed of the criteria and standards in which they are judged to be deficient, in sufficient time to be able to demonstrate the contrary;
- be able to maximise their own evidence to support their own position;
- be able to include a gatekeeper against discrimination if any is suspected;
- be helped to find their own support, both from peers and beyond,
- be fully informed of the subsequent assessment process, including methods and formal mechanisms (Evans 1990a: 36)

The processes of assessment

Whereas the last section has sought to answer one question: 'what are practice teachers looking for when assessing practice?', this section turns to two related questions: 'how can practice teachers put themselves in a good position to assess?' and 'how can they disseminate their assessment judgement effectively?'

The first question revolves particularly around the people who might become involved in the assessment and the processes which can be used to elicit the evidence upon which a judgement can be founded. The word 'elicit' begs an important question: whose responsibility is it to provide the evidence? The general consensus is that it is ultimately the student's, which is why in the NVQ/SVQ frameworks the language is of students' 'evidencing' the criteria. However, the practice teacher also clearly has some responsibility to seek the evidence which the student will generally supply: this leads to the language of assessment 'methods' (Evans 1990a; Shardlow and Doel 1996) and 'techniques' (Jarvis and Gibson 1985).

The second question gives rise to others, such as, 'who wishes to hear about the practice teacher's assessment judgement and for what reasons?' The main areas for exploration are, therefore, the nature of feedback to the student and writing reports for the educational programme.

Reliability

One of the key concepts in assessment is reliability (Rowntree 1987; Brown and Knight 1994). Reliability concerns the issue of consistency in measuring, or weighing up, the evidence. Greater reliability is thought to be achieved in three main ways: when different assessors agree with each other in their judgements, when the same assessor forms the same judgement on different occasions, and when different assessment methods or forms of evidencing confirm the same judgement.

Another term sometimes used to describe aspects of reliability is 'triangulation'. Phillips et al. (1994) tend to use it when different assessors agree, while Shardlow and Doel (1996) tend to use it when different methods agree. Brown and Knight (1994) describe the second option as 'test-retest' reliability.

Different assessors agree

There are a number of key people whose assessment opinions can greatly enhance the practice teacher's. Brooks and Sikes (1997) use the term 'significant others' for people who may have a significant role in assessing, while Phillips et al. (1994) use the term 'accredited witness' to refer to someone who has a particular competence to assess the student.

One significant person is the line manager of the team in which the student is placed. The line manager's contribution rests partly in the particular perspective they have of the student's work: often becoming involved in decision-making processes about the allocation of resources or in assessing risk, and hence able to assess the student's capacity to advocate on behalf of clients, give a succinct and accurate assessment and be able to prioritise. Their other valued perspective can often be their knowledge of relevant norms for standard setting, since they will usually have known quite a range of staff and will often have been in the position of employing newly qualified staff, hence providing a seamless link between standards at the point of qualification and at subsequent employment.

Other key people are practitioners who have had a specific role in the student's practice. This may have been as a co-worker or some other role which gave them direct access to the student's practice (see Chapter 2). They may have had some specific role in the student's learning and assessment, for example, a specialist worker who has supervised one specialist piece of work. Allen and Evans (1991) outline the contribution a specialist duty social worker regularly made to student learning and assessment in a particular Social Service Department. Another key practitioner is the location supervisor in the long-arm practice teaching arrangement, described in Chapter 5, who can easily be somewhat marginalised in the assessment process.

Experienced practice teachers can bring a particularly valuable additional judgement into a placement. CCETSW (1989) introduced a requirement that any marginal or failing student had to receive a second opinion from another practice teacher, usually experienced in assessing students. Branicki and Horncastle (1994) evaluated a small number of occasions when a formal second opinion was sought, concluding that it was valuable, although clear guidelines would assist the smooth operation of the procedure. It would seem unfortunate that the CCETSW (1995) subsequently abandoned this requirement, although many social work programmes have found it useful enough to persist with it.

All these people have a particular role to play in a student's placement. Moreover, it could be argued that there is a place for any other opinion from someone with a legitimate perspective on the relevant profession which can supplement the practice teacher's. One of the difficulties with the judgement that the practice teacher makes is that it is usually highly subjective, particularly on longer placements when practice teacher and student get to know each other well. Subjectivity is often frowned upon in the assessment. However, Rowntree (1987) argues persuasively that subjectivity is desirable within the assessment system, although it needs to be counterbalanced with some objectivity. Another person, be they from the same agency or another one, will inevitably not have the same subjective position as the practice teacher, although they will have their own subjectivity and as a colleague may sympathise with the practice teacher's (Wolf 1995; Thompson et al. 1990).

One of the difficulties with involving different people in assessing the student's practice is that they do not usually have access to the same practice. In some residential and day care settings, a number of staff and clients may witness the same piece of practice by the student. However, often different people will access the student's practice at different times and hence it will be a different example of practice. It is reasonable to expect some internal consistency to the student's practice, especially when different examples of practice occur close together and in similar contexts. However, permanent records of the student's practice can make the same practice event available to different assessors at different occasions and in different locations. Some practice in most professions is written. However, other forms can be tape-recorded, on either audio or video (see Chapter 6)

Same assessor at different times

It is sometimes tempting to leave the provision of evidence for summative ('selection') assessment until quite late in a placement, particularly if the practice teacher and the student are concerned not to inhibit the development of their working relationship. This can be a risky strategy if the clients become less available suddenly, or the student becomes unwell. On several courses, I have known students leave acquiring a required tape-recording of practice until the last moment and then discover that the client does not turn up or the recorder does not function properly or even that they forget to switch it on, in their anxiety.

Shardlow and Doel (1996) suggest that it is a key principle to assess students throughout a placement, thus giving adequate evidence of consistency in the student's practice. They suggest a form of sampling through time on the basis of some rationale. One useful structure for sampling the student's practice would seem to be the three main phases of the placement: beginning, middle and end (see Chapter 5). In the beginning phase, sampling of the student's practice would give some baseline information to add to the student's self-assessment and upon which learning plans can be constructed. In the middle phase, the sample could check how that learning is being achieved and discuss how it might be furthered. In the end phase, final judgements about the student's standard and the degree of improvement can be made. These three phases suggest a development in the function of assessment similar to the three suggested by Yorke (1998) – diagnostic, formative and summative. One form of sampling is direct observation and the three direct observations required by CCETSW (1995) could be structured to occur in the three different phases.

Different assessment methods agree

Several writers (Hayward 1979; Evans 1991; Beaumont 1996) emphasise the importance of employing a range of different assessment methods. If a consistent impression of the student's ability is gained from different sorts of evidence gained in different ways, then the reliability of the judgement is increased. However, this is not the only advantage of using a range of ways of acquiring evidence. Hayward (1979) on the basis of her major study of social work assessment suggests four other advantages:

- It allows for a greater range of abilities to be demonstrated and rewarded.
- It creates less strain and anxiety and allows greater freedom to experiment.
- Students seem to perform differently at different tasks.
- Students can develop their own tailor-made learning and work habits.

Validity

Validity is another key concept in the literature on assessment (Rowntree 1987; Brown and Knight 1994). It concerns the extent to which the evidence provided is actually of the area of professional ability which the assessors wish to assess. One common form of evidence in practice assessment is the student's self-report, largely because the practice teacher is not usually able to be present at much of the student's practice. As evidence of the actual practice performance it is not particularly valid: the student may have been unaware of crucial aspects of the practice, or forgotten them or even sanitised their account, intentionally or unintentionally. However, the self-report may provide very valid evidence of some learning-to-learn skills such as reflective learning or of some aspects of their repertoire, such as their knowledge or values. Whether oral or written, the self-report will also provide valid evidence of the student's communication skills, although not of communicating to clients.

Since professional competence or ability is complex and wide-ranging, and in the analysis above comprises three major components and their interrelationships, no one assessment method is likely to provide valid evidence for the whole of that competence. In this section, some key ways of providing evidence will be explored for the validity that they offer.

Direct access to practice performance

The four main ways of accessing directly a student's practice performance –

observation, jointwork, live supervision and tape-recording - have been explored in some detail in Chapter 6 'Reflective apprenticeship'. Their particular strength as assessment methods is that they give highly valid evidence of the performance element of professional competence. However, the validity is somewhat limited by the position of the practice teacher or the recording device, since they define what can or cannot be observed. Moreover, live supervision and jointwork sacrifice some assessment validity in the cause of increased learning, since the practice teacher does not concentrate solely on the student's part in the practice, since they also have a part to play.

Another limitation on the validity of this method is that it usually gives evidence of the behavioural aspects of performance only. Schon's (1987) powerful notion of the reflection which occurs during practice suggests that observation alone will not give evidence of the cognitive and affective processes which occur within the student during the practice, never mind those occurring within the client. I have experienced some rather misguided attempts by assessors to infer some of these internal processes from the observable behaviour. It is possible that these aspects of the practice could be accessed by some form of commentary by the student, for example, when the practice is largely or solely non-verbal and the student describes what is in their mind as they perform certain actions. This would seem to occur in medicine and nursing at times. The most universal way of accessing these internal aspects of practice, however, would seem to be through verbal reporting after the practice. This can be particularly valuable if all three parties to the directly accessed practice - student, practice teacher and client - can participate.

As suggested in Chapter 6, direct access to practice performance is most effective if supplemented by dialogue between the student and the practice teacher at any point before, during and after the practice. This dialogue extends the validity of the evidence to cover the two other elements of professional competence - the repertoire and the learning-to-learn skills. Before the practice, the student can explain what aspects of knowledge they bring to this context and what ways of practising they intend to transfer from past contexts. During the practice they can analyse and evaluate the practice so far. After the practice, they can continue to demonstrate these reflective learning skills and indicate how they are beginning the process of transferring knowledge and skills from that context to future contexts.

As Phillips et al. (1994) suggest dialogue can be of particular value in the assessment process. Through dialogue, the practice teacher can elicit ideas from the student as well as simply receive them. It can also be a means of the student correcting the practice teacher's misinterpretations of the practice process: details of behaviour and inaccurate assumptions about the student's intentions. One danger in dialogue, however, is that it can confuse exactly whose ideas are being assessed. The practice teacher's motivation to help the student learn may influence them to lead the student's thinking or to consider that a peremptory assent to an idea of the practice teacher's constitutes an item of knowledge newly acquired by the student. Notwithstanding these dangers, the benefits of dialogue in expanding the validity of direct access is considerable.

Practice outcome

In many occupations the practice performance will lead to a product. A cabinet-maker, for example, will produce an item of furniture which can be assessed for its intrinsic attractiveness, solidity and so forth, in addition to an assessment of the various processes employed by the cabinet-maker to produce it. The assessment of product plays an important role in the NVQ framework (Training Agency 1988). The equivalent element in the caring professions is the outcome of the practice: has the client's need been fulfilled? The outcome of practice can provide valid evidence of the student's ability to make something happen. In Butler and Elliott's (1985) analysis of five skill areas which apply to all the caring professions, they include 'processing work through time'. Students may start well with an accurate assessment but do not always persist until something improves or, sometimes, until further deterioration is prevented.

This practice outcome is the acid test of professional activity and yet it often seems neglected in assessment. One of the main reasons for this neglect is probably the difficulties which beset the assessment of outcomes. Is it the student's practice which has brought about the change or other influences on the client? Was the client well placed to improve or were there intrinsic difficulties severely restricting their progress? In many cases, the practice teacher may know the client's propensity to improve, particularly if the client is well known to the practice agency or the practice teacher. In my view, the considerable gains in validity which practice outcome affords outweigh the degree of uncertainty surrounding it. Assessing practice as a practice teacher, an academic tutor and an external assessor, I have always been somewhat reassured when a student has generally been associated with more positive outcomes than not, even when I am not entirely sure how.

The evaluation of practice outcomes is generally considered an important part of the work process for all the caring professions (Lippitt et al. 1958) and contained within the literature of each. If the student is involved in evaluating practice outcomes, therefore, they not only contribute to their own self-assessment, they also learn a skill which will help them learn and develop throughout their future career. By encouraging the student to evaluate their practice outcomes first, the practice teacher can thus assess one of the student's learning-to-learn skills as well as the effectiveness of their practice performance.

Client feedback

The client's view of both professional practice performance and its outcome is an important one. Most caring professionals would probably consider it good practice to seek the client's perspective both during and at the end of their practice. Some may even seek it as part of a follow-up procedure after the practice is complete (Evans and Kearney 1996). The importance of the client's view rests in their subjective response to the practice, as one of its two main participants, which the practitioner cannot know without asking. Seeking client feedback about the student's practice, therefore, provides valid evidence of this missing aspect of the practice performance. A recent study in social work education (Swift 1997) has confirmed the value of this perspective.

Another advantage of seeking client feedback about the student's practice is the empowerment of consumers in professional education. Not only would their feedback help students in their learning, but a contribution to an assessment system which results in the selection of students into the profession would, in my view, appropriately relax the current exclusiveness of professions in making these decisions. As with evaluating practice outcome, however, there are difficult variables. Has the client been unreasonably biased for or against the student by something they have done or because of some discriminatory attitude? Is the client saying something simply because they want the student to pass or fail? Notwithstanding, these difficulties the validity offered by this perspective would seem worth the seeking. Moreover, if eliciting authentic client evaluation is part of good practice, the student will need to learn how to do it effectively. I have found it particularly valuable to assess students by observing and discussing contacts when one aim of the contact is to evaluate outcomes to date and seek the client's view of progress. One such event can give valid evidence of many aspects of practice performance, as well as these two important learning-to-learn skills.

Seeking client feedback raises a number of technical questions. First, whom should the student ask? This is quite clear with an adult client who is able to express a clear opinion. If the client is a young child or someone with a severe learning difficulty or mental health difficulty, it may be more appropriate to ask a close relative as well or instead. A second question concerns what the student should ask about. Should the student ask for feedback just about outcomes and processes of that practice or about wider aspects of service delivery? In a project with social work students (Evans et al. 1988), we found it useful to develop a principle that feedback should be congruent with the aims and processes of the practice and not extend beyond it. Another question concerns who should seek the feedback, student or practice teacher? Again, the principle of congruence would indicate that the student is the better placed as the practitioner, although there may be some circumstances when the practice teacher may wish to seek feedback not in the student's presence or even after the placement is finished. A final issue is whether feedback should be oral or written. The congruence principle would suggest oral feedback, but the assessment system might require the feedback to be written as a piece of evidence which can be removed from the placement. If the client is aware of the reason for feedback and gives informed consent, it is unusual for them to refuse written feedback.

Self-assessment

The general literature on assessment (Rowntree 1987; Brown and Knight 1994) advocates the role of student self-assessment. Moreover, it would seem to be a growing method of assessment in professional education. Burnard (1988) and Vaughan (1992) support the use of self-assessment in nurse education, while Brooks and Sikes (1997) report the development of records of professional achievement (ROPA), a student self-assessment tool, in initial teacher education. The Self Assessment in Professional and Higher Education (SAPHE) project based at the University of Bristol is investigating the development of self-assessment in law and social work education, although it has yet, at the time of writing, to report its findings.

The great advantage of self-assessment is that it helps the student develop reflective skills of self-analysis and self-evaluation which preserve a level of autonomy within the assessment system and actively promote learning. Boud (1990) claims that self-assessment

> ... is fundamental to all aspects of learning. Learning is an active endeavour and thus it is only the learner who can learn and implement decisions about his or her own learning: all other forms of assessment are therefore subordinate to it (Boud 1990: 109)

The validity of self-assessment evidence is, thus, the access it gives not to practice performance but to the student's reflective learning, part of their learning-to-learn skills. A further considerable advantage of self-assessment is that, like client feedback and evaluating practice outcome, it is a process which is transferable beyond the qualifying programme and into lifelong learning in the workplace.

The practice placement offers considerable scope for self-assessment, largely because of its individual learning pathway and its many opportunities for dialogue between student and practice teacher. Self-assessment can start with the development and agreement of individual learning objectives for the placement. Throughout the placement, the student can be encouraged to articulate their own sense of standard as well as assess their practice against agreed criteria. In discussions about practice, it is tempting for the practice teacher to offer their own evaluation of the student's practice, particularly if the student lacks confidence in their judgement or feels that it is up to the practice teacher to judge. However, if the practice teacher seeks the student's self-assessment first, they can then comment on the student's self-evaluative skills as well as the original practice. The opportunities for such discussion include supervision sessions, reflective apprenticeship situations and three-way meetings with the academic tutor. Sometimes it can seem like a dereliction of duty not to offer a judgement immediately when asked, but students and tutors usually understand the reason. Self-assessment can also be encouraged at the end of the placement in written reports or oral reviews of the whole process.

Practice portfolios

Portfolios are becoming increasingly valued as a way of assessing practice-based material. It has been a major assessment method in the NVQ framework since its inception. Some caring professions are also showing an interest in portfolios for qualifying education. The English National Board (1997) have recently required the use of portfolios in the assessment of nurses, health visitors and midwives, although they would seem to be intended to include theoretical as well as practice-based work. Portfolios are beginning to be developed in social work education, as an appropriate assessment method for placements although not yet required by the CCETSW (1995).

Portfolios are used for a number of purposes, including as a method of aggregating and storing all the assessment material produced during the course of the qualifying programme. The term is used here, however, referring to a specific method for producing evidence of practice for assessment. For this purpose, a portfolio has three main components: a compilation of evidence drawn from practice, sometimes called exhibits (Chaney 1998); a reflective account commenting on the evidence, and a way of indicating how the evidence and the account are mapped against the assessment criteria or competences, sometimes a matrix or grid. Other items in the portfolio may include the placement agreement, basic details of the placement setting and basic details of the student.

The portfolio can, thus, be seen to offer valid evidence of all three major elements of professional competence in one method. The evidence section focuses particularly on practice performance and some aspects of repertoire, while the reflective account gives evidence of learning-to-learn skills and other aspects of repertoire not apparent in the practice evidence. Thomas and Taylor (1998) interestingly relate the different types of evidence in the portfolio to the Kolb (1984) learning cycle. Thus concrete experience is evidenced by case notes, minutes, reports and audio/video recordings; reflective observation by diaries, log books, supervision notes; abstract conceptualisation by references to theoretical literature and generalisations comprising the student's own practice wisdom, and active experimentation by action plans and agendas.

One of the major difficulties with portfolios (Brown and Knight 1994) is the tendency for students to be over-inclusive in their selection of evidence, often including standard documents in use in the agency but which are not evidence of the *student's* ability. In my experience, programmes usually offer advice as to what constitutes useful evidence, including tapes of practice performance, recording done in the course of practice, key reports, evidence of outcomes, client feedback and reports from people who have had access to their practice. They can also offer guidance as to the maximum and minimum of evidence. The practice teacher can play a key role in helping the student recognise for themselves what constitutes good evidence of their practice ability, namely in developing self-assessment skills.

It is helpful to conceive the evidence within the portfolio as a subset of the activities of the placement – a sample, in Shardlow and Doel's (1996) terms – which is chosen to represent the whole of the placement as faithfully as possible. One considerable strength of the practice portfolio is, therefore, that it makes a significant proportion of the placement experience available outside the placement. It can thus be used as a source of reliability, since another practice assessor can access the same evidence as the practice teacher. An external assessor can do the same, thus extending the judgement of standard into a national community.

Whilst both reliability and validity are key principles in assessment, they are not always compatible (Gipps 1995). Multiple-choice tests, for example, would produce reliable results over a range of assessors, but, as Wolf (1995) indicates, bear little relevance to the complex activities of a profession. Brown and Knight (1994) suggest that there has been a shift towards validity in assessment at the expense of reliability. In my view, validity is of paramount value in the assessment of caring professions, since professions must attempt to guarantee a level of competent performance to the public. None the less, there are aspects of reliability which can also be achieved in the practice setting if the practice teacher takes the appropriate steps.

Disseminating assessment judgements

Once the practice teacher has arrived at a suitably valid and reliable judgement about a student, they will need to communicate it to other people, particularly the student and the student's educational programme.

Feedback to students

Feedback has a major role in student learning. Not only can it help the student adjust and develop sufficiently to meet the necessary pass standard, it can also provide genuine learning about strengths and weaknesses, whether or not passing is an issue. As with all other aspects of the practice teacher's activities, giving feedback can be more or less helpful.

In a study of social work students' attitudes to assessment, in both practice and academic settings (Evans 1990a), students indicated that they appreciated feedback which was frequent, close to the time of the work assessed, individualised, involving dialogue and clearly written. Frequent and individualised feedback should be relatively easy to achieve in the placement context, given regular supervisory contact between the practice teacher and the individual student. However, Brodie's (1993) study of the actual content of supervision sessions suggests that a disappointingly small proportion of time was allocated to feedback. In some ways, this is not surprising given the number of other pressing tasks which student and practice teacher are keen to engage in, particularly in relation to future practice. For feedback to become a frequent topic of supervisory contact, both practice teacher and student need to be convinced of its valuable contribution, not only to the student's learning but also to their confidence in the work setting. Moreover, it is helpful if they agree processes for frequent feedback. Some students and practice teachers, for example, agree to have a brief period of mutual feedback at the end of every formal supervision session. It has been my practice to record assessment judgements during the course of supervision sessions, to note whether I have conveyed those judgements orally to the student or not and to make the written record available to the student at any time.

It is generally helpful if the student and the practice teacher conceive of feedback as more than a linear, one-way process. Dialogue between them can enrich the quality of the feedback and its usefulness (Brown and Knight

1994; Phillips et al. 1994). The practice teacher may well have misconstrued the student's intentions or actions and this can be rectified through discussion. Dialogue also gives the student an opportunity to respond to the practice teacher's feedback. Bond and Holland (1998) discuss the possibilities of enhancing the student's assertiveness in response, rather than passively accepting or aggressively rejecting all feedback. This might include differentiating areas of agreement from areas of disagreement. Depending on the student's response to the feedback, the practice teacher will often be able to reshape it in order to maximise the student's learning.

The student is likely to receive much of their oral feedback in formal supervision sessions. These are usually reasonably close in time to the work being judged: close enough for many details to be readily recalled. However, the various processes of reflective apprenticeship, outlined in Chapter 6, have the additional advantage of allowing feedback and dialogue immediately after a practice event, when details are vividly retained in the memory of both student and practice teacher and when dialogue can be based on clear recollection rather than hazy impression.

As well as making similar suggestions regarding the processes of feedback, Gibbs et al. (1986) also indicate the nature of helpful feedback. They suggest, for example, that feedback should be both affective and cognitive. Simple phrases such as 'I liked the way you did X' can introduce an affective element into the feedback dialogue. This is particularly important in the contexts not only of caring professions which recognise the importance of feelings but also of the developing relationship between the practice teacher and the student which facilitates effective learning (see Chapter 6).

Gibbs et al. (1986) also advise a balance between positive and negative comments and some indication of how to improve. These three components are at the heart of constructive criticism, see Figure 7.3.

indicating strengths ⟶ indicating weaknesses ⟶ indicating ways of improving

Figure 7.3 Constructive criticism

Constructive criticism is built upon a strong foundation of positive feedback, in the sense of indicating the student's strengths. This is not merely a behaviourist technique of rewarding the desired rather than punishing aspects to be avoided. It is also a humanistic process, communicating a positive regard (Rogers 1983) for the student in that work context. Hinchliff (1992) similarly emphasises the importance of encouragement and praise to the student and suggests the occasional need for an unconditional 'excellent' which is not hedged about with qualifications. Most students wish for more praise than they receive. Often it is the practice teacher's eagerness to help the student learn how to eradicate weaknesses which reduces their emphasis on strengths which need no alteration. It is a reasonable rule of thumb to consider at least doubling the amount of positive feedback the practice teacher is giving their student.

It is only after strengths have been clearly acknowledged that many students can readily accept the practice teacher's identification of their weaknesses. Thus, positive feedback usually precedes negative feedback chronologically. This chronology is often followed in therapeutic contexts and is fundamental to Winnicott's (1964) notion of 'disillusionment' in child care. The sequence can be over the broader progression of the placement – praising strengths before beginning work on weaknesses – or in structuring the feedback after a given practice event or in both the general and the specific. Self-assessment can be particularly effective in delineating areas of weakness in a helpful way. The student may identify a weakness which can be explored and expanded in dialogue to incorporate the practice teacher's sense of the student's weakness, which may overlap with but also differ from the student's. It is often helpful initially to encourage the student to reflect on a given area, when unsure how they may receive a critical comment.

The identification and acceptance of a weakness in the student, however, is not always sufficient to ensure learning. It is helpful if the practice teacher can indicate to the student how they might have practised more effectively in the practice event under discussion or even how they might practise effectively in future, comparable circumstances. The student is then not left with a sense of what *not* to do, but with a construction of what to do.

Unhelpful feedback usually entails a lack of appropriate balance between the positive and the negative. Destructive criticism, in contrast to constructive criticism, usually consists of a concentration on weaknesses with little reference to strengths, as the students in Walker et al.'s (1995) and Fernandez's (1998) studies indicate. Hinchliff (1992) also mentions the harmful effect of belittling a student. However, the balance can also shift too much towards the positive. This imbalance is understandable in the context of the close relationship which often develops between the practice teacher and the student and of the practice teacher's natural pleasure in the student's new accomplishments. However, it deprives the student of a valuable opportunity for further learning, no matter how accomplished they have become. Having read a considerable number of practice teachers' assessment reports for educational programmes, I would suggest that a sizeable majority err on the side of excessive praise and not damning criticism.

Despite the preceding general comments on helpful and unhelpful feedback, the distinction between the two inevitably rests on specific situations: one student's helpful criticism is another student's traumatic condemnation. Bond and Holland (1998) usefully suggest that responses to criticism will be determined largely by previous experiences of criticism, for example, within the family or in prior educational contexts. Brown and Knight (1994) also indicate how students' different approaches to learning will predispose them towards a particular form of feedback, charting different forms of feedback against Entwistle's (1993) four approaches to learning: deep, surface, strategic and apathetic.

Given these individual differences between students, it would seem useful for a practice teacher and a student to discuss the processes of giving feedback, not just to establish its importance, but also to determine how it can most effectively be given and received. If feedback is an important source of learning then the student needs to learn how to learn in this way and the practice teacher needs to learn how to teach this particular student. Students can usefully increase their awareness of what sort of feedback they most value and on what occasions and how to successfully seek feedback. This is a learning-to-learn skill which can be transferred usefully into later employment.

Informing the educational programme

The principal medium for the practice teacher to communicate their assessment judgement to the educational programme is generally assumed to be the written report. This report has no doubt developed in many caring professions as a response to the considerable difficulties inherent in transferring the evidence, particularly of the student's practice performance, from an agency setting into the educational setting and from there to external assessors. The practice teacher is enjoined to make various statements about the student's practice standard, often against various criteria.

This method of relaying an assessment judgement has two major flaws. One flaw emphasised by Doel (1987) is the process of summarising opinions gathered over the period of a placement in one judgement given at one point in time. This weakness is somewhat alleviated through the use of interim reports, required, for example, in social work qualifying education (CCETSW 1995) which give a summarised judgement at a second point in time. One particular advantage of an interim report is that it can clearly target specific criteria which a weaker student must meet by the end of the placement. The other flaw concerns the fact that the student's own work in practising becomes mediated by the practice teacher's work in writing about it. This contrasts with the assessment of the student's academic work which is available for direct scrutiny by the educational programme, including its external assessors, without the mediation of an internal assessor. This second flaw would seem to be the greater, since a reliance on one opinion, uncorroborated by the evidence upon which it is based, could be a major source of error and discrimination. This weakness will only be overcome as efforts are made to develop methods, such as the portfolio, which transfer evidence of the student's practice out of the practice setting and into the educational programme.

Nevertheless, educational programmes in the caring professions are still requiring such reports. Indeed, the CCETSW (1995) still insist, at the time of writing, on such reports as a requirement of all social work qualifying programmes. The inherent flaws in the process require some dexterity on the part of practice teachers. In communicating a clear judgement of standard against overt criteria, the practice teacher will need to specify the student's standard at the end of the placement and not simply indicate changes in standard, usually improvements, achieved during the period of the placement (Williamson et al. 1989). Moreover, because there is often no corroborating evidence from the student available, the practice teacher will need somehow to persuade the educational programme that their judgement is well founded. This can often entail citing concrete examples of the students' practice in place of the student doing so.

The process of constructing written reports to the educational programme can follow that of giving oral feedback to the student in many respects. Indeed, these reports are usually intended for the student as well as the programme. After arriving at an assessment judgement, it is useful for the practice teacher to discuss this with the student, partly to ensure they have not misconstrued the student's practice in some way and partly to allow the possibility of reshaping the statements for learning purposes. Such negotiations, however, can clearly not include the practice teacher's judgement as to whether the student has reached a satisfactory standard or not. After negotiation, the report can be drafted, read by the student and re-negotiated with the previous proviso. Some programmes encourage the student to submit their own critical comments on the practice teacher's report.

Whilst the emphasis is often on this written report, there are also other important opportunities for the practice teacher to communicate their judgement to the educational programme. The most common of these is at a meeting with the student and their academic tutor towards the end of the placement (see Chapter 4). The academic tutor will usually be well placed to relay a judgement to the formal assessment board and the external assessors. Once again it is the power of dialogue which gives this exchange its value.

The practice teacher can ascertain how the tutor responds to their opinion, if necessary reinforcing it with other evidence. Moreover, in dialogue the practice teacher may discover a reservation which the tutor has about the student's ability and may be able to provide clear and reassuring evidence in that respect. If no such meeting occurs, practice teachers can take it upon themselves to speak to some other member of the educational programme and not just rely on the limitations of a linear, written communication.

Conclusion

An agenda for practice learning

The Introduction outlined three aims for this book which could also form a wider agenda for the development of practice learning in the coming years. This brief section, therefore, comprises a form of coda which attempts to remind the reader of three major themes, at the same time seeking to develop them outside the confines of the book.

Emphasising the importance of practice learning

Anyone who believes it to be the case can emphasise the importance of practice learning: individually or collectively, within their work sphere and particularly to people in a position to ensure its development. Whilst individual advocacy can be effective, the history of minority perspectives and interests, to which practice learning would seem to belong, would suggest that collective action on the part of a number of committed individuals will often bear greater fruit. There have been a number of incidents of practice teachers combining as an informal group within an agency to achieve improved conditions for practice learning, such as workload relief and financial recognition. Moreover, the National Organisation for Practice Teaching (see Appendix), as apparently the only lobbying organisation specifically for practice learning in education for the caring professions, has achieved a number of successes in lobbying CCETSW, the regulatory body of its dominant profession.

It is not necessary to move outside our work sphere to promote practice learning, since there is currently no work sphere in which practice learning enjoys a highly privileged or protected existence. My own position within a higher education institution offers considerable scope for representing the interests of practice learning: on committees about placements, planning the curricula for educational courses for the professions and improving the training for practice teachers. Within practice agencies, where the belief in the efficacy of practice learning is perhaps strongest, there are similarly varied opportunities. Team members, including line managers, may need convincing, before they are prepared to reorientate priorities a little towards the provision of effective learning for students, and hence to future generations of clients, without compromising too much the needs of current clients. How many agency upper managers have developed a strategy for students to learn professional practice within the agency, including policies on the nature of student work in the agency, practitioner involvement in student learning and appropriate resource allocation? It may be that they are as likely to be influenced by a groundswell as by any other source.

Whilst it is often reassuring and enjoyable to discuss aspects of practice learning with like-minded individuals, it is also necessary for the growth of practice learning to take the message to others who influence the development of professional education. Sometimes, people in high places have a similar sense of the importance of practice learning. There are, for example, at least one Member of Parliament, several directors of Social Service Departments and professors of education who have expressed an interest in the role of practice learning. At other times, the collective group needs to present its case to less sympathetic listeners, but in a way which harmonises with other concerns.

Developing the practice and theory of practice learning

Most people actively involved in developing the practice of practice learning would seem to belong to what could be called a 'practitioner culture' (see Chapter 4) in which the transmission of ideas for practice is often oral rather than written. For ideas of good practice in practice learning to be effectively developed, exchanged and disseminated, therefore, there would seem to be a need for a range of forums for oral exchange. These include support groups, workshops, conferences and training courses, at local, regional and national levels.

Training has a particular role in this, but even less is known about effective training for practice teachers than other forms of professional learning. Two large studies within social work education (Walker et al. 1995; Marsh and Triseliotis 1996) have suggested that the current mode of training in social work leading to the CCETSW's (1996a) Practice Teaching Award, which lasts a minimum of 150 hours and incorporates a student placement, is largely ineffective. However, their data was gathered at an early stage in the development of these courses, nor were the courses a major focus of the research design. Moreover, that finding conflicts with much anecdotal evidence from students placed with trainee practice teachers and from those trainees themselves. It would seem contrary to the basic principle that course design should be congruent with course content for practice teaching courses not to contain a practice teaching component, that is, to require the trainee to teach a student in a practice setting. This form of training, however, is at some remove from the short, theoretical two- or three-day courses which some professions still give their practice teachers.

The development of theories of practice learning and of a research programme which might inform that theory is still at an early stage. There is still considerable ignorance about a range of quite fundamental issues concerning practice learning. What is the optimum number of placements to prepare a student for a profession? What is the optimum length of placements? How should placements be structured within an educational programme – concurrently with time in the higher education institution or in full-time blocks? Do the answers to these questions vary according to different professions and if so, according to which variables? Moreover, insufficient is known about what constitutes effective practice learning: the learning environment provided by the agency as a whole; whether the practice teacher should be a specialist educator, a part-educator/part-practitioner or predominantly a practitioner; aspects of the practice teaching process such as modelling or the supervision session. In these areas, too, effectiveness will vary according to the student, the practice teacher, the setting and probably the profession.

The development of both the practice and the theory of practice learning will not itself be effective if it is not rooted in current practice learning practices. The requirements of income generation in general and the Research Assessment Exercise in particular have led to a growing interest within higher education institutions in training practice teachers and in researching and writing about practice learning. However, there is a danger of a credibility gap for academics in this field, similar to the gap which can occur in educating students in and writing about professional practice. Whilst the English National Board (1997), for example, has sought to overcome the latter gap by insisting all nurse lecturers spend one day a week in practice, a similar strategy is unlikely to be employed for academic teachers in practice learning. A more feasible strategy might see academic staff working in partnership with practice staff in the development of the practice and theory of practice learning. The new *Journal of Practice Teaching in Social Work and Health* may require an approach of this sort in meeting the different aims of establishing its credentials as a journal and helping practice teachers to practise.

Ensuring the position of practice learning

One way of seeking to ensure the position of practice learning in the education of the caring professions is to embed it firmly within overall activities of the practice agencies. Central to this process would seem to be acknowledging it overtly as a significant agency activity. There has been a tendency for some agency upper managers to conceal the investment in practice learning in their agencies out of concern that there might be opposition to the expenditure of public money on this training activity rather than on service provision. This would still appear to be somewhat the case in the National Health Service, although the Personal Social Services took the step in the late 1980s of estimating the cost of practice learning, which clearly enabled a period of funding at a slightly higher level. Once identified, practice learning costs can then be included in agency budgets and business plans (Peddar 1998).

Another way of embedding practice learning in practice agencies is by firmly including students as part of the agency establishment and not simply as ghostly figures which somehow flit through the agency. This entails estimating on a routine basis how many students will be within the agency, where they will be placed and what arrangements are necessary to ensure that they can function as temporary agency members in those places. These would include processes such as: making police checks; issuing identity cards, computer identity codes and necessary equipment (uniforms, desks, phones and so on); and allocating appropriate staff, administrative as well as practice teachers, to aid their contribution to the agency. Moreover, as an agency-based process impacting directly on service provision, it would seem important that practice learning should be monitored within agency quality assurance systems, rather than left to higher education institutions, who would then be poorly placed to implement necessary changes.

It is a debatable issue whether any approach in an organisation is best reinforced by appointing specialists, by ensuring that most of the workforce is capable of taking that approach, or by a combination of the two. Practice learning is no exception to this debate. Some agencies write into the contracts of all their professionally qualified staff a requirement to be available to be a practice teacher, irrespective of commitment, aptitude and skills as an educator. Others employ staff with a specialist interest in practice learning, for example, clinical teachers and practice learning coordinators. Sometimes the specialists influence the practice teaching of the non-specialist staff through training, support and consultations. In the absence of any knowledge about the relative effectiveness of these different ways of organising practice learning in agencies, market forces have precipitated the gradual decline of specialist practice learning posts. However, it is likely that agency expertise has been diminished by the loss of these posts and any effort to reinstate some of them may pay dividends in the development of the next generation of practitioners.

Territorial boundaries of all sorts have had a considerable impact on the delivery of an effective service, and this is no less the case in practice learning. Professional boundaries are strong in practice learning, partly since practice teachers would seem to gain much of their motivation from a desire to encourage quality practice in their particular profession and partly because of the crucial role placements play in determining entry into a particular profession. However, as been suggested above, the processes of practice learning are largely common to all the caring professions. There would appear to be four main areas for interprofessional work in practice learning: a basic sharing of practical and theoretical knowledge, practice teacher training and the ongoing support which can often stem from such training, constructing placements which help students transcend professional and agency boundaries, and lobbying activities at a local or national level.

A second major boundary affecting the development of practice learning separates different levels of occupational learning. The practical and theoretical knowledge of work-based learning and assessment which have been hitherto developed within the S/NVQ frameworks for mainly what Winter (1992) calls 'lower-level' occupations has relevance for practice learning in the higher-level occupations. Whilst education and training in employment clearly differs from education based in a higher education institution, the focus on learning for and from practice shares many similarities. This will also doubtless be the case as the caring professions develop processes for continuing professional development after qualification. Already in the personal social services, staff are involved in practice learning across the continuum of training: in work-based assessment and verification, in practice teaching qualifying students and in mentoring post-qualifying candidates. Each activity better informs the others and many skills are transferable across the continuum.

The final boundary to be transcended in practice learning is the national border. While international forums exist for sharing ideas about professional practice and some aspects of education for the caring professions, there would appear to be no forum concentrating on exchanging ideas about practice learning. Isolated articles from other countries appear in professional education journals and Doel and Shardlow's (1996) book on social work practice learning is an important initiative in this direction. However, there does not yet appear to have been an international conference on practice learning at the time of writing.

Ultimately, however, the position of practice learning will only ever be assured through satisfactory levels of funding. In the unlikely eventuality of increased government funding for practice learning, it would seem more likely that the two main partners in education for the caring professions – the higher education institutions and the practice agencies – may be persuaded to channel a higher proportion of their income into practice learning. Some procedures have already been in place to enable higher education institutions to redirect funds to agencies for practice learning. The LEA mandatory grant has had a higher band to cover 'laboratory' learning and such a transfer was specifically required in initial teacher education (DfE 1992). However, such initiatives have not been as successful as they might in the transfer of funds. Practice agencies are beset with increasing demands for service provision with sometimes decreasing resources to meet them. They are only likely to channel more resources into practice learning if they can see clear benefits in terms of recruitment and retention of staff or quality and quantity of service provision. This places an onus once more on energetic advocacy of the importance of practice learning or research-based evidence of its effective contribution to agency services.

As the writer, I have had the power to determine all the items on this particular agenda. However, it may well be that the readers' AOB will produce a much more effective set of items. I shall be most interested to hear of them directly from readers or to chart their progress in the literature and elsewhere.

Appendix

The National Organisation for Practice Teaching's (NOPT) Vision Statement (1986):

The Purpose of NOPT is:

To promote Practice Teaching and to Represent and Advocate for the Interests of Practice Teachers within Social Work Education

and,
To Advise and Support its members to be the Guardians of Good Social Work Practice

by,

- Promoting quality Practice Teaching and Learning within a framework of Social Work Values and Anti-Oppressive Practice

- Ensuring that Practice Teaching is seen as central to Social Work Education and lobbying for adequate resources to maintain this position

- Ensuring that Social Work Education creates reflective individuals able to make independent professional judgements

- Providing a national forum for discussion of the major issues in Social Work Education, collecting and disseminating relevant information to members and others and working in collaboration with other bodies for the advancement of Practice Teaching

- Providing a range of services to support individual members in relation to their professional development in Practice Teaching

The NOPT's Administrator is:

Janet Sewart
227 Bramhall Moor Lane
Hazel Grove
Stockport
SK7 5JL

tel: 0161 483 3788
e-mail: janet.sewart@mcmail.com
nopt@mcmail.com

References

Adams, R. (1990) *Self-Help, Social Work and Empowerment* (London: Macmillan Education Ltd).

Adler, S. (1991) 'The Reflective Practitioner and the Curriculum of Teacher Education', *Journal of Education for Teaching*, 17 (2).

Ahmed, S., Hallett, C., Statham, D. and Watt, S. (1988) 'A Code of Practice', *Social Work Education*, 7 (2): 7–8.

Allen, C. and Evans, D. (1991) 'Learning Duty in an Area Office', National Organisation for Practice Teaching *Newsletter*, 2, March.

Allmark, P. (1995) 'A Classical View of the Theory-Practice Gap in Nursing', *Journal of Advanced Nursing*, 22: 18–23.

Allott, M. and Robb, M. (eds.) (1998) *Understanding Health and Social Care* (London: Sage).

Anderson, G., Boud, D. and Sampson, I. (1998) 'Qualities of Learning Contracts', in Stephenson, J. and Yorke, N. (eds) *Capability and Quality in Higher Education* (London: Kogan Page).

Anglia Polytechnic University and Essex Social Services Department (1994) *The ASSET Programme*, Handbook (London: HMSO).

Anglia Regional General Practice Education Committee (1996) *Anglia General Practice Training Handbook* (Cambridge: ARGPEC).

Anonymous (1994) *Black Consultancy in Practice Teaching*, a report produced by Probation Tutors, Practice Teachers and Placement Co-ordinators in the East Midlands.

Atkins, S. and Murphy, K. (1993) 'Reflection: A Review of the Literature', *Journal of Advanced Nursing*, 18: 1188–92.

Ayer, A.J. (1956) *The Problem of Knowledge* (Harmondsworth: Penguin).

Back, D. and Booth, M. (1992) 'Commitment to Mentoring', in Wilkin, M. (ed.) *Mentoring in Schools* (London: Kogan Page).

Baldwin, M. (1992) 'Induction Programmes for Students on Placements', *Journal of Training and Development*, 2 (4): 7–13.

Bandura, A. (1977) *Social Learning Theory* (Englewood Cliffs, NJ: Prentice Hall).

Bartholomew, A., Davis, J. and Weinstein, J. (1996) *Interprofessional Education and Training* (London: Central Council for Education and Training in Social Work).

Bastian, P. and Blyth, E. (1989) *Joint Appointments in Social Work Education* (London: Central Council for Education and Training In Social Work).

Bateson, G. (1973) *Steps to an Ecology of Mind* (London: Paladin).

Baty, P. (1997a) 'TTA is an Insult to the Profession, Dearing Told', *Times Higher Education Supplement*, 4 April.

Baty, P. (1997b) 'Sir Ron Accused of School Bias', *Times Higher Education Supplement*, 7 March, p. 2.

Beaton, A. (1989) 'The Politics of Student Assessment in Social Work', unpublished paper.

Beaumont, G. (1996) *Review of 100 NVQs and SVQs* (London: NCVQ and SCOTVEC).

Becher, T. (1994a) 'Freedom and Accountability in Professional Curricula' in Becher, T. (ed.) *Governments and Professional Education* (Buckingham: SRHE and Open University Press).

Becher, T. (ed.) (1994b) *Governments and Professional Education* (Buckingham: SRHE and Open University Press).

Bell, L. (1991) 'The Love of the Long-Arm', National Organisation for Practice Teaching *Newsletter*, 3 August.

Bell, L. and Webb, S.A. (1992) 'The Invisible Art of Teaching for Practice: Social Workers' Perceptions of Taking Students on Placement', *Social Work Education*, 11 (1): 28–46.

Benner, P. (1984) *From Novice to Expert* (New York: Addison Wesley).

Beresford, P. (1994) *Changing the Culture; Involving Service Users in Social Work Education, Paper 32.2* (London: Central Council for Education and Training in Social Work), Paper 32.2.

Beresford, P. (1996) 'Meeting the Challenge: Social Work Education and User Involvement', in Trevillion, S. and Beresford, P. (eds) *Meeting the Challenge : Social Work Education and the Community Care Revolution* (London: National Institute of Social Work).

Beresford, P. and Croft, S. (1990) 'A Sea Change', *Community Care*, 4 October: 30–31.

Berlin, I. Sir (1956) *The Age of Enlightenment* (New York: Mentor Books).

Bines, H. (1992) 'Issues in Course Design' in Bines, H. and Watson, D. (eds) *Developing Professional Education* (Buckingham: Society for Research into Higher Education and Open University Press).

Birch, W. (1986) 'Towards a Model for Problem-based Learning', *Studies in Higher Education*, 2 (1).

Birdwhistell, R.L. (1970) *Kinesics and Context* (Harmondsworth: Penguin Books).

Bloom, B.S. (ed.) (1956) *Taxonomy of Educational Objectives: Cognitive Domain* (New York: McKay).

Boe, S. (1996) 'The Experiences of Students and Practice Teachers: Factors Influencing Students' Practice Learning', in Doel, M. and Shardlow, S. (eds) *Social Work in a Changing World* (Aldershot: Arena).

Bogo, M. and Vayda, E. (1987) *The Practice of Field Instruction in Social Work* (Toronto: University of Toronto Press).

Bond, M. and Holland, S. (1998) *Skills of Clinical Supervision for Nurses* (Buckingham: Open University Press).

Boud, D. (1990) 'Assessment and the Promotion of Academic Values', *Studies in Higher Education*, 17 (2): 101–111.

Boud, D., Keogh, R. and Walker, D. (eds) (1985a) *Reflection: Turning Experience into Learning* (London: Kogan Page).

Boud, D., Keogh, R. and Walker, D. (1985b) 'Promoting Reflection in Learning: A Model', in Boud, D., Keogh, R. and Walker, D. (eds) *Reflection: Turning Experience into Learning* (London: Kogan Page).

Boud, D. and Miller, N. (eds) (1996) *Working with Experience* (London: Routledge).

Boutland, K. and Batchelor, J. (1993) *The Patterns that Connect: Action Research into Models of Network Placements for Social Work Students* (Bath: Bath University Practice Learning Centre).

Boyd, E.M. and Fales, A.W. (1983) 'Reflective Learning – Key to Learning from Experience', *Journal of Humanistic Psychology*, 23 (2): 99–117.

Bradbury, G. (1984) 'Learning Styles and C.S.S. Student Supervision', *Social Work Education*, 4 (1): 35–36

Brandon, J. and Davies, M. (1979) 'The Limits of Competence in Social Work: The Assessment of Marginal Students in Social Work Education', *British Journal of Social Work*, 9: 295–347.

Branicki, M. (1997) 'Specifics of Supervision', National Organisation for Practice Teaching Annual Workshop Paper, available from NOPT (see Appendix).

Branicki, M. and Horncastle, J. (1994) 'The Role of the Second Opinion Practice Teacher', *Issues in Social Work Education*, 14 (2): 64–82.

Brewer, S.O. and MacCowan, P. (1992) 'Long Arm Supervision', National Organisation for Practice Teaching *Newsletter*, February.

Bridge, G. (1996) 'Minimising Discrimination: A Case for Excluding Interviews from Selection for Social Work Courses', *Social Work Education*, 15 (4): 5–15.

Bridges, D., Elliott, J. and McKee, A. (1995) *Competence Based Higher Education and the Standards Methodology: Final Report* (Norwich: University of East Anglia, the Employment Department and the Engineering Council).

Brodie, I. (1993) 'Teaching from Practice in Social Work Education: A Study of the Content of Supervision Sessions', *Issues in Social Work Education*, 13 (2): 71–91.

Brookfield, S. (1996) 'Helping People Learn What They Do. Breaking Dependence on Experts', in Boud, D. and Miller, N. (eds) *Working with Experience* (London: Routledge).

Brookfield, S.D. (1987) *Developing Critical Thinkers* (Buckingham: Open University Press).

Brooks, V. and Sikes, P. (1997) *The Good Mentor Guide* (Buckingham: Open University Press).

Brown, A. (1992) *Groupwork*, 3rd edn (Aldershot: Ashgate).

Brown, A. and Bourne, I. (1996) *The Social Work Supervisor* (Buckingham: Open University Press).

Brown, S. and Knight, P. (1994) *Assessing Learners in Higher Education* (London: Kogan Page).

Bryant, R. and Noble, M. (1987) 'Putting Placements in Perspective', *Social Work Education*, 8 (1): 30–33.

Burger, K. and Greenwell, S. (1989) *Perspectives of Community Care* (Bath: University of Bath).

Burgess, H. and Jackson, S. (1990) 'Enquiry and Action Learning: A New Approach to Social Work Education', *Social Work Education*, 9 (3): 3–19.

Burgess, R., Campbell, V., Phillips, R. and Skinner, K. (1998) 'Managing Unsuccessful or Uncompleted Placements', *Journal of Practice Teaching*, 1 (1): 4–12.

Burgess, R., Crosskill, D. and Carose-Jones, L. (1992) *The Black Student's Voice* (London: Central Council for Education and Training in Social Work).

Burn, K. (1992) 'Collaborative Teaching', in Wilkins, M. (ed.) *Mentoring in Schools*

(London: Kogan Page).
Burnard, P. (1988) 'Self Evaluation Methods in Nurse Education', *Nurse Education Today*, 8: 229–33.
Burnard, P. (1992) *Know You! Self Awareness for Nurses* (London: Scutari Press).
Burnham, J. (1986) *Family Therapy* (London: Tavistock).
Burrows, D.E. (1995) 'The Nurse Teacher's Role in the Promotion of Reflective Practice', *Nurse Education Today*, 15: 346–50.
Butler, B. and Elliott, D. (1985) *Teaching and Learning for Practice* (Aldershot: Gower).
Carew, R. (1979) 'The Place of Knowledge in Social Work Activity,' *British Journal of Social Work*, 9: 349–64.
Carr-Hill, R. (1995) 'Welcome? To the Brave New World of Evidence Based Medicine', *Social Science and Medicine*, 41 (11): 1467–68.
Cavanagh, S.J., Hogan, K. and Ramgopal, T. (1995) 'The Assessment of Student Nurse Learning Styles Using the Kolb Learning Style Inventory', *Nurse Education Today*, 15: 177–83.
CCETSW (Central Council for Education and Training in Social Work) (1980) *Regulations and Guidelines for Courses Leading to the Certificate in Social Service (CSS)*, Paper 9.5 (London: CCETSW).
CCETSW (Central Council for Education and Training in Social Work) (1984) *Certificate in Social Service – The Durham Papers*, Paper 9.7 (London: CCETSW).
CCETSW (Central Council for Education and Training in Social Work) (1987) *Care for Tomorrow: The Case for Reform of Education and Training for Social Workers and Other Care Staff* (London: CCETSW).
CCETSW (Central Council for Education and Training in Social Work) (1989) *Rules and Requirements for the Diploma in Social Work*, Paper 30 (London: CCETSW).
CCETSW (Central Council for Education and Training in Social Work) (1991) *Improving Standards in Practice Learning*, revised edn (London: CCETSW).
CCETSW (Central Council for Education and Training in Social Work) (1995) *Assuring Quality in the Diploma in Social Work – 1. Rules and Requirements for the Diploma in Social Work* (London: CCETSW).
CCETSW (Central Council for Education and Training in Social Work) (1996a) *Assuring Quality for Practice Teaching: Rules and Requirements for the Practice Teaching Award* (London: CCETSW).
CCETSW (Central Council for Education and Training in Social Work) (1996b) *Assuring Quality for Agencies Approved for Practice Learning* (London: CCETSW).
CCETSW (Central Council for Education and Training in Social Work) (1996c) *Guidance on the 'Long Arm' Model of Practice Teaching* (London: CCETSW).
Centre for the Advancement of Interprofessional Education (1997) 'Interprofessional Education: What, How and When?', Centre for the Advancement of Interprofessional Education *Bulletin* 13 (Summer).
Chaiklin, S. (1993) 'Understanding the Social Scientific Practice of Understanding Practice' in Chaiklin, S. and Lave, J. (eds) *Understanding Practice Perspectives on Activity and Context* (Cambridge: Cambridge University Press).
Chaiklin, S. and Lave, J. (eds) (1993) *Understanding Practice: Perspectives on Activity and Context* (Cambridge: Cambridge University Press).
Chaney, G. (1998) 'Portfolios – Models and Reality', unpublished paper (Peterborough: Central Council for Education and Training in Social Work External Assessor Conference).
Clapton, G. (1989) *Support Groups for Individual Practice Teachers*, National Organisation for Practice Teaching, available from NOPT (see Appendix).

Clapton, G. (1996) 'Practice Teaching in a Cold Climate', *Professional Social Work*, November.

Clow, C. (1998) 'Managing Endings in Practice Teaching', in Lawson, H. (ed.) *Practice Teaching – Changing Social Work* (London: Jessica Kingsley Publishers).

Cohen, L., Manion, L. and Morrison, K. (1996) *A Guide to Teaching Practice* (London: Routledge).

Collins, S. (1985) 'Working Agreements in Fieldwork Placements – an Evaluation', *Social Work Education*, 4: 15–18.

Collins, S. (1998) 'Empowering Social Work Students in the College Setting', *Social Work Education*, 17 (2): 203–18.

Construction Industry Training Board (1995) *Modern Apprenticeships Framework for the Construction Industry* (King's Lynn: CITB).

Conway, J. (1994) 'Reflection, the Art and Science of Nursing and the Theory – Practice Gap', *British Journal of Nursing*, 3 (3): 114–18.

Cooper, L. (1995) 'Social Justice and Rationing in the Allocation of Field Practicums', *Social Work Education*, 14 (2): 30–43.

Coulshed, V. (1986) 'What Do Social Work Students Give to Training? A Survey', *Issues in Social Work Education*, 6 (2): 119–28.

Coulson, M. (1993) *Catalysts or Victims of Change?* (London: Central Council for Education and Training in Social Work).

Crain, W. (1992) *Theories of Development* (Englewood Cliffs, NJ: Prentice Hall).

Cross, K.P. (1981) *Adults as Learners* (London: Jossey-Bass).

Curnock, K. (1975) *Student Units in Social Work Education* (London: Central Council for Education and Training in Social Work).

Curnock, K. and Hardiker, P. (1979) *Towards Practice Theory* (London: Routledge & Kegan Paul).

Curnock, K. and Prins, H. (1982) 'An Approach to Fieldwork Assessment', *British Journal of Social Work*, 12: 507–32.

Curzon, L.B. (1985) *Teaching in Further Education*, 3rd edn (London: Holt, Rinehart & Winston).

Danbury, H. (1986) *Teaching Practical Social Work* (Aldershot: Gower/Community Care).

Davies, M. (1984) 'Training: What We Think of it Now', *Social Work Today*, 24 January: 12–17.

Davies, M. and Wright, A. (1989) *Probation Training: A Consumer Perspective* (Norwich: Social Work Monographs).

Davies, R. (1998) *Stress in Social Work* (London: Jessica Kingsley Publishers).

Davies, S. et al. (1995) *An Investigation into the Changing Educational Needs of Community Nurses, Midwives and Health Visitors in Relation to the Teaching, Supervising and Assessing of Pre- and Post-Registration Students* (London: English National Board for Nursing, Midwifery and Health Visiting).

Davies, S. et al. (1996) 'How Can Nurse Teachers be More Effective in Practice Settings?', *Nurse Education Today*, 16: 19–27.

Davis, J. and Walker, M. (1985) *Planned and Integrated Practice Learning. An Evaluative Study of Social Work Student Placements* (London Borough of Hammersmith and Fulham Social Service Department).

Dearing, R. (1997) *Higher Education in the Learning Society*, Report of the National Committee of Inquiry into Higher Education (London: HMSO).

DfE (Department for Education) (1992) *Initial Teacher Training (Secondary Phase)*, Circular 9/92 (London: DfE).

DfEE (Department for Education and Employment) (1996) *Higher Level Vocational Qualifications* (London: DfEE).
DfEE (Department for Education and Employment) (1997) *Teaching: High Status, High Standards. Requirements for Courses of Initial Teacher Training,* Circular 10/97 (London: DfEE).
DfEE (Department for Education and Employment) (1998a) *The Learning Age: Higher Education for the 21st Century. Response to the Dearing Report* (London: DfEE).
DfEE (Department for Education and Employment) (1998b) *The Learning Age: Further Education for the New Millennium. Response to the Kennedy Report* (London: DfEE).
Department of Employment (1981) *A New Training Initiative; A Programme for Action,* Cmnd 8455 (London: HMSO).
Department of Health (1997) *The New N.H.S.: Modern, Dependable* (London: The Stationery Office).
DHSS (Department of Health and Social Security) (1978) *Social Services Teams: The Practitioner's View* (London: HMSO).
de Souza, P. (1991) 'A Review of the Experiences of Black Students in Social Work Training', in *One Small Step Towards Racial Justice* (London: Central Council For Education and Training in Social Work).
de Souza, P. (1992) 'The Black Students' Experience', in Burgess, R.M., Crosskill, D. and LaRose-Jones, L. (eds) *The Black Students' Voice* (London: Central Council for Education and Training in Social Work).
Dewey, J. (1933) *How We Think* (Boston: D.C. Heath).
Dillon, J.T. (1990) *The Practice of Questioning* (London: Routledge).
Doel, M. (1987a) 'The Practice Curriculum', *Social Work Education,* 6 (3): 6–12.
Doel, M. (1987b) 'Putting the "Final" in the Final Report', *Social Work Today,* 2 February: 13.
Doel, M. (1993) *Teaching Social Work Practice* (Sheffield: University of Sheffield).
Doel, M. and Shardlow, S. (eds) (1996) *Social Work in a Changing World: An International Perspective on Practice Learning* (Aldershot: Arena).
Dowling, E. (1979) 'Co-therapy: A Clinical Researcher's View', in Walrond-Skinner, S. (ed.) *Family and Marital Psychotherapy* (London: Routledge & Kegan Paul).
Dunne, M., Lock, R. and Soares, A. (1996) 'Partnership in Initial Teacher Training', *Educational Review,* 48 (1): 41–54.
Durkin, K. (1995) *Developmental Social Psychology: From Infancy to Old Age* (Oxford: Blackwell).
Earnshaw, G.J. (1995) 'Mentorship: the Students' View', *Nurse Education Today,* 15: 274–79.
Eisner, E. (1985) *The Art of Educational Evaluation* (Lewes: Falmer).
Elliott, J. (1997a) 'Symposium on Reflective Practice', British Educational Research Association Annual Conference, University of York.
Elliott, J. (1997b) 'Evidence-based Practice', Paper to British Educational Research Association, Manchester, May 1997.
Elliott, N. (1990) *Practice Teaching and the Art of Social Work* (Norwich: University of East Anglia Social Work Monographs).
Else, J. (1992) 'Learning Logs and Reflection Skills', *Training and Development,* March: 23–24.
Employment Department (1991) *Development of Assessable Standards for National Certification,* Guidance Note 8 (Sheffield: Employment Department).
England, H. (1986) *Social Work as Art* (London: Allen and Unwin).
England, H. (1997) 'Where Have All the People Gone?', in Evans, D. (ed.) *'Where Have*

All the People Gone?' National Organisation for Practice Teaching 19th Annual Workshop Proceedings.

ENB (English National Board for Nursing, Midwifery and Health Visiting) (1993) *Regulations and Guidelines for the Approval of Institutions and Courses* (London: ENB).

ENB (English National Board for Nursing, Midwifery and Health Visiting) (1994) *Creating Lifelong Learners* (London: ENB).

ENB (English National Board for Nursing, Midwifery and Health Visiting) (1996) *Shaping the Future: Practice-focused Teaching and Learning* (London: ENB).

ENB (English National Board for Nursing, Midwifery and Health Visiting) (1997) *Standards for Approval of Higher Education Institutions and Programmes* (London: ENB).

Entwistle, N. (1988) *Styles of Learning and Teaching* (London: David Fulton Pub. Ltd).

Entwistle, N. (1993) 'Recent Research on Student Learning and the Learning Environment', Birmingham, Paper presented to the Standing Conference on Educational Development.

Eraut, M. (1994) *Developing Professional Knowledge and Competence* (London: The Falmer Press).

Eraut, M. (1997) 'Evidence-based Practice', Paper to British Educational Research Association, Manchester, May 1997.

Eraut, M., Alderton, J., Boylan, A. and Wraight, A. (1995) *Learning to Use Scientific Knowledge in Education and Practice Settings: An Evaluation of the Contribution of the Biological, Behavioural and Social Sciences to Pre-Registration Nursing and Midwifery Programmes* (London: English National Board for Nursing, Midwifery and Health Visiting).

Erikson, E.H. (1963) *Childhood and Society*, 2nd edn (New York: W. W. Norton & Co.).

Evans, D. (1987a) 'The Centrality of Practice in Social Work Education', *Issues in Social Work Education*, 7 (2): 83–101.

Evans, D. (1987b) 'Live Supervision in the Same Room: a Practice Teaching Method', *Social Work Education*, 6 (3): 13–17.

Evans, D. (1990a) *Assessing Students' Competence to Practice* (London: Central Council for Education and Training in Social Work).

Evans, D. (1990b) 'Black Consultants for Predominantly White Practice Settings', National Organisation for Practice Teaching *Newsletter*, 1, December.

Evans, D. (1992) 'More Comments on the Long Arm Debate', National Organisation for Practice Teaching *Newsletter*, February.

Evans, D. (1993) 'A Model of Practice Teaching', National Organisation for Practice Teaching *Newsletter*, 7, July.

Evans, D. (1996) 'Can We Afford to Develop Quality rather than Quantity?', *Professional Social Work*, January.

Evans, D. (1997) 'A Comparative Study of the Practice Component in Qualifying Education for the Caring Professions', unpublished paper, University College Suffolk.

Evans, D., Cava, H., Gill, O. and Wallis, A. (1988) 'Helping Students Evaluate Their Own Practice', *Issues in Social Work Education*, 8: 113–36.

Evans, D. and Kearney, J. (1996) *Working in Social Care: a Systemic Approach* (Aldershot: Arena).

Evans, D. and Langley, J. (1996) 'Practice-based Assignments – Social Work Education as a Case Study', Paper presented to Higher Education for Capability Conference, January.

Faiers, M. (1987) 'The Importance of Being Relevant', *Community Care*, 16 April:

20–21.
Fernandez, E. (1998) 'Students' Perceptions of Satisfaction with Practicum Learning', *Social Work Education*, 17 (2): 173–201.
Fish, D. (1995) *Quality Mentoring for Student Teachers* (London: David Fulton Publishers).
Fisher, T. (1990) 'Competence in Social Work Practice Teaching', *Social Work Education*, 9 (9): 9–24.
Folliard, J. (1983) 'Practice Teaching: a Neglected Cause?', *Community Care*, 14 March.
Ford, K. and Jones, A. (1987) *Student Supervision* (London: Macmillan/British Association of Social Workers).
Foucault, M. (1980) *Power/Knowledge: Selected Interviews* (New York: Pantheon).
Foulds, J., Sanders, A. and Williams, J. (1991) 'Co-ordinating Learning: the Future of Practice Teaching', *Social Work Education*, 10 (2): 60–68.
Franks, R. (1997) 'Practice Makes Perfect', Master of Education Dissertation, University of Sheffield.
Freire, P. (1970) *Pedagogy of the Oppressed* (New York: Herter & Herter).
Fryer, R.H. (1997) *Report of the National Advisory Group for Continuing Education and Lifelong Learning*.
Furlong, J. (1997) Personal Communication.
Gadamer, H.G. (1975) *Truth and Method* (London: Sheed & Ward).
Gardiner, D. (1989) *The Anatomy of Supervision* (Milton Keynes: Open University Press).
Gardiner, D.W.G. (1985) 'Assessment of Students' Performance in Practice: Some Issues to Consider', unpublished paper, Central Council for Education and Training in Social Work.
Gibbs, G., Habeshaw, S. and Habeshaw, T. (1986) *53 Interesting Ways to Assess Your Students* (Technical and Educational Services Ltd).
Gipps, C. (1995) 'Reliability, Validity and Manageability in Large-scale Performance Assessment', in Torrance, H. (ed.) *Evaluating Authentic Assessment* (Buckingham: Open University Press).
Glasman, D. (1998) 'An ABC of Feelings', *Community Care*, 22–28 January.
Gould, N. (1989) 'Reflective Learning for Social Work Practice', *Social Work Education*, 8 (2): 9–19.
Gould, N. (1996) 'Introduction: Social Work Education and the "Crisis of the Professions"', in Gould, N. and Taylor, I. (eds) *Reflective Learning for Social Work* (Aldershot: Arena).
Gould, N. and Taylor, I. (eds) (1996) *Reflective Learning for Social Work* (Aldershot: Arena).
Gray, J. and Gardiner, D. (1989) 'The Impact of Conceptions of "Learning" on the Quality of Teaching and Learning in Social Work Education', *Issues in Social Work Education*, 9 (1&2): 74–92.
Greenwood, J. (1993) 'Reflective Practice: a Critique of the Work of Argyris and Schon', *Journal of Advanced Nursing*, 18: 1183–87.
Gross, R. (1996) *Psychology*, 3rd edn (London: Hodder & Stoughton).
Habermas, J. (1968) *Knowledge and Human Interests* (Boston: Beacon Press).
Habermas, J. (1984) *The Theory of Communicative Action* (Boston: Beacon Press).
Haggar, H., Burn, K. and McIntyre, D. (1993) *The School Mentor Handbook* (London: Kogan Page).
Hallett, C., Butterworth, T., Collister, B., Orr, J. and William, A. (1993) *The Provision of Learning Experiences in the Community for Project 2000 Students* (London: English

National Board for Nursing, Midwifery and Health Visiting).
Hallett, C.E., Williams, A. and Butterworth, T. (1996) 'The Learning Career in the Community Setting. A Phenomenological Study of a Project 2000 Placement', *Journal of Advanced Nursing*, 23 (3): 578–86.
Hanmer, J. and Statham, D. (1988) *Women and Social Work: Towards a Women-centred Practice* (London: Macmillan).
Hanson, P. (1986) *The Joy of Stress* (London: Pan Books).
Haralambos, M. and Holborn, M. (1990) *Sociology: Themes and Perspectives*, 3rd edn (London: Unwin Hyman).
Harper, J. (1969) 'Group Supervision of Students', *Social Work (U.K.)*, 26 (4): 18–22.
Harre-Hindmarsh, J. (1997) Personal communication.
Harre-Hindmarsh, J. (1998) Personal communication.
Hasenfeld, Y. (ed.) (1992) *Human Services as Complex Organisations* (London: Sage).
Hawkins, P. and Shohet, R. (1989) *Supervision in the Helping Professions* (Buckingham: Open University Press).
Hayward, C. (1979) *A Fair Assessment*, Study 2 (London: Central Council for Education and Training in Social Work).
HCPEF (Health and Care Professions Education Forum) (1997) *A Comparative Study of the Arrangements for Clinical Placements Across 10 Health and Care Professions: Recommendations for Improved Practice* (London: HCPEF).
HMSO (Her Majesty's Stationery Office) (1992) *The Nurses, Midwives and Health Visitors Act* (Amended) (London: HMSO).
Heron, J. (1975) *Six Category Intervention Analysis*, Human Potential Research Project (Guildford: University of Surrey).
Higher Education Quality Council (1997) *Graduate Standards Programme*, Final Report, Vol. 1 The Report (London: HEQC).
Hill, A., Jennings, M. and Madgwick, B. (1992) 'Initiating a Mentorship Training Programme', in Wilkin, M. (ed.) *Mentoring in Schools* (London: Kogan Page), 116–32.
Hill, D. (1997a) 'What? All Kids and No Theory?: Newly Qualified Teachers and Final Year Student Teachers and Their Evaluation of Their ITE Courses Validated under the 1989 CATE Criteria: A Tale of Little Discontent. Implications for the School-focused, "National Curriculum for Teacher Training"', British Educational Research Association Annual Conference, University of York.
Hill, D. (1997b) 'No Bollocks, no Width? New Labour and its Confirmation of the Conservative Restructuring of Initial Teacher Education 1984–97', British Educational Research Association Annual Conference, University of York.
Hinchliff, S. (ed.) (1992) *The Practitioner as Teacher* (London: Scutari Press).
Hinds, D. (1998) 'Supervision – A Framework for Development', unpublished paper, British Educational Research Association, Oxford 1998.
Hirst, P.H. and Peters, S.R. (1970) *The Logic of Education* (London: Routledge & Kegan Paul Ltd).
Hislop, S. et al. (1996) 'Situating Theory in Practice: Student Views of Theory – Practice in Project 2000 Nursing Programmes', *Journal of Advanced Nursing*, 23: 171–77.
Honey, P. (1994) *Learning Log* (Maidenhead: Dr. Peter Honey).
Honey, P. and Mumford, A. (1986) *Using Your Learning Styles*, 1st edn (Maidenhead: Dr. Peter Honey).
Honey, P. and Mumford, A. (1995) *Using Your Learning Styles*, 3rd edn (Maidenhead: Dr. Peter Honey).

Honey, P. and Mumford, A. (1996) *Building a Learning Environment* (Maidenhead: Dr. Peter Honey).
Howe, D. (1987) *An Introduction to Social Work Theory* (Aldershot: Wildwood House Ltd).
Howe, D. (1992) 'Theories of Helping, Empowerment and Participation', in Thoburn, J. (ed.) *Participation in Practice Involving Families in Child Protection* (Norwich: University of East Anglia).
Howe, D. (1996) 'Relating Theory to Practice', in Davies, M. (ed.) *The Blackwell Companion to Social Work* (Oxford: Blackwell).
Hughes, L. and Heycox, K. (1996) 'Three Perspectives on Assessment in Practice Learning', in Doel, M. and Shardlow, S. (eds) *Social Work in a Changing World: an International Perspective on Practice Learning* (Aldershot: Arena).
Hugman, R. (1991) *Power in the Caring Professions* (London: Macmillan).
Hulatt, I. (1995) 'A Sad Reflection', *Nursing Standard*, 9 (20): 22–23.
Humphries, B. (1988) 'Adult Learning in Social Work Education: towards Liberation or Domestication', *Critical Social Policy*, 23 (Autumn): 4–21.
Humphries, B., Panchania-Wimmer, Searle, A. and Stokes, I. (1993) *Improving Practice Teaching and Learning* (Leeds: Central Council for Education and Training in Social Work).
Hunter, D.J. (1996a) 'Evidence-Based Medicine: the Illusion of Certainty', *IFMH Inform.*, 7, (3): 1–3.
Hunter, D.J. (1996b) 'Rationing and Evidence-Based Medicine', *Journal of Evaluation in Clinical Practice*, 2 (1): 5–8.
Hurst, B. and Wilkin, M. (1992) 'Guidelines for Mentors', in Wilkin, M. (ed.) *Mentoring in Schools* (London: Kogan Page).
Hyland, T. (1994) *Competence, Education and NVQs: Dissenting Perspectives* (London: Cassell).
Jack, R. (1986) 'Two-way Stretch', *Community Care*, 24 July.
James, C.R. and Clarke, B.A. (1994) 'Reflective Practice in Nursing: Issues and Implications for Nurse Education', *Nurse Education Today*, 14: 82–90.
Jarvis, P. and Gibson, S. (1985) *The Teacher Practitioner in Nursing, Midwifery and Health Visiting* (London: Chapman and Hall).
Johns, C. (1995) 'Framing Learning through Reflection within Carper's fundamental Ways of Knowing in Nursing', *Journal of Advanced Nursing*, 22: 226–34.
Johnson, S. and Shabbaz, A. (1989) 'Integrated Practice Placements – A Model for Development', *Practice*, Autumn/Winter.
Johnson, T.J. (1972) *Professions and Power* (London: Macmillan).
Joint University Council Social Work Education Committee (1997) 'Comparison of Two Surveys on the Impact of CCETSW Practice Learning Funding Changes', unpublished paper.
Jones, C. (1995) 'Demanding Social Work Education: An Agenda for the End of the Century', *Issues in Social Work Education*, 15 (2): 3–17.
Jessup, G. (1991) Outcomes: NVQs and the Emerging Model of Education and Training (Lewes: Falmer Press).
Jowett, G., Banks, R., Lukhezo, M. and Medhurst, S. (1989) 'Subject to Scrutiny', *Social Work Today*, 23 November: 18–19.
Kadushin, A. (1968) 'Games People Play in Supervision', *Social Work*, 13 (3): 23–32.
Kadushin, A. (1976) *Supervision in Social Work* (New York: Columbia University Press).
Kadushin, A. (1992) *Supervision in Social Work*, 3rd edn (New York: Columbia

University Press).
Kearney, J. (1989) 'Screen Memories', M.Sc. Dissertation, University of Edinburgh.
Kemshall, H. (1993) 'Assessing Competence: Scientific Process or Subjective Inference?', *Social Work Education*, 12 (1): 36–45.
Kennedy, Baroness (1998) *Learning Works* (London: Further Education Funding Council).
Kim, H.S. (1993) 'Putting theory into practice: problems and prospects', *Journal of Advanced Nursing*, 18: 1632–39.
Kingston, P. and Smith, D. (1983) 'Preparation for Live Consultation and Live Supervision When Working without a One-way Screen', *Journal of Family Therapy*, 5: 219–33.
Kirschenbaum, H. and Henderson, V.L. (eds) (1990) *The Carl Rogers Reader* (London: Constable).
Kolb, D.A. (1984) *Experiential Learning* (Englewood Cliffs, NJ: Prentice Hall PTR).
Kolb, D.A. (1985) *Learning Style Inventory: Technical Manual* (Boston: McBer).
Knapp, P.H. (1963) *Expression of the Emotions in Men* (International Universities Press Inc.).
Knowles, M. (1978) *The Adult Learner: a Neglected Species*, 2nd edn (Houston: Gulf).
Knowles, M. (1986) *Using Learning Contracts* (San Francisco: Jossey-Bass).
Lauder, W. (1994) 'Beyond Reflection: Practical Wisdom and the Practical Syllogism', *Nurse Education Today*, 14: 91–98.
Lave, J. and Wenger, E. (1991) *Situated Learning: Legitimate Peripheral Participation* (Cambridge: Cambridge University Press).
Lawson, H. (1998) 'Inside the Long-Arm Model of Practice Teaching: the Experiences of Students, Practice Teachers and On-Site Supervisors', in Lawson, H. (ed.) *Practice Teaching – Changing Social Work* (London: Jessica Kingsley Publishers).
Le Riche, P. and Tanner, K. (1998) *Observation and its Application to Social Work* (London: Jessica Kingsley Publishers).
Lippitt, R., Watson, J. and Wesley, B. (1958) *The Dynamics of Planned Change* (New York: Harcourt Brace).
Lishman, J. (ed.) (1991) *Handbook of Theory for Practice Teachers in Social Work* (London: Jessica Kingsley Publishers).
Loewenberg, F.M. (1984) 'Professional Ideology, Middle Range Theories and Knowledge Building for Social Work Practice', *British Journal of Social Work*, 14: 309–22.
Longman (1984) *Dictionary of the English Language* (Harlow: Longman).
Lorenz, W. (1998) 'Trends in European Social Work Education', unpublished paper, Peterborough, Central Council for Education and Training in Social Work External Assessor Conference.
Lyon, D. (1994) *Postmodernity* (Buckingham: Open University Press).
MacLeod, M.L.P. (1996) *Practising Nursing – Becoming Experienced* (New York: Churchill Livingstone).
Macleod Clark, J., Maben, J. and Jones, K. (1996) *Project 2000, Perceptions of the Philosophy and Practice of Nursing* (London: English National Board for Nursing, Midwifery and Health Visiting).
McGill, I. and Beaty, L. (1995) *Action Learning*, 2nd edn (London: Kogan Page).
McIntyre, D. and Hagger, H. (1993) 'Teachers' Expertise and Models of Mentoring', in McIntyre, D., Hagger, H. and Wilkin M. (eds) *Mentoring* (London: Kogan Page), 86–102.
Marsh, P. and Triseliotis, J. (1996) *Ready to Practise? Social Workers and Probation*

Officers: Their Training and First Year in Work (Aldershot: Avebury).
Maslow, A. (1954) *Motivation and Personality* (New York: Harper and Row).
Meadows, S. (1993) *The Child as Thinker* (London: Routledge).
Megginson, D. and Boydell, T. (1979) *A Manager's Guide to Coaching* (London: British Association for Commercial & Industrial Education).
Mezirow, J. (1981) 'A Critical Theory of Adult Learning and Education', *Adult Education*, 32 (1).
Mezirow, J. (1990) (ed.) *Fostering Critical Reflection in Adulthood* (San Francisco: Jossey-Bass).
Mountford, B. (1993) 'Mentoring and Initial Teacher Education', in Smith, P. and West-Burnham, J. (eds) *Mentoring in the Effective School* (Harlow: Longman).
Murphy, R. and Torrance, H. (1988) *The Changing Face of Educational Assessment* (Milton Keynes: Open University Press).
Narayanaraja, P.N. (1996) Personal communication.
NCVQ (National Council for Vocational Qualifications) (1986) *The National Council for Vocational Qualifications: Its Purposes and its Aims* (London: NCVQ).
NCVQ (National Council for Vocational Qualifications) (1989) *The Extension of the N.V.Q. Framework above Level 4*. Consultative document (London: NCVQ).
Newell, R. (1992) 'Anxiety, Accuracy and Reflection: the Limits of Professional Development', *Journal of Advanced Nursing*, 17: 1326–33.
NHS (National Health Service) (1996) *Education and Training Planning Guidance, 1997/98* (EL (96) 46) (Leeds: NHS).
NHS (National Health Service) (1997) *The New N.H.S.: Modern, Dependable* (London: NHS).
NOPT (National Organisation for Practice Teaching) (1998) 'Taking Practice Teaching to Lithuania', NOPT *Newsletter*, April.
O'Brien, D. and Watson, D. (1993) 'Nurse Education: a Social and Historical Perspective', in Reed, J. and Procter, S. (eds) *Nurse Education: a Reflective Approach* (London: Edward Arnold).
O'Neill, J. (1995) 'On Schools as Learning Organizations: A Conversation with Peter Senge', *Educational Leadership*, 52 (7): 20–23.
Owens, C. (1995) 'How the Assessment of Competence in Dip. S.W. is Changing the Culture of Practice Teaching', *Social Work Education*, 14 (3): 61–78.
Paley, J. (1987) 'Social Work and the Sociology of Knowledge', *British Journal of Social Work*, 7: 169–86.
Palmer, A.M., Burns, S. and Bulman, C. (eds) (1994) *Reflective Practice in Nursing* (Oxford: Blackwell).
Papell, C.P. (1996) 'Reflections on Issues in Social Work Education', in Gould, N. and Taylor, I. (eds) *Reflective Learning for Social Work* (Aldershot: Arena).
Patrick, D. and Geddie, W. (eds) (1930) *Chambers Encyclopaedia, Vol. 1* (London: W. & R. Chambers Ltd).
Payne, C. and Scott, T. (1982) *Developing Supervision of Teams in Field and Residential Social Work* (London: National Institute of Social Work).
Payne, M. (1977) 'An Apprenticeship Model of Social Work Education', *Social Work Today*, 9, 27 September.
Payne, M. (1991) *Modern Social Work Theory* (London: Macmillan).
Peddar, J. (1998) 'The Use of Business Planning in Practice Teaching', *Journal of Practice Teaching in Social Work and Health*, 1 (1): 24–32.
Perry, W. (1970) *Forms of Intellectual and Ethical Development in the College Years* (New York: Holt, Rinehart & Winston).

Peters, R.S. (1977) *Education and the Education of Teachers* (London: Routledge & Kegan Paul).
Pettes, D.E. (1979) *Staff and Student Supervision. A Task Centred Approach* (London: Allen & Unwin).
Phillips, R. (1998) 'Disabled Students: Barriers to Practice Learning', *Journal of Practice Teaching in Social Work and Health*, 1 (1): 13–23.
Phillips, T. (1997) 'Assessment and Reflective Practice: Contending Discourses in Nursing Education. Towards Prospective Practice', British Educational Research Association Annual Conference, University of York.
Phillips, T., Bedford, H., Robinson, J. and Schostak, J. (1994) *Education, Dialogue and Assessment: Creating Partnership for Improving Practice* (London: English National Board for Nursing, Midwifery and Health Visiting).
Phillips, T., Schostak, K., Bedford, H. and Leamon, J. (1996) *Evaluation of Pre-Registration Undergraduate Degrees in Nursing and Midwifery Programmes* (London: English National Board for Nursing, Midwifery and Health Visiting).
Phillipson, J., Richards, M. and Sawdon, D. (eds) (1988) *Towards a Practice Led Curriculum* (London: National Institute for Social Work).
Pilalis, J. (1986) 'The Integration of Theory and Practice: A Re-examination of a Paradoxical Expectation', *British Journal of Social Work*, 16: 79–96.
Pink, D. (1991) 'Black students' views of existing CQSW courses and CSS schemes', in Northern Curriculum Development Project (ed.) *Setting the Context for Change* (London: CCETSW).
Pithouse, A. (1987) *Social Work: the Social Organisation of an Invisible Trade* (Aldershot: Gower Publishing).
Polychronis, A., Miles, A. and Bentley, P. (1996) 'The Protagonists of "Evidence-based Medicine": Arrogant, Seductive and Controversial', *Journal of Evaluation in Clinical Practice*, 2 (1): 9–12.
Powell, J.H. (1989) 'The Reflective Practitioner in Nursing', *Journal of Advanced Nursing*, 14: 824–32.
Preston-Shoot, M. (1989) 'A Contractual Approach to Practice Teaching', *Social Work Education*, 8 (3): 3–15.
Qualifications and Curriculum Authority (1998) *Assessing NVQs* (London: QCA).
The Quality Assurance Agency (1998) *An Agenda for Quality* (London: QAA).
Reed, J. and Procter, S. (eds) (1993) *Nurse Education: a Reflective Approach* (London: Edward Arnold).
Resnick, L.B. (1987) *Education and Learning to Think* (Washington, D.C.: National Academy Press).
Richards, M. (1984) 'Pulled in All Directions', *Community Care*, 18 October: 18–21.
Richards, P. (1995) 'Compound Fractures', *Times Higher Education Supplement*, 20 January.
Richardson, B. and Stewart, S. (1997) 'A Study of the Process of Developing Reflective Practice in Occupational Therapy and Physiotherapy Students', British Educational Research Association Annual Conference, University of York.
Richardson, G. and Maltby, H. (1995) 'Reflection-on-Practice: Enhancing Student Learning', *Journal of Advanced Nursing*, 22: 235–42.
Roberts, H. (1998) 'Look Who's Talking', *Community Care*, 29 January–4 February.
Rogers, C. (1983) *Freedom to Learn for the 80s* (Columbus, OH: Charles E. Merrill Publishing Co.).
Rogers, C. R. (1974) *On Becoming a Person* (London: Constable).
Rogers, G. (1996) 'Comparative Approaches to Practice Learning', in Doel, M. and

Shardlow, S. (eds) *Social Work in a Changing World: an International Perspective on Practice Learning* (Aldershot: Arena).
Rosenblatt, A. and Mayer, J. (1975) 'Objectionable Supervisory Styles: Students' Views', *Social Work*, 2: 184–89.
Rowntree, D. (1987) *Assessing Students: How Shall We Know Them?*, 2nd edn (London: Harper & Row Ltd).
The Royal New Zealand College of General Practitioners (1997) *General Practice Vocational Training Programme*, Handbook 1997 (RNZCGP).
Ryle, G. (1949) *The Concept of Mind* (London: Hutchinson House).
Sacco, T. (1996) 'Towards an Inclusive Paradigm for Social Work', in Doel, M. and Shardlow, S. (eds) *Social Work in a Changing World: an International Perspective on Practice Learning* (Aldershot: Arena).
Sackett, D.L. and Haynes, R.B. (1995) 'On the Need for Evidenced-based Medicine', *Evidenced-based Medicine*, 1 (1): 5–6.
Saltzberger-Wittenberg, I., Henry, G. and Osborne, E. (1983) *The Emotional Experience of Learning and Teaching* (London: Routledge).
Sawdon, D. (1986) *Making Connections in Practice Teaching* (London: National Institute for Social Work).
Sawdon, D. and Sawdon, C. (1987) 'What Makes a Good Practice Learning Experience', *Social Work Education*, 6 (3): 3–5.
Schon, D. (1983) *The Reflective Practitioner* (London: Temple Smith).
Schon, D. (1987) *Educating the Reflective Practitioner* (San Francisco: Jossey Bass).
Secker, J. (1992) 'More than Tea and Sympathy', *Community Care*, 2 July: 22–23.
Senge, P. (1990) *The Fifth Discipline: the Art and Practice of the Learning Organisation* (New York: Doubleday/Currency).
Senior, P. (ed.) (1994) *Creative Practice Teaching Materials for Probation Placements* (Sheffield: Sheffield Hallam University).
Shardlow, S. and Doel, M. (1996) *Practice Learning and Teaching* (London: Macmillan).
Shaw, I. and Walton, R. (1978) 'What Use is Social Work Training?', *Community Care*, 18 January: 22–23.
Sheldon, B. (1978) 'Theory and Practice in Social Work: A Re-examination of a Tenuous Relationship', *British Journal of Social Work*, 8: 1–22.
Shields, E. (1994) 'A Daily Dose of Reflection', *Professional Nurse*, August: 755–58.
Sibeon, R. (1991) *Towards a New Sociology of Social Work* (Aldershot: Avebury).
Skilbeck, M., Connell, H., Lowe, N. and Tait, K. (1994) *The Vocational Quest* (London: Routledge).
Smith, D. (1997) 'Facilitating Reflective Practice in Professional Preservice Education: Challenging some Sacred Cows', Unpublished paper, University of Sydney Faculty of Education.
Smith, R.M. (1984) *Learning How to Learn: Applied Theory for Adults* (Milton Keynes: Open University Press).
Solomon, R.L. (1993) *The Passions: Emotions and the Meaning of Life* (Indianapolis: Hackett Publishing Co.).
Sparkes, J. (1998) 'What Type of Student do You Have to Teach?', *Times Higher Education Supplement*, 6 February, Teaching: iv & v.
Star, B. (1979) 'Exploring the Boundaries of Video-tape Self-confrontation', *Journal of Education for Social Work*, 15 (1): 87–94.
Steinaker, N. and Bell, M. (1979) *The Experiential Taxonomy: a New Approach to Teaching and Learning* (New York: Academic Press).
Stephenson, J. (1998) 'The Concept of Capability and its Importance in Higher

Education', in Stephenson, J. and Yorke, M. (eds) *Capability and Quality in Higher Education* (London: Kogan Page).
Stephenson, J. and Yorke, M. (eds) (1998) *Capability and Quality in Higher Education* (London: Kogan Page).
Swain, H. (1996) 'Doctors Have a Good Feel', *Times Higher Education Supplement*, 11 October.
Swift, P. (1997) 'Service User Feedback', in Evans, D. (ed.) *National Organisation for Practice Teaching, Annual Workshop Proceedings 1997*, available from NOPT (see Appendix).
Syson, L. and Baginsky, M. (1981) *Learning to Practise* (London: Central Council for Education and Training in Social Work).
Targett, S. (1995) 'Employers Reveal no Interest in NVQs', *Times Higher Education Supplement*, 22 December.
Taylor, J. and Woods, M. (1998) *Early Childhood Studies: an Holistic Introduction* (London: Arnold).
Taylor, P. and Baldwin, M. (1991) 'Travelling Hopefully: Anti-racist Practice and Practice Learning Opportunities', *Social Work Education*, 10 (3): 5–32.
Taylor, W. (1969) *Society and the Education of Teachers* (London: Faber & Faber Ltd).
Teacher Training Agency (1997) *National Standards for Headteachers* (London: TTA).
Tennant, M. (1997) *Psychology and Adult Learning*, 2nd edn (London: Routledge).
Thomas, G. (1997) 'What is the Use of Theory?', *Harvard Educational Review*, 67 (1): 75–104.
Thomas, J. and Taylor, P. (1998) 'The Portfolio Approach to Learning', in Evans, D. (ed.) *National Organisation for Practice Teaching, Annual Workshop Proceedings 1998*, available from NOPT (see Appendix).
Thompson, A. (1998) 'The Search for Certainty', *Community Care*, 12–18 February: 16–17.
Thompson, N. (1995) *Theory and Practice in Health and Social Welfare* (Buckingham: Open University Press).
Thompson, N. and Bates, J. (1996) 'Learning from Other Disciplines', Unpublished monograph, North East Wales Institute of Higher Education.
Thompson, N., Osada, M. and Anderson, B. (1990) *Practice Teaching in Social Work* (Birmingham: Pepar).
Thompson, S. and Marsh, P. (1991) 'The Management of Practice Teaching', Sheffield: *Research in Social Work Education*, No. 3.
Times Higher Education Supplement (1998) 'Millennium Magic Blunkett Style?', 27 February, News: 10–13.
Tomlinson, J. (1989) 'The Enigma of Theory v. Practice', *Education*, 10 March: 236–37.
Tomlinson, P. (1995) *Understanding Mentoring* (Buckingham: Open University Press).
Torrance, H. (ed.) (1995) *Evaluating Authentic Assessment* (Buckingham: Open University Press).
Toussaint, P., Yeardley, A. and Leyden, L. (1989) *Live Supervision* (London: London Borough of Hackney).
Training Agency (1988) *Development of Assessable Standards for National Certification. Guidance Note 3: the Definition of Competences and Performance Criteria* (Sheffield: Training Agency).
Trotter, J. and Gilchrist, J. (1996) 'Assessment Dip. S.W. Students: Anti-discriminatory Practice in Relation to Lesbian and Gay Issues', *Social Work Education*, 15 (1): 75–82.
Tsang, Nai-Ming (1993) 'Shifts of Student Learning Styles on a Social Work Course', *Social Work Education*, 12 (1).

Tysome, T. (1994) 'Teacher Scheme "Failing"', *Times Higher Education Supplement*, 8 July.

Tysome, T. (1995) 'NVQs Pass Tough Admissions Test', *Times Higher Education Supplement*, 30 June, p. 6.

United Kingdom Central Council for Nursing, Midwifery and Health Visiting (1997) *Framework of Standards for the Preparation of Teachers of Nursing, Midwifery and Health Visiting* (London: UKCCNMHV).

Vaughan, J. (1992) 'Assessing Learning Needs', in Hinchliff, S. (ed.) *The Practitioner as Teacher* (London: Scutari Press).

Walker, H. (1996) 'Liberated Practice Teaching: the Experience of Self-Selection in Finding Placements,' in Doel, M. and Shardlow, S. (eds) *Social Work in a Changing World: an International Perspective on Practice Learning* (Aldershot: Arena).

Walker, J., McCarthy, P., Morgan, W. and Timms, N. (1995) *In Pursuit of Quality: Improving Practice Teaching in Social Work* (Newcastle-upon-Tyne: Relate Centre for Family Studies).

Wallace, D. (1996) 'Experiential Learning and Critical Thinking in Nursing', *Nursing Standard*, 10 (31): 43–47.

Walrond-Skinner, S. (1974) 'Training for Family Therapy', *Social Work Today*, 5, 30 May.

Warnock, M. (1996) 'The Sage of Discovery', *Times Higher Education Supplement*, 13 December: 23.

Waterhouse, L. (1987) 'The Relationship Between Theory and Practice in Social Work Training', *Issues in Social Work Education*, 7: 3–19.

Watson, D. (1992) 'The Changing Shape of Professional Education', in Bines, H. and Watson, D. (eds) *Developing Professional Education* (Buckingham: The Society for Research into Higher Education and Open University Press).

Wegerif, R. (1997) 'The Question of Faith', *The Friend*, 5 September.

Weinstein, J. (1992) *Placement Survey of Local Authority Placements and Provision in England and Wales* (London: Central Council for Education and Training in Social Work).

Weinstein, J. (1994) *Sewing the Seams for a Seamless Service* (London: Central Council for Education and Training in Social Work).

Whiffen, R. and Byng-Hall, J. (eds) (1982) *Family Therapy Supervision* (London: Academic Press).

White, E., Riley, E., Davies, S. and Twinn, S. (1993) *A Detailed Study of the Relationships between Teaching Support, Supervision and Role Modelling for Students in Clinical Areas within the Context of Project 2000 Courses* (London: English National Board for Nursing, Midwifery and Health Visiting).

Wijnberg, M.H. and Schwartz, M.C. (1977) 'Models of Student Supervision: the Apprentice, Growth and Role Systems Models', *Journal of Education for Social Work*, 13: 107–13.

Wilkin, M. (ed.) (1992) *Mentoring in Schools* (London: Kogan Page).

Wilkin, M. (1997) 'Texts on Mentoring of Student Teachers', Unpublished paper.

Williams, A. (ed.) (1994a) *Perspectives on Partnership – Secondary Initial Teacher Training* (London: The Falmer Press).

Williams, A. (1994b) 'Roles and Responsibilities in Initial Teacher Training – Student Views' in Williams, A. (ed.) *Perspectives on Partnership – Secondary Initial Teacher Training* (London: The Falmer Press): 93–108.

Williams, B. (1996) 'Probation Training: the Defence of Professionalism', *Social Work Education*, 15 (3): 5–19.

Williams, J.E. and Best, D.L. (1994) 'Cross-cultural Views of Women and Men', in Lonner, W.J. and Malplass, R.S. (eds) *Psychology and Culture* (Boston: Allyn & Bacon).
Williamson, H., Jefferson, R., Johnson, S. and Shabbaz, A. (1989) *Assessment of Practice – a Perennial Concern?* (University of Wales College Cardiff: Social Research Unit).
Winnicott, D.W. (1964) *The Child, the Family and the Outside World* (Harmondsworth: Penguin).
Winnicott, D.W. (1971) *Playing and Reality* (London: Routledge).
Winter, R. (1992) *Outline of a General Theory of Professional Competence* (Chelmsford: Anglia Polytechnic University).
Witkin, H. (1950) 'Perception of the Upright when the Direction of the Force Acting on the Body is Changed!', *Journal of Experimental Psychology*, 40: 93–106.
Witkin, H., Goodenough, D. and Cox, P. (1977) 'Field Dependent and Field Independent Cognitive Styles and their Educational Implications', *Review of Educational Research*, 47 (1): 1–64.
Wolf, A. (1995) *Competence-Based Assessment* (Buckingham: Open University Press).
Yelloly, M. and Henkel, M. (eds) (1995) *Learning and Teaching in Social Work* (London: Jessica Kingsley Publishers Ltd).
Yorke, M. (1998) 'Assessing Capability', in Stephenson, J. and Yorke, M. (eds) *Capability and Quality in Higher Education* (London: Kogan Page).

General Index

Index of Authors Cited